CHICKEN SOUP FOR THE SISTER'S SOUL

Inspirational Stories About Sisters and Their Changing Relationships

Jack Canfield
Mark Victor Hansen
Patty and Nancy Mitchell
Heather and Katy McNamara

Backlist, LLC, a unit of
Chicken Soup for the Soul Publishing, LLC
Cos Cob, CT
www.chickensoup.com

Contents

3. SIBLING REVELRY

4. OVERCOMING OBSTACLES

5. OH BROTHER!

6. SISTERS BY HEART

7. SPECIAL MEMORIES

8. INSIGHTS AND LESSONS

Introduction

"She's always there for me," "I can call her day or night," "I can tell her anything," "I'd be lost without her." These are just some of the phrases we found repeated in the thousands of inspiring, heartfelt and humorous stories that were submitted to us for *Chicken Soup for the Sister's Soul.* Whether connected by genetics or the heart, our sisters know us in a way no one else can. We're cut from the same cloth, molded by a unique shared experience. Our sisters know what it was like to grow up where we grew up, when we grew up and with whom.

We are at once girlfriends, shopping companions, confidants, rivals, sounding boards and more. These invisible ties stretch and bend through times of closeness and distance, yet, in all but the fewest cases, we remain inextricably connected.

We conceived of this book as a gift to our own sisters; however, we hope that it inspires you to recognize the essential role your sisters play in your lives. You've probably noticed that when you're going through a challenging time, your natural inclination is to reach out to another woman. When we talk with our biological sister, or a chosen sister of our heart, we feel less alone. Knowing that we can count on our sister in a time of crisis or to celebrate good news brings great comfort. With our sisters, we can ramble through our internal landscape—no agenda, no planned outcome—just to listen and be listened to.

What's more, our sisters are a storehouse of our most treasured memories: snuggling under the covers in the middle of the night, taking baths together, rehearsing for school plays and piano recitals, experiencing family vacations, shared secrets, first bras, first menstruation, first boyfriends.... These collages of memories create the foundation upon which every sister relationship rests.

Sisters share. We share the joy of a first love, the pain of rejection. We often entrust one another with our most private thoughts: to them we can confess to ludicrous things we've done, along with never-uttered aspirations and dreams. Our connection with our sister is strengthened because we share the gifts that are reaped from having survived a family's darkest hours. Sisters often share our burdens as well as our joys; the pain along with the triumphs.

And let us not forget our brothers. Even though we can rarely discuss uniquely feminine issues with brothers in the same way we can with women, we still share a unique biological and emotional connection. So we've devoted a chapter especially for brothers, those special souls who first helped teach us about the opposite sex by showing us how to climb trees, how to wrestle as well as any boy, and how to follow instead of lead on the dance floor.

The stories in *Chicken Soup for the Sister's Soul* are all about love, overcoming obstacles, family, growing up, moving away from home, becoming parents, losing parents and the bond between generations. We hope that you will cherish these stories as much as we do. We're thrilled to celebrate this unique relationship. We hope this collection will reveal the magic of sisterhood and inspire you to appreciate how truly blessed you are to be and have a sister.

1

A SISTER'S LOVE AND SUPPORT

Where we love is home,
Home that our feet may leave,
But not our hearts.

Oliver Wendell Holmes

Revenge of the Fifth-Grade Girls

An older sister helps one remain half child, half woman.

Anonymous

A mother cannot force her daughters to become sisters. She cannot make them be friends or companions or even cohorts in crime. But, if she's very lucky, they find sisterhood for themselves and have one true ally for life. My daughters did not seem likely candidates for sisterly love. They are as different as night and day, and as contrary as any two girls living under the same roof can possibly manage.

My youngest daughter, Laura, is smart, athletic and good at most everything she tries. But for her, friendships are tricky. When, at seven years old, she was thrust into the world of lunch pals and sleepovers, she struggled to survive.

Catherine, on the other hand, sits at the top of the elementary school pecking order. A bright, popular and beautiful fifth-grader, she is usually surrounded by a bevy of adoring girlfriends. When you are in second grade, a word or nod from a fifth-grade girl is the greatest thing that can happen. But Catherine and her friends seldom noticed her sister's valiant attempts to be noticed.

One hectic morning, while getting ready for school, both girls began begging for a new hairstyle. Sighing, I gathered brushes, combs and pins and quickly created new looks. I braided Laura's wispy locks into a snazzy side-braid. I combed Catherine's shiny black hair into a sleek, French twist. They twirled in front of the mirror, pleased with what I'd done.

Laura bounced out the door, swinging her braid proudly. But at school, one girl pointed at her and whispered to the other girls. Then the girl walked up to Laura and asked in a scathing tone, "What's with the stinking braid?"

Laura crumbled. After getting permission from her teacher, she went to the bathroom, where she sat and cried in an empty stall. Then she splashed cold water on her face and bravely returned to the classroom—braid intact.

That afternoon, she broke my heart with her sad tale. *How could I have sent her out wearing a stinking braid? How could I have set her back in her meager attempts to fit in with the other girls?* I fought back my tears as I drove my girls home. Hearing her sister's sorrow, Catherine sat in stony silence, and as I often do, I wished they had the kind of bond that would allow them to reach out to each other. I barely noticed Catherine spent more time on the phone than usual that evening.

The next afternoon, when I pulled to the front of the carpool line, I discovered a small miracle had occurred. There stood Laura, surrounded by the smartest, cutest, most popular fifth-grade girls. My tiny daughter glowed with utter astonishment as they twirled her around, complimented her and focused a brilliant light of attention upon her. And, to my amazement, every single one wore a side-braid, exactly like the one Laura had worn the day before. *Ten stinking braids*, I thought, as I tried to swallow the lump lodged in my throat.

"I don't know what happened!" exclaimed Laura, clambering into the van. "I looked up, and all the girls were wearing my braid." She grinned all the way home, arms wrapped around skinny knees, reliving her short life's happiest moment.

I glanced at Catherine in the rearview mirror, and I think she winked at me. I'm not sure.

Carolyn Magner Mason

A Gift of Love

To be my best I need you swimming beside me.

Mariah Burton Nelson

"It's time," my sister whispered, and I was instantly awake, my heart pounding frantically in my chest. It was 4:00 A.M., and I wondered how I could have ever slept so late. After all, it was Christmas morning. I should have been awake hours ago.

We crept down the hall as quickly as we could. In the back of the house, our parents slept peacefully. I had been waiting for this day all year, marking off the days on my calendar as they passed, one by one. I had watched every Christmas special on TV, from Charlie Brown to Rudolph, and now that Christmas morning was finally here, I could hardly contain myself. I wanted to laugh, I wanted to play and, perhaps most of all, I wanted to rip open my presents.

As we approached the den, my sister put a single finger to her lips and whispered, "Santa might still be here." I nodded in complete understanding. At six, I knew all about Santa and his magic. At eleven, my sister was trying to give me my dream.

When we finally walked into the den, my first instinct was to rush toward the presents that were stacked oh-so-carefully around the room, but something made me hesitate. Instead of rushing forward, I stared in wonder at the room, wanting this single moment to last as long as it could. My sister stood quietly beside me, and we stared at the beautiful tree that we had decorated together weeks before. The lights shimmered, the ornaments sparkled, and our golden angel sat just slightly off-center on the top of the tree. It was the most perfect sight I'd ever seen.

On a nearby table, the cookies that we'd left for Santa were gone, and a small note read, "Thank you. Merry Christmas!"

My eyes widened in amazement at the note, for I was sure that I had finally found real proof of the jolly man's existence. Yet before I could truly marvel over the letter, my sister was handing me a small package. "It's from me," she whispered with a shy smile.

With trembling fingers, I slowly opened the package, carefully preserving the green bow. Inside, I found my sister's favorite necklace. It was a small heart on a golden chain. She had received the present from our grandfather two years before. My eyes filled at the sight. Santa's note was forgotten.

She put her arm around me. "He was going to give you one this year, but—" she stopped, and carefully wiped her eyes, "he just did not get a chance." He had died on Easter morning—the heart attack had been a harsh shock to our family. Our mother still cried quietly when she thought no one was watching. My sister squared her slender shoulders with a brave air. "So, I thought you might like to have mine."

I held the necklace as if it were made of the finest gold in the world. It seemed to shine even brighter than the lights on our tree.

"Let me help you," she said as she moved to put the necklace around my neck.

The small heart felt warm against my skin, almost like it was alive. In my mind, I could see my grandfather. He'd loved Christmas, and he had always given each of us a special surprise on Christmas day.

"Consider this his surprise," my sister told me as if she'd read my mind.

I grabbed her hand and held onto her with all of the strength that I possessed.

When our parents finally made their way into the den two hours later, they saw a beautiful Christmas tree, a dozen unopened gifts, and two sisters holding each other tight.

Cindy Beck

Spit Promises

*It is the friends that you can call at 4:00 A.M.
that matter.*

Marlene Dietrich

With five years difference in our ages, people still said
how uncanny it was for us to look so much alike. My sister and I shared a lot of the same facial features and, of
course, we both have long, red hair. Well, at least I had
hair until I started chemotherapy. My long red locks fell
from my head in clumps as the treatments went on.

I touched my now-bald head. Fresh tears sprang to my
eyes. People would not say we looked alike now. My sister
Marlanea was flying in from Montana to see me. She did-
n't know how bad I was going to look. I wanted to prepare
her for the shock or protect her from what she was going
to see. I had always watched over her, trying to keep her
safe and out of harm's way. She was born on my fifth
birthday. Our mother said she was my birthday present. I
took that seriously, and I loved her with all my heart.

We went through our growing-up years inseparable.
We were each other's best companions. Our parents used

to tell us that we should have been twins for how much we resembled each other, for how close we were.

We even thought alike. When we were shopping, we would buy each other small gifts—from T-shirts to coffee cups—but most of the time we bought each other the same thing. We shared a connection that was beyond most people's understanding.

Now adults, we live in different states. She called me on the phone, and all I said was "Hello." Instantly, she said, "I know something is wrong. Tell me. What is it?"

No longer amazed at her uncanny ability to tell when something is wrong, I told her, at eight o'clock that morning, I had to put our family pet to sleep. Together in silence, we cried. Tears I could not shed earlier that morning now flowed freely as I talked on the phone with my sister.

Since finding out that I have cancer, she has called almost daily. Concern always in her voice, but cheerful nonetheless. She has sent me a funny card every week, a bright ray of hope that makes me believe life will be okay again.

During one tearful phone conversation she told me she knew for sure that I would not die from this intruder called cancer.

"Oh how do you know?" I asked through my tears.

"Because when we were really small, we made a spit promise that we could only die if the other sister was ready to die, too. And I'm not ready to die yet so neither can you."

We never discussed what would happen if we broke a spit promise. But we both knew that it had to be serious.

I heard her cab pull up in front of my house. My sister, my friend, had arrived.

With trembling hands I reached up and touched my bald head once more before I opened the door to my best friend—my sister.

There she was, the sun shining behind her, lighting her up like the angel I had always thought her to be. There she was in her tight jeans and a T-shirt, wearing a hat that read, "I'm having a bad hair day." We both smiled.

"Hello sister," I said.

"Hello sister," she replied.

She raised her hand and removed her hat. My sister had shaved her head. We stood there crying and laughing and hugging.

"We still look like sisters," was all she said.

"I love you," was all that I could say.

I shut my eyes and said a silent prayer, *Thank you God for my life. Thank you God in heaven for my sister. Thank you Mother for my gift.*

Dawn Braulick

For Better or For Worse®

by Lynn Johnston

Diane's Walk

For attractive lips, speak words of kindness. For lovely eyes, seek out the good in people. For poise, walk with the knowledge you'll never walk alone.

Audrey Hepburn

Diane and her sister were only eighteen months apart in age, but complete opposites. Diane was outgoing and daring. A smile often crinkled her freckled nose and lit up her wide brown eyes. Both in and out of school, she could be found surrounded by a group of giggling, boisterous friends. Her sister, though, was quiet and shy. Her eyes were blue, and hidden behind a pair of glasses. She preferred to spend her time alone reading.

These two very different girls shared a yellow upstairs bedroom. They fought and argued, threatened and cried. They even drew a line of demarcation down the middle of their yellow room. Life was not harmonious.

But time passed and the girls grew up. They went to college. Diane got a job and her own apartment near Washington, D.C. Her sister married young and had two children. Their lives flowed in separate directions.

Then, when they were in their fifties, Diane's sister was diagnosed with breast cancer.

Diane felt powerless and frustrated. She wanted to do something to help. When she heard about an organized walk that would raise breast cancer research money, she signed up without hesitation, determined to make a difference.

Diane wrote letters to her friends, neighbors and relatives, asking them to sponsor her. And she began training after work and on the weekends. All autumn she walked—short distances at first, then farther and farther. She donned a backpack, stuck a pompom on her orange baseball cap, and added miles as the weeks went on. She walked in the rain, in the snow, through slush and cold. Five miles. Ten. Spring arrived. Fifteen miles, then twenty in a day. She walked over five hundred miles, just to get ready.

And she collected donations from her many friends to find a cure for breast cancer. She raised over $7,000.

The weekend of the walk, her sister and brother-in-law drove from out of state to cheer her on. And Diane, a fifty-four-year-old woman who had never done anything like that before, walked the entire sixty-mile course to the finish line in downtown Washington, D.C.

While the flags at the base of the Washington Monument fluttered in the sunshine, and the music swelled over the crowd and into the warm spring air, Diane's sister stood watching as wave after wave of walkers in blue T-shirts marched triumphantly over the hill. But she saw only one person—the woman in the orange pompom cap who had walked so far for her.

This story of love and generosity is true. I know, because those were my blue eyes searching the crowd from behind my glasses, and Diane, the woman in the orange pompom cap, is my sister.

C. Michele Davis

A Promise to Roxanne

For there is no friend like a sister
In calm or stormy weather;
To cheer one on the tedious way,
To fetch one if one goes astray,
To lift one if one totters down,
To strengthen whilst one stands.

Christina Georgina Rossetti

"Breakfast!" I call and within seconds, the floor above me shakes as feet gallop down the steps. And as I turn, I see the photograph. It's of the boys sitting with their mother. Her arms are around them. *Roxanne*, I think, *your arms are still around them.*

Although my brother Ross was the oldest, Roxanne, the middle one, was always my rock. "Be strong," she'd tell me after our parents divorced. Somehow, there was something spiritual about Roxanne. Her words of comfort always made me feel better.

Justin was her first child; two years later, Shaun was born. And when I'd watch Roxanne cuddle with them, I'd think, *Someday I want to have two boys, too.*

But Roxanne's life wasn't perfect. She got divorced and I moved in to help so she could go to work and school.

"Aunt Rhonda, watch me!" Justin would cry from his bicycle. And Shaun would crawl onto my lap with his teddy bear. Later, I moved out and into a life of my own. And Roxanne met a man I didn't care for before finding Tony, who loved her and the boys. To my joy, they married. But something was happening to Roxanne.

"I fell asleep in class today," she'd say. "And my fever won't go away." Finally she went to the doctor.

"It's advanced AIDS," the doctor said. A shocked hush fell over the room. Ross and Mom went to embrace her while I stood there shaking in disbelief.

But though Roxanne cried, she didn't look surprised. That man she'd dated, the one I didn't like, he had been an IV drug user.

"Don't cry for me," she said, "look at all I've enjoyed." Then she turned to me, as if she'd already thought about it. "Rhonda, I want you to take my boys."

Oh Roxanne, I thought. *You won't die. They'll find a cure!* I went home and cried through the night.

All we told the boys was that their mother was sick. We wanted to spare them the grief for as long as possible. But maybe it was the not knowing that made them angry. It wasn't long before they started playing hooky. From Roxanne's window I'd watch them with their new friends, kids you could tell were trouble. "These are difficult years," I told Justin. "But don't give in. Remember who you are." My heart constricted. *They're the sons of a mother who's dying,* I thought.

Then one day while I was away on business, I got a call from Roxanne: "Justin stole a car, and someone gave Shaun marijuana!"

When I raced to her house, Roxanne's cheeks were wet

with tears. "I'm too sick to care for them, and Tony is caring for me. They need you now!"

"Now?" I stood trembling.

"I want them to be good boys," she wept. "I want them to be fine young men." I looked into her sad, pleading eyes. She needed me. How could I let her down?

I wasn't there when Roxanne told the boys that they were losing their mother and would be leaving their home. But in the darkness of my living room, I imagined their tears, and wondered, *Can I ever be enough to help them?*

I didn't have time to worry; two weeks later I was awarded custody. Nights were hard, especially after the boys had spent the day with Roxanne. Shaun's arms would wrap around me and I could feel his tears against my shoulders. "I'm afraid, and I want to go home," he'd cry.

"It's okay," I'd whisper. "Your mom and I love you." Out of the corner of my eye, I saw Justin just standing there in his pajamas. He'd told me firmly that he wouldn't cry.

As Roxanne worsened, I knew I had to be strong for them. "Homework first," I'd say flipping off the TV. "But Mom lets us!" they'd protest. "No church!" they said. "Yes, church," I replied.

And though at first they went with long faces, over time, they looked forward to seeing their new friends. There were fewer battles, and visits with Roxanne were calmer. I'd watch as they sat on the bed chatting about school. Roxanne would take them in her arms, and from over their shoulders, her eyes would meet mine and she'd mouth the words "Thank you."

It was at church that I met Jerry. When Roxanne met him, she must have thought, *This man may raise my children.* I was thinking the same thing. That spring, he was the one to play ball with the boys when Roxanne was too ill for them to visit. "I asked God for this one more summer," she told me in June. "It brings me peace to know how their life is going to be when I am gone." Five days after autumn began, Roxanne joined God.

In the weeks that followed, the boys and I talked about heaven. "She's our guardian angel," they'd tell me. And we shared stories about Roxanne. *Memories will keep her alive,* I'd think.

Soon our tears were replaced with hugs. And the next June, the boys stood at my side as Jerry and I took our vows.

Today, if we're out and someone says to the boys, "Your parents. . ." I always correct them. "We're Aunt Rhonda and Jerry," I say. I could never take Roxanne's place—and I don't want to. I just want to raise the boys to be the fine young men she wanted them to be.

"I'm working tonight," Justin reminds me now at breakfast. He's sixteen and saving for college.

"Love you," Shaun says, leaving the table. He's fourteen and wants to be a marine biologist. I know his dreams may change a million times. But he has dreams!

"Your mom would be so proud of you," I sometimes say as the boys head out the door. They smile, and in their fresh, confident grins, so full of the promise of life, I see my sister still, and I know she's watching over them.

We've come so far, I think, and I know we've never walked alone. God has guided our family. And Roxanne, we *all* feel your arms around us.

Rhonda Adkins
As told to Carla Merolla
As appeared in Woman's World

Are You Sure?

The heart has its reasons, which reason knows nothing of.

Blaise Pascal

One day in second grade, I raised my hand and asked to be excused from class. I walked down a corridor to the fourth-grade class, knocked on the door and asked to talk with my sister. In tears, I whispered to her, "I forgot my lunch."

Without hesitation my sister said, "Wait here." She grabbed her brown bag, walked back to where I was standing and handed me half of her peanut butter and jelly sandwich, half of her crackers, half of her grapes— even half of her oatmeal cookies!

"Here, take this," she said.

"Are you sure?" I asked. "Even your cookies?"

She smiled and nodded yes.

"Thank you," I said, hugging the lunch as I returned to my room.

Years later, I stood up for her in her wedding, and she stood up for me in mine. Shortly after that I was diagnosed with endometriosis. I began the journey of medications and surgeries, hoping to get some relief from the pain and to preserve my ability to bear children.

Meanwhile, this same sister became pregnant. While she was preparing for birth, I was preparing for my fourth surgery; a hysterectomy.

This time my loss was bigger than a lunch, and my sister couldn't rescue me. Still, when she and her husband asked my husband and me to become legal guardians of their newborn daughter if something should happen to them, across the years my heart could hear her say, "Here, take this."

"Are you sure?" I asked.

She smiled and nodded yes.

"Thank you," I whispered, hugging their beautiful daughter close to me.

Penny Perrone

Pictures

Blessed are those who believe and see through the eyes of a child.

Author Unknown

I never had a sister, just two younger brothers. Now that we are adults, we get along well, even though it seems as though I spent much of my childhood trying to get rid of them. I wasn't exactly what you would call a benevolent older sister. But with a sister, I thought it would have been different. I envied the relationship that a few of my friends had with their sisters. When I had two daughters of my own, I hoped that they would have what I had only dreamed of.

It didn't start out that way at first. When the girls were young, although they got along most of the time, they weren't exactly soul mates. Maybe it was the difference in their ages—Shoshana was nearly five when Ilana was born—or maybe just a difference in personalities. As they got older, my dream of a special relationship between these two sisters seemed less important. After all, they were beautiful, bright children, and while they were not unusually close, they clearly loved each other.

But then, when I had almost forgotten the dream, things began to change.

It was June and Shoshana was fourteen, about to enter high school. Like many of the other teenagers in our small community, she had decided to attend a school in Chicago. The school had an excellent academic reputation, which helped offset our apprehension about sending our little girl nearly 100 miles away from home, with her coming home only on the weekends.

It was hard at first to think of our child so far away, but my husband and I knew it would be good for her, and we gradually got used to the idea.

But Ilana didn't.

Actually, I didn't know that at the time. I was preoccupied with Shoshana's needs, and I didn't really stop to think about the effect this would have on Ilana. She was only nine, and it didn't occur to me that she would have such strong feelings on the subject. After all, in only four more years Shoshana would be going off to college anyway. It just didn't seem like such a big difference to me. But it was to Ilana.

I wish I could say that I knew this because I had many long, heartfelt discussions with Ilana on this subject or because Ilana confided in me, or because she told Shoshana how she felt. But that would be a lie. I only found this out by accident.

One morning, about a week before Shoshana was scheduled to leave for her new school, I went into Ilana's room to put away some clean laundry. I found Ilana sitting on the floor, surrounded by several piles of photo - graphs. I looked more closely, I saw that they were the pictures from our family's summer camping trip. I hadn't even seen the pictures yet. They must have arrived in the mail just that morning. I was mildly annoyed that Ilana had just taken them up to her room without telling me, but what I saw next made me really angry. Ilana had taken scissors and glue, and was carefully cutting out the figures on some of the pictures and pasting them onto a sheet of pink construction paper.

"What are you doing?" I yelled. "Stop that! Why are you cutting up those pictures?"

I didn't wait for an answer. I just grabbed the pictures and stormed out of the room. I was too angry to talk to Ilana at that moment. I just threw the pictures on the dresser in my room and stormed off.

Ilana stayed in her room the rest of the morning. When it got to be lunchtime, I decided that I should go up and talk with her. By now, I was more curious than angry. I wanted to know why she had been cutting up the pictures.

When I opened the door to Ilana's room, I saw that she had fallen asleep on the bed. Lying beside her was the pink construction paper. I picked it up and turned it over. About half of the paper was covered with a collage of photographs that Ilana had cut out and assembled from the family vacation pictures, as well as a few older pictures from several years ago. Every picture was of her and Shoshana. Here they were, as infant and toddler, in the bathtub together. Here they were, in front of the mirror, with my lipstick and high heels. And in another, Shoshana was holding onto the back of Ilana's bike as she learned to ride without training wheels. I remembered that day. Ilana had come running into the house, beaming with pride. "I did it, Mommy!" she exclaimed. "Shoshana taught me!"

I sat down on the bed, and Ilana stirred and opened her eyes. "Hi, honey," I said gently.

Her lower lip quivered. "I'm sorry, Mommy," she said.

"I know, honey," I said. "It's okay. I'm sorry I got so

angry. "What were you making, anyway?" I asked her.

She took the pink paper from my hand and studied it. "It's for Shoshana," she said finally. "She can hang it up on the wall in her new room."

"That's a good idea," I agreed.

Then she looked up at me. "She's going to be really far away now. And she's going to be really busy; she'll have a lot of homework and a lot of new friends."

I reached out and hugged her. I knew what she was thinking, but it was too painful to say it out loud. *How could I reassure her that things wouldn't change so much? How to tell her with confidence that her sister wouldn't forget about her?* After all, I wondered those very same things myself. I didn't have the words to comfort her, but Ilana's next question provided the answer.

"Do you think she'll like it?" she asked. "I shouldn't have used pink. Shoshana hates pink. I like pink; that's why I picked it, but it's not for me."

"I think she'll love it," I answered gently. "She'll look at it every day and she'll think of you because you like pink." And I knew she would.

When Shoshana moved into her new room, it took her several weeks before she was settled in, and found places for all of her things. But she hung up the pink paper the very first day.

And Ilana was right: Shoshana was very busy those first few months. We spoke on the phone every night, but we only saw her on weekends, and then she had homework and wanted to spend time with her friends. But she had that pink paper to remind her. And she remembered well. I found this out by accident, too. One evening, a few weeks after the start of the school year, I walked into the den. Ilana was sitting at the computer and she started giggling.

"What's so funny?" I asked. Ilana pointed to an e-mail from Shoshana.

"Remember the time I was teaching you to ride without training wheels?" the message began. "I let go of the bike, and you couldn't steer and you rode right through Mrs. Parker's flower bed. You squashed all of her tulips." By Thanksgiving, Ilana had a stack of e-mails an inch high from her sister. Each one started out with a reference to one of the pictures.

It took a physical distance between them to bring them closer emotionally. During the four years that Shoshana was away, Ilana became a teenager herself. The two girls found that they had more in common than just memories and a shared childhood. But it was precisely those memories and those shared experiences that formed the basis for their friendship, and that gave them something to build on. All of those years, when I had all but forgotten about the bond that I hoped they would develop, it was happening right under my nose and I didn't even recognize it.

When Shoshana went away to college, Ilana was just starting high school. She and Shoshana continued their frequent e-mail conversations. Ilana printed out and saved every one. And when Shoshana moved into her new dorm room, the first thing she hung up on the wall was the pink picture.

Last summer Shoshana got married. Ilana was her maid of honor. We have a whole album of beautiful pictures, including many of our two daughters together. But Ilana gave Shoshana and her new husband a picture of her own. It's a lovely picture of the two sisters, taken in front of our house on a soft spring morning. And on the frame, there is a lovely inscription: "A sister is a supportive companion, loyal and loving, protective and kind. A keeper of secrets, a one of a kind. A true friend in thought, and provider of memories."

When Shoshana and her husband moved into their

new apartment I went over to help them unpack and settle in. The apartment was in chaos, filled with suitcases, partially opened gifts and half-eaten pizza. Shoshana had just started unpacking, and she had carefully laid out the important things the young couple would need as they started their new life together— toothbrushes, linens, a frying pan.

And of course, Ilana's pink picture.

We fill many roles throughout life, but just because we become something new—wives and mothers, for example, we never stop being what we were as children— daughters and sisters. Shoshana is a wife now. One day, God willing, she'll be a mother. But she is wise enough to know that the adult she is today owes much to the child she once was. She fills her home with the things of her own choosing that make her happiest, that bring her joy and remind her of those she loves and who love her. She and her sister still have time together, to giggle and share secrets and just be sisters with their own private language. There is enough love between them to share with others. Shoshana and her husband are in the process of writing their own history, of making memories together that they will share with their children and grandchildren in the years to come.

If she is very lucky, my daughter Shoshana will, one day, come across a child of hers cutting up pictures on the bedroom floor. And if I know Shoshana, she'll look at an old faded pink paper that will be framed and hung on the wall of some room in her house and she'll do what I should have done.

She'll smile to herself and softly close the door.

Phyllis Nutkis

Happy Mother's Day!

When my kids become unruly, I use a nice, safe playpen. When they're finished, I climb out.

Erma Bombeck

So you're having a baby, we know it's a boy,
A sweet, cuddly creature to hug and enjoy,
He will be your own blood, and he'll love and adore you,
But have no illusions of what lies before you.

As the time for my nephew to come quickly nears,
As a sister who's now been a mom for ten years,
I can tell you some things that I've learned and for free,
As the battle-scarred, happy, proud mother of three.

First you'll have to invest in a big, roomy car,
And the more they can hold then the better they are,
For your stroller and car seat and big Portacrib,
For your bag with the diapers, some clothes and a bib.

Some HandiWipes, pins and some lotion for rash,
Plastic bags for wet diapers, wet clothes and the trash,

To distract him some crackers, a rattle, a toy,
And those plugs for his mouth that us mothers enjoy.

A luxurious pillow for a small baby seat,
Some cozy, wee booties for small baby feet,
You'll need blankets and then by the time that you're
    through,
You are lucky if there is a space left for you.

You will have some important decisions to make,
About whether your diapers are real or are fake,
Ecologically speaking, our state is now drastic,
So you should use cloth and relinquish the plastic.

But then sometimes you might become selfish and mean,
As the smell of the diaper pail makes you turn green,
And say, "Screw all the birds and the earth on the wane,
If I pin one more diaper I may go insane."

So you opt for the plastic, ignore those who chide,
And prepare your kid's supper with care and with pride,
You grind up the apples direct from the tree,
So your baby is healthy, preservative-free.

This insanity lasts for about ninety days,
Then the mother will stop these ridiculous ways,
At the market no critics can hurt or disturb her,
As she happily fills up her wagon with Gerber.

First new babies wear cotton alone on their skin,
'Cause it breathes and allows life's good things to get in,
They wear rompers and booties from Dior—the top,
And ensembles that cost ninety dollars a pop.

When the baby is seven months old Mom dispenses,
With all of the fancy stuff, comes to her senses,
She watches the kid destroy all that he nears,
Now she does all her shopping at Penney's and Sears.

Your inaugural shopping trip with your new child,
Will be challenging, dangerous, exciting and wild,
You'll spend hours in search of a restroom through halls,
'Cause all babies get hungry when near shopping malls.

They are also inclined to save up for this outing,
With all of their cares and their woes and their shouting,
And the people will whisper, they'll point and they'll sneer,
"What a terrible mother, the poor little dear."

You will find that the biggest of all of your cares,
Will be how to get baby and stroller upstairs,
Bag and baby in one arm, the stroller behind,
Without losing the bag or the kid or your mind.

When you've shopped and you're driving back home
    down the street,
You will notice the baby's asleep in his seat,
He is blissfully napping and make no mistake,
That at home when you're tired, he'll be wide awake.

There are numerous things that you really should know,
About what he will do as he starts in to grow,
About playmates and potties and school PTAs,
Birthday parties and Christmas and kid holidays.

You will need more advice because you're a greenhorn,
But perhaps we should wait till at least the kid's born,
But I'm anxious to know who this new soul will be,
Who is coming to you, by extension to me.

Will he be like our family or like your hubby's kid?
Will he be a high-strung type or sweetly placid?
Will he be like our brother was, pensive and sad,
Will he be a cantankerous type like our dad?

Will he have your warm nature, so patient and true,
Well, we know he'll be swell since he's coming from you,
And for now, my sweet sister, I write just to say,
Please enjoy your last peaceful and calm Mother's Day!

Victoria E. Thompson

We Chose to Be Friends

A sister is nagging and needling, whispers and whisperings, bribery and thumpings, borrowings, breakings, kisses and cuddlings, lendings, surprises, defendings and comfortings, welcoming home.

Pam Brown

When my sister was four years old, she thought it would be a good idea to climb onto the top of a Dumpster. A group of us kids were playing nearby when I heard her screaming. I ran to grab her, and like the mothers who suddenly have enough strength to lift entire cars off their trapped children, my instincts took over. I was her sister, and I was only six, but the sight of blood and the sound of her earsplitting screams made me move at a superhuman pace. Without stopping to think, I immediately hijacked a skateboard from one of the other kids, positioned my sister on it and set out as fast as my little legs could travel for the next three blocks. I ran the whole way home, crouching down low enough so that I could push her and keep her balanced on the board at the same time. My leg and arm muscles ached as I navigated the sidewalks, shoving that sister-laden board over every crack and rut—a big sister on a big mission. I was out of breath as I rounded the final corner to our apartment building. When I reached the stairs, I yelled up to my mom with a scream she claims can still give her chills.

Tawna ended up being fine. I, on the other hand, relished being the hero for a while. Over the years, my mom loved to tell the story of my little sister's rescue. I guess I *had* been pretty resourceful for a six-year-old. But she was my first best friend, and I would have done anything for her.

And it went both ways. At my ninth birthday party, a posse of us girls, my little sister furiously trying to keep up behind us, roller-skated to the top of a steep street in our neighborhood. It bewilders me how much less daunting that "slope" is today, but back then it was a monster. I rolled, no *flew*, down that hill. I felt invincible. Until my skate caught on a pebble and I was launched through the air. The rest is pretty blurry. When I finally landed, Tawna stepped right in and organized my trek to safety. Like ants collectively marching food toward their ant hill, the girls stood me upright and wheeled me all the way home on my skates.

I nearly broke my arm, but I was fine. Tawna was applauded for her fine wheeling skills. She loved the attention but hadn't helped me for that reason. I was her first best friend, and there was no limit to what she would do for me.

Of course, ours was more complicated than the typical friendship. There was that whole imaginary-line-in-the-back-seat-of-the-car thing. You know the one, constructed to keep your wayward sibling contained on *her side*. There was the hair pulling and name calling, sure. And the pleas for mercy when a tickling match would go on so long it became torture. We even went through a stage whereby we were constantly compelled to try to bite each other's noses off. And then there was my personal favorite threat, "Ooooh . . . I'm gonna *tell.*" All to the soundtrack of my parents' repeated cries of, "Knock it off, you two!"

But there were other, kinder, moments, too. When we were little and both of us happened to be crying, for instance, one of us would stop and let the other cry. It wasn't like we took turns or anything; we just seemed to naturally figure out who needed to cry more.

I let her borrow my cool clothes (which really weren't so cool now that I look back), and I would give her fashion tips since I was convinced she shouldn't go to school representing our good name looking like a Cabbage Patch Kid. She patiently indulged me when I needed to analyze every last gesture of that guy in second period—even though guys still had "cooties" to her.

When I lost my first love she held me tight and told me I would be okay. She wanted to yell and scream at him for hurting me—but didn't. When friends treated her badly, I let her vent her anger and told her it would all work out. I wanted to tell those "friends" a thing or two about friendship—but didn't. When I graduated high school, she cried because she was proud of me and because she was losing me. When she was crowned homecoming queen I smiled because I knew she had finally outgrown that Cabbage Patch look and because I wasn't the only one to recognize her inner beauty and quiet strength.

We carry each other's secrets and hold each other's deepest hopes. We pick each other up when we are down. And we do our best to wheel each other to safety. We have somehow been able to parlay a close sibling bond into a symbiotic friendship. And that makes me proud. We had to be sisters. We chose to be friends.

Tasha Boucher

Playing Cupid

*What is the best gift you ever received? Better
still, what is the best gift you ever gave? Perhaps
you will recall that in each instance, the best gift
was the one that was tied with the heartstrings of
the giver, one that included part of self.*

Wanda Fulton

I was lying on the slick tile floor of my college dorm
room chatting with my younger sister (by a year and a
half) about the latest gossip in our little community while
twirling the black phone cord around my fingers. Deep in
the mire of love, she was gushing about an all-important
upcoming date—she and Mr. Be-All-End-All's first anni -
versary of dating. She was in a state—would he remember, would he forget? If he did forget, what did that mean
about their relationship? And God help him if he messed
this up. A helpless romantic myself, I filed away this tid-
bit of information, not having the heart to mention that of
course he was going to forget. He was a guy. He might
have a general idea of when they started dating, but the
odds were good that he didn't have that all-important

date scribbled in his diary, surrounded by intertwining hearts and other symbols of true love.

I took pity on the poor boy. After all, my sister was head over heels in love—the least I could do was give him the small break that was in my power. As was my custom, I headed for home the following Friday, which, as the fates would have it, was *the* day. Making a last stop on my way out of the college town, I purchased a bouquet of mixed flowers and gently stowed them away for the five-hour drive.

Pulling into the gravel parking lot of our little high school, I headed in to say "hi" to friends and see how my sister's day had evolved—as it turned out, not so well. It seemed as though her significant other had blown it off completely. No card, no whispered sweet nothings, no acknowledgment. The way I saw it, no surprise, but I knew she was crushed and I was all set to play Cupid.

Leaving my sister, I sought out the tarnished hero. Not in such high spirits himself, he greeted me with a somber expression. Casually, I mentioned that I knew the importance of the day and that I just happened to have a lovely arrangement of flowers sitting unclaimed in my vehicle, and that if he could think of a good use for them, he was more than welcome to nonchalantly remove them from their spot of waiting.

A lifeline thrown to him, he was off for the vehicle—and I was off to distract my sister. The rest I would learn later that evening as my reenchanted sister told her story over and again for any and all who would listen. He hadn't forgotten! He had merely acted that way to surprise her. She had talked to me after school, and then he had asked her to go for a ride with him. They had gone up to his parents', and he had a bouquet of absolutely beautiful flowers waiting for her. Could we believe it?! Wasn't it just too perfect?!

Didn't we think they were just beautiful?

I nodded, I smiled, I acknowledged her as the luckiest girl in the world, but I'm not sure whose heart was fuller, hers or mine.

One thing puzzled her—she wasn't sure how he had gotten the flowers (the closest flower shop being a half-hour drive from home). She was guessing his mother had made the trip—he wouldn't tell. My little sister was confused, but nonetheless ecstatic. He had *remembered!*

Her knight in shining armor had regained his luster, and the day would go down in her diary as a successful step in their relationship.

That was eight years ago. On August 1, my sister and Mr. Be-All-End-All (who, by the way, is a true romantic in his own right) celebrated their third wedding anniversary, and the following day, we all gathered for the celebration of my niece's first birthday.

The part I played in their romance was miniscule, but it made my sister happy, and that's really the only thing that matters.

Chera Lee Bammerlin

My Family Was Separated

My family was separated and placed into foster care when I was five years old. We grew up living in separate homes, never knowing each other. As I grew older, the only memory that remained of my family was of a tall, slender woman always being there to comfort me. In my mind, this woman was my mother. I believed that some-day she would return and life would be normal again. She was in my prayers throughout my childhood.

On Thanksgiving Day, which was also my forty-fifth birthday, there wasn't much to celebrate. My son was moving to another state, and I was feeling not only older but also sad to be losing the closeness of the only family I knew. A card arrived in the mail with a return name and address of someone I didn't recognize. Opening it, I found a Thanksgiving wish with a short note reading, "I was thinking of you on your birthday, Mom." The memories of the tall, slender woman flashed through my mind. My feelings felt like a roller coaster going from anger to extreme happiness in moments. *If this was my mother, why had she abandoned us? Why didn't she ever come to get me? Why would she be writing now, after all these years?* At the same time, I wanted to hear her voice and feel her warmth.

For two weeks, the card lay on the table tearing at my heart. Finally, summing up the courage to call information, I got her number. Holding my breath and trying to calm my heart, I dialed. On the fifth ring, I felt relief that no one was answering. Then, just as I was about to hang up, a voice from the past said, "Hello." Unsure of what to say, I asked to whom I was speaking. It turned out to be my older sister who was cleaning out our mother's apartment. Two weeks after sending the card, Mom had died.

As we talked, reacquainting ourselves, I asked what my mom looked like. My sister was surprised that I didn't remember. She told me Mom was a very short, stocky lady. *Then who was the tall, slender woman that I remember?*

As we continued our conversation, our family and our life began returning to me.

My older sister was seven when our mother left us. For two years, she was the one caring for us, keeping us safe, cooking our meals and drying our tears. She was the one holding me at night when nightmares woke me, singing me songs, wiping my tears when I was scared. It was my sister who told me to run and lock myself in the bathroom as she tried to keep foster care from taking us away.

We talked for hours that night, reminiscing about the past. She had found our brother and baby sister, and we made plans to reunite after forty years of separation. Neither one of us wanted the night to end, but as dawn approached we finally gave in. "By the way," I asked before hanging up, "how tall are you?"

She answered, "Five-foot-nine, why?"

"Because you were the tall, slender woman who made the difference in my life." She was crying as I said, "Good night, I love you."

Nora Steuber-Tamblin

Comfort Zones

It is in the shelter of each other that people live.

Irish Proverb

Some years back I pored over black and white family photos in order to decipher mysteries of my past. My sister Kathleen and I didn't smile much. In each photo, whether we wore corduroy overalls or Grandma's finest hand-sewn dresses, my sister's arm is secured around my shoulders. Her tiny body posture shouts, "This is my sister. Leave her alone!" *From what,* I wondered, *was she protecting me?*

Then I began to remember.

I was no fan of bedtime. When we left our closet door open, the clothes by day became ghosts by night. The sprawling sweet potato vine in the pink bird cage planter reached for me. I covered my eyes. I didn't dare get up because of the snapping turtles under my bed. And when Dad came home, I'd lie there and listen to my parents fight. The thunder of Dad's belligerence. The lightning of Mom's terror. Plugging my ears didn't silence the storm. I tried to muffle my sobs in the pink comforter that Grandma made with the cherries hand-stitched on top.

Soon it was Kathleen's voice I heard. Standing next to my bed, she whispered, "Don't be afraid. Come and get in bed with me." I inched out of bed, careful not to disturb the turtles.

We climbed into my sister's twin bed. "Don't pay any attention to them. They won't hurt you."

"But I'm afraid they'll hurt each other."

"They won't. Moms and dads just get mad at each other sometimes."

"Do they hate each other?"

"I don't know, but they don't hate us." She was sixteen months wiser than I was.

She parted the pink- and white-striped café curtains and pointed toward the neighbor's house. "Hey, look! She didn't shut them yet."

Our neighbor's cuckoo clock hung on her wall in direct view of our bedroom window. Night after night, we'd hope with all our might that Barbara wouldn't pull her massive draperies before the cuckoo appeared.

"Look, they're getting closer."

The exquisite carved boy in lederhosen and girl in pinafore inched toward each other for a kiss. When their lips met, the cuckoo announced the hour. On summer nights we heard him. We always laughed. The show was over when Barbara pulled her drapes.

"Let's go to sleep now." Kathleen yawned, prompting a similar response in me. I'd fall asleep in the crook of her arm. Some mornings I'd wake up in the same position. She never complained.

Decades later when I was on the verge of my own divorce, my sister invited me to live with her. "You need a comfort zone right now." I agreed.

We were both teachers, and every day after school we walked six miles. I vented; she listened.

"I can always tell when you're upset," she'd say. "You start walking so fast I can't keep up with you. Why don't you just pretend the pavement is his face?"

I laughed. Then I walked hard and fast on the pavement portrait. Anger exited my body via the soles of my Nikes. "I love it!"

"I know how well it worked for me."

We lived close enough to hear each other's heart beat for nine months. At the end of the school year, she followed her heart to the ocean. Mine led me to the mountains. We've acknowledged we'll probably never live in the same state again.

When she came to visit last year, she followed me up a mountain on a horse—a major accomplishment for one with a lifelong fear of heights.

"I'm so proud of you, Kathleen!"

"I only thought I was going to die a couple times."

"You did? I didn't know that."

"Just like you didn't know I was scared to death when Mom and Dad fought."

"You were?"

"Sure, but I felt important and needed when you were scared. I couldn't let you down."

"I always thought you were the brave older sister." I hugged her hard.

Yesterday I had a touch of the blues. My family and friends seemed so far away. As I was trying to get over myself, the phone rang.

"Hi Sweetie!" I felt the arm around my shoulder as surely as if she were standing in the room with me. We talked for an hour. When I hung up, I was wrapped in her familiar comfort zone.

CLOSE TO HOME   JOHN McPHERSON

Seeing Everything

You can be boring and tedious with sisters, whereas you have to put on a good face with friends.

Deborah Moggach

"Connie," I whisper loudly, "wake up." By the way she moves, I can tell my younger sister is waking. I tap her on the forehead. She ignores me. "You're breathing too loud!" These words always work.

"What do you want? You want me dead? I have to breathe!" Connie always wakes up grumpy. "I want to sleep."

Connie doesn't know I have stuffed my dirty socks and underwear in her pillowcase. It is beyond me how she can rest her head on the pillow without noticing the lumps. I turn the pillow and place the dirty clothes on the bed side, not head side. I make sure not to do this too often, otherwise Connie will check her pillow before getting in bed. It's a lousy thing to do, and I'm not really *sorry* about waking her. I'm *sorry* I can't sleep, and she doesn't notice. I want Connie to wake up and talk with me. Our best conversations take place when the room is dark and the house is quiet. I don't understand how Connie can sleep and she doesn't understand why I put the dirty clothes in her pillowcase.

"Check your pillowcase, Connie." This always makes her angry.

"Why do you do this to me?" Connie asks while she pulls out my dirty socks.

"Because I love you." This isn't a lie, but the dirty clothes make it appear as such. I know it's a cruel thing to do, and it will definitely upset her. Most things, no matter how horrible or cruel, seem to pass without Connie expressing any emotion.

Connie looks me in the eyes and says, "You're sick."

Within an hour, I want to wake Connie and apologize, but her loud, sporadic breathing lets me know she is asleep and angry. She won't believe I am sorry because I will stuff her pillowcase again.

Connie sleeps. I don't. She doesn't know how long my nights are. I share a bed with a little sister who has loud, almost braggart breaths coming out of her mouth all night. I can't wake Connie and apologize because Dad apologizes that way, says he's sorry after doing something horrible, and then does it again. Connie and I talk about this before falling asleep.

"He doesn't mean it. He'll do it again, won't he?" I ask Connie.

"Probably. But Mom believes him."

"Do you, Connie?"

"No. He'll do it again."

Connie looks like she's falling asleep, but there's one more thing on my mind, the same thing that is on my mind every night.

"Connie, did I act like Dad today?"

"No! Quit asking me that."

In bed, I know Dad apologizes about being in jail

because he doesn't apologize for being drunk and screaming those horrible words at us. He breaks all the dishes and kitchen windows, but apologizes about being in jail because he knows it will hurt us when the neighbors and kids at school bring this up. They always find out through the newspaper and the radio.

He doesn't know how quiet the house is when he's in jail. On those nights we don't have to worry about him driving home drunk, or coming home at all. We don't set a place for him at the table. We even invite a neighbor friend over because we know the meal will be fun. And Dad will get a break from the factory and us. He doesn't need to apologize, but he will. Dad apologizes because when he's in jail he remembers his father who was always in jail and how that humiliated him.

Connie always says I didn't act like Dad, but Connie only speaks the truth in the middle of the night when the room is dark. During the day, when I've upset her, she'll say, "You're just like Dad!" But at night, she speaks the truth, and we lie in bed silently wondering when our lives will change, quietly hoping we'll always have each other for these nocturnal reassurances.

Diane Payne

Swing Set

When my oldest daughter, Anny, was a little girl, we had a swing set in the backyard. It was the kind with ladders on each side and bars across the top. A child was supposed to hang down from the bars, making her way across by putting one hand on a bar, then the other hand on the next bar and so on. At two years old, Anny's arms weren't strong enough nor long enough to enable her to do this alone. But she loved to pretend to do it with a parent holding her from beneath. It was extremely hard for me to play this game with her because it necessitated my hoisting her two-year-old frame onto my shoulders. I preferred to push her on the swing or play with her in the sandbox, reserving the bars for a special "Daddy/Anny only" activity.

But one day when Daddy was not around, Anny and I were playing outside on the swing set. For some reason, I left her alone for just a minute while I went inside. I wasn't gone very long but as I passed the kitchen window, I looked out to see my daughter standing next to the ladder. She appeared to be deep in thought, and for some reason, I waited to see what she would do next. She stood there a long time as if debating whether or not to climb up. She did. But then when she reached the top, she seemed to hesitate, knowing that without a parent underneath her, she wouldn't be able to swing from bar to bar in the conventional way. So she tried something else.

Carefully, Anny climbed on *top* of the bars. Crawling along on her hands and knees, she made her way over them instead of trying to swing under them. It was a process that took her about six feet off the ground—high enough for her to get hurt if she fell.

To this day, I don't know why but I did not run out to stand beneath my daughter, waiting to catch her if she fell. Instead I stayed where I was, in the kitchen, and just watched her through the window. It was one of the hardest things I've ever done.

Years later I was to always see that little girl on the swing set in my oldest daughter. She would always think long and hard before attempting anything new. But if she wanted to do it, she would try. Her methods aren't always conventional. Often, she has to find a different, more creative way to accomplish things because the usual way is out of her reach. Not everything comes easily to Anny, but she tries. And sometimes she is very successful.

Years later when Anny was six and her little sister Rachael was three, that swing set again showed me what my children were made of. But this time, it also showed me what the relationship between these two sisters was and what it would be for the rest of their lives.

Anny had long since mastered the art of going across the bars of that swing set—over them, under them—forwards and backwards. But Rachael was still at the stage where she needed Daddy's shoulders to take her across. And she seemed in no hurry to try anything adventurous on her own.

But it happened again. I left the two of them alone and went inside. This time when I saw them through the

kitchen window, I didn't even think about rushing outside to intervene.

I saw Rachael approach the ladder with trepidation and
heard Anny encouraging her. "Come on, Rach, you can do
it. I'll be right here and I'll catch you if you fall. But you
won't."

Gradually, Rachael climbed up to the top. Then, putting
one tiny hand on the first bar, she looked down.
Something that she saw in her sister's face below her gave
her confidence. She looked back to the bars in front of her
and swung out.

And fell six feet to the ground, on top of her sister.

My heart jumped into my throat, but in another second
Rachael and Anny both stood up, brushing the dirt off
their hands and laughing. "That didn't hurt!" shouted
Rachael, gleefully. "Of course not," agreed her sister.
"Now try again."

It took Rachael only one more try to get across the bars
by herself. I breathed again and went back outside, where
both my daughters made me watch to see what "Rachael
can do all by herself!" I applauded the achievement of
both the student and the teacher.

That's how it continued to be between these two. The
older one worked hard at something until she got it.
Often it did not come easily and she had to find an alter-
nate way of accomplishing her goal. The younger one
only had to work a little at something before she achieved
her goal, largely because she has always had enough self-
confidence to believe that she could accomplish anything
she attempted. And a large part of that confidence came
from having a big sister who was always there telling her
"Come on Rachael! You can do it!"

Apart from encouraging her sister (and the subsequent
other two), Anny also felt it was her position in the family
to preserve her sister's innocence. As the big sister, she

was the one to awaken in the middle of the night to make sure the Tooth Fairy had not forgotten Rachael the first time Rachael lost a tooth. And when her baby sister Elliana's goldfish died, Anny was the one to replace it before Elli could realize that it had suffered an untimely demise. Anny has always wanted to preserve the sweet fictions of her sisters' childhoods even as she, herself, has become an adult.

I have watched these sisters from my unique vantage point as their mother. And as in the case with the swing set, I have often had to stifle the urge to intervene. The sisters fight and argue, make up and share secrets, and often they exclude me from their world.

These moments belong to sisters and not to mothers, however much I may wish to be part of them. But I know that these moments cement the bonds of sisterhood and will carry these children into adulthood, into a place where I won't be someday. But that's okay.

After all, I helped create this relationship, nurtured it and fostered it. I really do have an important place in it.

I know where it is, where it must be. It is there, behind the kitchen window, watching.

Marsha Arons

Anny and Rachael in high school.

2

THE BOND BETWEEN SISTERS

Your sister is the only creature on earth who shares your heritage, history, environment, DNA, bone structure and contempt for stupid Aunt Girdy.

Linda Sunshine

Sister's Song

We heard a song, we heard it in harmony.

Maxene Andrews, of the Andrews Sisters

The Oklahoma City (OKC) bombing had devastated our community; but six weeks later at the largest high school in OKC, we were having our baccalaureate service as usual in a neighborhood church. There was still a heartfelt obligation to affirm this end-of-year ceremony for our students. At our "Little United Nations," as I liked to call it, we were a strong community of faith and our young Vietnamese Catholics would worship beside our African-American Baptists, in this, their next to the last ceremony before they danced off into the world of college and jobs.

Of course, court rulings involving separation of church and state meant the students and parents were totally in charge of this event. The students had to meet on their own for the rehearsal and to set the tone of the program. Even though it was difficult to "let go" of a service of this nature, as the building principal I had done just that. From the past history of the school I knew that this release of responsibility had normally worked out fine as the students were mature and Northwest Classen was known for its wonderful end-of-year activities. It was a difficult time for everyone. Several students had loved ones injured and killed in the bombing.

As the principal, my role was minimal, but I was able to participate in helping students pin collars on their robes in the waiting area, help quiet the nervous jitters, and supervise as they lined up for this most important event—which many viewed as a dress rehearsal for commencement.

Finally, all was in readiness, and I slid silently into a back pew as the students began to proudly march down the center of the sanctuary. Many a parent's eyes dripped tears as a son or daughter quietly walked in line with their classmates to the front rows of the church, which had been reserved for the graduating class of 1995.

The program began normally with a routine of introductions and speeches. Finally, it was time for one of the most coveted parts of the ceremony—the senior solo. Several students each year would try out for this spot, but only one was chosen.

One of our beautiful young ladies walked proudly to the lectern and prepared to sing. Her song was an old hymn and one that seemed especially appropriate after this recent tragedy—"His Eye Is on the Sparrow." However, as she began to sing, something appeared to be wrong. She began to stumble through the first verse of the song, and tears started running down her face. Suddenly from the back of the church, the song echoed from another voice. Her older sister had seen her distress and had come to her aid. She calmly walked down the center aisle of the church, keeping her eyes steadfastly on her sister, as she continued to sing along. She took her place next to her sister and placed her arm around her shoulder. They sang triumphantly, the original singer buoyed by the love and courage of her family member, until the song was finished.

There were other parts to the program, of course. A young minister encouraged the graduates with the theme of, "The sun will come up tomorrow, no matter what happens." The senior speakers were refreshing and challenged their young colleagues to seek significant tasks to the greater glory of mankind.

For me, however, the epiphany of that program will forever be the story of the two young women—especially the one who didn't stop to think of the possible embarrassment of walking down a long aisle from the back of the church to rescue her sister. Because at that one gleaming moment in their family history, the only thing that mattered was that her sister needed her, and she was prepared to answer the call and claim the victory of that moment.

Rita Billbe

Voices

Empathy is your pain in my heart.

Author Unknown

I answered the phone, for what seemed to be the hundredth time that July afternoon, with my typical phone greeting announcing the name of the company where I worked and identifying myself. The person at the other end paused, and I heard a barely audible voice say my name. A voice that I would recognize anywhere because it sounded hauntingly similar to mine. A voice that I had been hearing ever since I could remember. A voice that had called for me as a playmate. A voice that had scolded me in sibling anger. A voice that had soothed away tears. A voice that had sung again and again in harmony with mine.

Immediately I asked, "What's wrong?"

A voice I knew so well could not hide the fear. A voice that had shared whispers and secrets. A voice that had given information reserved for the most special friends. A voice that had spilled out hardships and joy, sorrow and delight. A voice that could laugh and light up a room. A voice that I had often envied and looked up to. A voice that I had learned to respect, love and cherish.

The voice on the other end of the phone line that was now silent. I waited, as I had often learned to wait on this voice. A voice that I had developed a patience for because I had found that it sometimes needed me to wait. A voice that was often soft, even silent, but always had something important to say.

I could hear a slight tremor as the voice of my sister began to speak. My heart raced in anticipation. Her words were carefully chosen so that I wouldn't be too upset. But the words didn't matter to me. I would have known even if she had been speaking a different language. Her voice gave it away. Something was terribly wrong.

"It's Lauren," she said simply.

And then she broke. I could hear the quiet sobbing at the other end as my mind searched to fill in the missing pieces. Just saying the name of her ten-month-old daughter had caused her to lose the only fragment of composure that she had left. So I waited on her voice.

"We're at the hospital. She had an ear infection. She couldn't stop vomiting. They did a CT scan. There's some sort of a dark spot—a mass on her brain. They're trans - ferring her to Columbus for more tests. The ambulance will be ready in just a few minutes. I can't get in touch with Mom and Dad." All in broken speech. Spitting out words. That voice managed to convey to me the reality that was even worse than what my imagination had already con- jured up.

"Which hospital in Columbus? I'll meet you there."

The words that I heard myself say sounded much more calm than I felt. But that had always been my job. Even though I was the youngest child, I had always felt a need to be the strong one for my sister. She always seemed to be so much more emotional. Somehow weaker and more frail. As the middle child, she had been the peacemaker between our older brother, Mark, and myself while we were growing up. Yet somehow she had always seemed to be less independent, more in need of support.

Cindy and I had always been different. We liked it that way, most of the time. Except when I wanted to be just like her because she, with the two years she had on me, represented something so much more wise and mature. Usually, though, we accepted our differences and allowed each other freedom to be unique.

One of those unique qualities was our temperament. She was the sweet, innocent one with lots of friends and many boyfriends. I was the tomboy who fought with Mark, climbed trees and couldn't get a boy to notice me until I was sixteen. Her senior year in high school, she was voted onto the Prom Court. My senior year highlight was competing in the state track finals.

We had a few things in common, though, the most prominent of which was music. Because our family had a slight musical orientation, we had been encouraged to sing and play instruments since before we could really remember. So through piano lessons, band instruments and school and church choirs, music became a part of us.

Cindy sang alto. She was a natural. Everyone said it. Even before I really knew what an alto was, I knew it was my sister. And I was proud of her. (Except when I wanted to sing alto and found that I wasn't exactly gifted for harmony. But I got over that quickly.) It seemed rather convenient that I become a soprano. It made sense. What good is an alto without a soprano? And who better to be her soprano than me?

So we began to sing together. At our small church, in the car, at camp, with the family. Anywhere we happened to be. We realized that our voices blended well because they sounded a lot alike. Something hereditary, maybe. Then we began to sing together so often that we thought alike. So not only our sound, but our rhythm was the same.

I'm not sure when I realized that Cindy was my best friend. Because she was older than I, we had some different interests and different friends throughout our school years. We shared everything else though. Especially clothes. And when she went away to college, both of our wardrobes were tragically divided in half. I visited her often at college, and we wrote many letters to one another. By the time I had to choose where to go to college, it only made sense to follow my sister, if for no other reason than to regain my wardrobe!

College was the first time where we really had a choice whether or not to spend time together. We could have gone our separate ways, but it was only natural that we were together. We even roomed together for one semester. In fact, we were together so much that no one believed we were sisters, since we didn't look at all alike.

So when she got married, I was the maid of honor. When she had a baby, I spoiled her baby rotten. And when she found out that her daughter was sick, I was the one she called.

The six-hour drive from my home in southern Indiana to Columbus, Ohio, took about three hours that evening after her phone call, and I spent the entire drive in prayer. In my state of mind at the time, it was a miracle that I didn't get a traffic ticket, or have an accident. I couldn't even really remember the trip.

I only remember the look on my sister's face as I found her in the hospital room. The room was quiet as I entered, except for the beeping of the heart monitor. Cindy was standing by the bed, looking at her sleeping child, who was wearing the tiniest hospital gown that I had ever seen. She heard the door as I slipped in, and I saw a look of relief cross her face.

"I was worried about you," she said as I crossed the room to hug her.

She was worried about me. All that she had been through in the last few hours and she was worried about me. Typical of her to think of my safety. She was right, of course. I had driven like a maniac to get there. She knew me well.

The situation was at a standstill for the night. Lauren had been stabilized. Cindy had gained control of her emotions, and her husband, Roy, seemed to be as calm as he always was. A nurse was nearby. Nothing else was to be done until the next morning when more tests could be run.

Cindy and I slept in my car that night, or tried anyway. Only one parent was allowed to stay in the room, and she decided that it should be Roy. We put the seats as far back as they would go and tried to get comfortable. She told me the whole story of what had happened, and we cried, I think. I did, anyway. We were afraid. She told me that she was glad I came. Sometime in the wee hours of the morning, we fell asleep together from exhaustion.

I'm not sure that I will ever forgive myself for leaving. I stayed for a day, but felt like I needed to return to work as I felt fairly useless at the hospital anyway. Word had finally reached my parents, and they arrived early that next morning. Others came, too—relatives from both sides of this tiny child's family. So, with my sister's permission, I went home shortly before a scheduled MRI that would probably take hours.

I never stopped praying. Questions of why ran through my head, but mostly I just prayed for healing. I knew God, and I knew that he was capable of healing my niece if he chose, even though her illness was still undetermined. God knew.

That evening, when I heard my mother's voice on the telephone, I knew that the news was not good. Brain tumor. The size of an adult fist. Malignant.

"How is Cindy?" I needed to know.

But my mom didn't have to tell me. I knew. How would *any* mother be upon learning this about her ten-month-old child? My sister needed me, and I wasn't there. It didn't matter to me that other people were there for her. *I wasn't there.* No one understood her like I did. No one knew her voice the way I knew it.

The next few months were something of a blur. Hospital rooms. Surgeries. Nurses. Tests. IVs. Medications. Needles. Doctors. Chemotherapy. Treatments. Sickness. Pain.

Yet, over those months, I witnessed a change in Cindy that amazed me. She was no longer the fragile, dependent sister that I had once thought her to be. She became strong. She had to. Her daughter needed her strength. And I, along with others, learned a great deal from her strength.

Cindy and I laughed a lot through those days. My mom and I took turns spending time at the hospital with Cindy and Lauren while Roy was working. We cried sometimes, too, but mostly I remember the laughter. We had always laughed together often, but it seemed that then we had to more than ever. Just to get through.

And we wanted Lauren to laugh. To experience some joy in the midst of all of the pain. To hear laughter. To know happiness and fun. Yet Lauren helped us to laugh. Such a small child filled with so much pain and so much life. Although we celebrated her first birthday in the hospital during a round of chemotherapy, we were still able to laugh.

Though the doctors sometimes gave less-than-hopeful diagnoses, we never stopped hoping. When Lauren was released from the hospital the day before Christmas Eve after three major surgeries, along with countless months of chemotherapy, hospital visits, and other complications because of this or that treatment, our prayers were answered. Her brain tumor was completely removed, and she was recovering remarkably.

Cindy was tired from the last six months of such an ordeal, but I have never seen her happier or more thankful. The end was nowhere near in sight. This would affect Lauren for the rest of her life, and at this stage no one could be quite certain how. But we had witnessed a miracle, and for a while, everything was blissful.

Decisions had to be made and doctors consulted. Lauren was seventeen months old but thin and frail. She had become emaciated during her chemotherapy and developed throat complications from the tubular feedings. After her last surgery, her brain had accumulated too much fluid, so she endured yet another surgery to install a shunt to remove the fluid.

She was a fighter through it all. Her smiles and sweet disposition continued to charm and delight everyone who came into contact with her, especially her doctors and nurses. Every moment spent with her was cherished as well as entertaining. Though the medical care that her mother had to provide for her at home was often painful, she was immediately forgiving, with laughter not far behind. Her patience and endurance touched the lives of everyone around her. Stories of her frail strength spread to those who did not know her but had been keeping her in their prayers.

Doctors listed the odds of recurrence. Further treatments were decided upon. The insurance company was consulted but declined payment. The self-donor bone marrow transplant, for which her bone marrow had been harvested seven months before, was considered to be in developmental stages. The insurance wouldn't cover it. Without the treatment, the chance of reccurrence significantly increased.

Lauren didn't know that. I'm guessing that she only knew that the pressure and pain that she had been feeling were gone. Her personality and liveliness blossomed further. Her mother watched with caution, but obvious joy, as she saw her only child seemingly healthy again. For a month, Cindy was given that gift.

During that time Mark got married. Cindy and I were both in the wedding as "groomswomen." We stood up for our brother, on his side, as he married our new sister. And we sang, together, of course. I think it was the best that my sister and I have ever sung. We had witnessed the miracle of life. We knew more about love than we ever had before, and we sang about it—for my brother, for his wife, for Lauren, for ourselves. We sang, and we knew the meaning of happiness and thankfulness and hope and love.

Doctors wrote letters to convince the insurance company that this treatment was completely necessary; finally the decision was reversed. Lauren was scheduled for a round of massive chemotherapy to reduce the chances of cancer returning, but it would also kill all of her bone marrow. This would be followed by a painful bone marrow transplant and a long, grueling recovery.

Cindy was worried. We all were. Lauren's tiny twenty-month-old body had been through so much. I was worried about my sister. Her twenty-four-year-old mind had been through enough trauma to last a lifetime, and a great deal of strain had been placed on her two-year-old marriage as well. I knew that she would endure, but I didn't want to see that look on her face again. The look that a mother has when she can physically feel her child's pain.

I didn't know at the time that I would see an even more excruciating look in my sister's eyes. Lauren was not strong enough to make it through the chemotherapy. She died of kidney and liver failure on the second day of treatment. The harsh chemicals were too much for her little body. She died in her mother's arms.

Again, I was not there. Maybe it was better that way. But

when I answered the phone call that was not even meant for me, it was Lauren's father's voice that I heard this time.

"I lost my baby," he said in a broken voice that I hardly recognized.

No. No. No. For minutes that seemed like hours, I screamed in horror. I couldn't even hang up the phone. I wouldn't believe it. I couldn't believe it. The irony was too bitter. The reality too painful to bear. The treatment that was supposed to prevent further pain had taken her away. From my sister. From me. From life. No. It was simply too unfair.

Numbness developed over the next few minutes. I had been visiting my sister for the weekend, and it was just a short drive to the hospital. It seemed like the longest drive of my life. I wasn't even sure what I would say when I got there.

"Can I hug you?" came out of my mouth when I saw her.

To the others who were already there, it probably seemed like a strange thing to say, but she understood why. And she let me hug her. She didn't say anything. Not for quite a while, actually. I think it made the others in the room uncomfortable. I knew that her voice had nothing left to say.

Cindy sang at the funeral. Alone. A mother singing a final lullaby. Never have I heard a more beautiful voice. Heart-wrenchingly bitter. Agonizing. Loving. Aching. Unbelieving. Angry. Pained. Beautiful voice. The voice that I had heard all of my life. The voice that I thought I knew so well had acquired another dimension from the experience of life. The voice that had harmonized with me and laughed with me. I wondered if I would ever hear that voice laugh again.

The mark of grief never goes away. It holds a treasured memory. It cannot, nor should it, be forgotten. For a while, it defines our world. It holds questions that can only be answered after this life is through. Understanding will only come when finally there is no more pain.

Yet, for all of the pain that she has endured, Cindy never would have given up the joy of knowing Lauren. None of us who knew her would have. Even though she never heard Lauren's voice say, "I love you, Mommy," Lauren's love still lives in her mother's heart.

Cindy is still my older, wiser, more mature sister. Her closet still contains parts of my wardrobe. And she is still my best friend even though we have both changed and will continue to do so.

Her voice has changed with her. It is now a voice that is more aware. A voice that has seen pain and grief. A voice that is stronger. A voice that is somehow more confused and more understanding at the same time. A voice that knows about life and love. A voice that knows about holding on and letting go. A voice that has lost faith yet still hopes. A voice that laughs the laugh of experience.

Yes, Cindy and I still laugh together. We can laugh together differently than we laugh with anyone else. A special kind of laughter. A cherished, understanding laughter. At anything we happen to find funny when we are together. And when we are not together, we think of each other and share it later.

And we cry sometimes. We cried when Lauren's little brother was born. I was there this time.

And we sing together when we can. Our voices still blend well, I suppose. Maybe even better than before because of the experiences we have shared. Our thoughts blend together even when we are thousands of miles apart.

Now, when I hear my sister's voice, I hear something else along with it. It's quiet, barely audible, and it may be that no one can hear it but me. It has a slight heavenly overtone. I'm sure that it is the voice of an angel. The voice of an angel saying, "I love you, Mommy."

Julie D. Workman

We Sisters

Gossiping on the phone with your girlfriends for ten minutes will firm up the jaw and chin and is far better than plastic surgery.

Dr. Jane Curtain

Diana likes the brownies in the middle. I go for the corners first, then the edges. She loves muffin tops. I like the stumps better. Her hair is long and thick and curly. Mine is stringy, straight and baby-fine. We lament over one another's hair. She is right-handed, I am left. She is taller and looks like Dad, while I favor Mom. Still, when we sit across from each other in a downtown diner, we look into a mirror of mannerisms and expression. Our hands move in the same way. We both sip our coffee before we bite the toast. (Hers is pale, I order mine burned.) We catch ourselves acting like each other, and we smile wide, covering our lips with our fingertips . . . just like each other. We suppress a giggle. "Hmm," we say. Sometimes people ask if we are twins. We're not, but we are sisters.

Growing up, we were best friends. Running barefoot in our seersucker jammies under the streetlights, we chased lightning bugs and rinsed the day's dirt from our feet in the puddles on the sidewalk. Then, if one of us saw a bat, we shrieked our way back to the safety of the porch, hugging each other and giggling. I know we must have looked silly to anyone passing by, but we never thought about it then. I never looked silly to my sister.

We spent almost all of our time together. We had other friends, but none were as close as we were to each other. We shared everything then. We shared a room, a double bed, the bathtub, our clothes and our toys. We shared our secrets, our fears and our dreams. No confidence is stronger than a sister's.

Our Barbies acted just like us. Hers was older than mine, owned all the clothes and was bossy. My doll was a whiner and a real baby who stomped away in a huff if things didn't go her way. We never said so out loud, but we knew they were sisters.

I got married first. She was the first one I told of my engagement. She was the maid of honor. She told me first when she promised to marry as well. I was her maid of honor, too. We wondered whether I should be called the "matron of honor," but decided not. We thought of matrons as old, as big, as women past thirty. We were none of these, we sisters.

Diana was the first to know when I became pregnant. Some things, like the "tell me first" rule of sisters, never change. She carries photos of my sons in her wallet and shows them to anyone who will look. "See my baby nephews?" she asks. The boys are seventeen and fourteen years old. She doesn't have any children of her own, so she claims her sister's.

After I married, I moved away. Now we see each other only a few times a year. We still share our secrets, fears and dreams, but we have added our memories, our history and our hurts. We call each other by old nicknames. I can't recall that we ever used our given names. She is "Goon," and I am "Hoot." Our husbands, who always call each other by their given names, look at us as though we haven't a wisp of a brain between us. Mine in particular is confused by this sometimes-unflattering name-calling. But that's to be expected. He doesn't have a sister.

Her husband just gets out of the way. He doesn't understand the long embraces and the tears we share when we meet and part. He doesn't understand the language we speak only with our eyes. He doesn't read the volumes spoken with a glance, a gesture, a secret silence. I'm not surprised. He's not a sister.

We call each other three or four times a week. We don't talk that often because we try to call when the other is not home. We leave messages that sound like code. See, we don't need to say a lot. We just need to connect and know that the other knows that they were being thought about. If I told you that I can tell when the message light on the phone is a call from her, you might think I'm nuts. Unless, of course, you have a sister.

We try to get away together. Just us from time to time. We need the kind of rest that comes from conversation that requires no explanations. It is comfortable predictability that is closer than a marriage. She is my right side. I am her left. I think you know what I mean, if you have a sister.

Now if you'll excuse me, I hear the phone. Betcha I know who it is.

Ann Marie Rowland

A Sister Is . . .

Someone special, a friend so true,
Exactly the same, yet different from you;
She knows your thoughts without a word,
Understands your feelings before they're heard;
May drift apart but remains near,
In her heart she holds you dear;
Your secrets safe, your faults untold,
A bond of trust she will uphold;
So cherish her as she does you,
For remember you are a sister, too.

Lisa Baillargeon

The Diary

When we were thirteen our parents got us twin beds. Know what we did? We put a violin case in her bed, covered it up, and the two of us slept in mine. By fifteen, it got doggone crowded in there.

Abigail Van Buren, of her sister Ann Landers

Armed with two overpacked suitcases, we arrived at the airport just in time for my flight. "Well, here we are, the airport," my sister said with a sigh. As I watched her unload my luggage, I could see the sadness in her eyes. This was not easy on her either. We had both been dreading this moment for the past week. One last hug and a final good-bye and I would be on my way to a new life abroad, leaving my beloved sister behind.

All my life I had loved airports. To me they were some kind of magic gateway to the world, a place from which to start great holidays and adventures. But today it seemed like a cold and heartless place.

As we made our way to the gate, we passed through a busload of frustrated holiday goers and their screaming children. I looked at my sister, and even though her eyes were filled with tears, she was trying to keep a brave face. "You better go or you'll miss your flight," she said.

"I am just going to walk away and not look back," I said, "that would just be too hard."

As I held her one last time, she whispered, "Don't worry about me, I'll be just fine."

"I'll miss you," I replied, and with those last words I was off. As promised, I did not look back, but by the time I reached the customs office I was sobbing. "Cheer up, love," the tall customs officer said with a smile. "It's not the end of the world, you know." But to me it was the end of the world as I had known it.

While boarding the plane I was still crying. I did not have the energy to put my bag in the overhead locker, so I stuffed it on the empty seat next to mine. As I settled into my chair, a feeling of sadness overwhelmed me. I felt like my best friend had just been taken away from me.

Growing up, my sister and I would do everything together. Born barely fifteen months apart we not only looked alike, we were alike. We both had that same mix of curiosity and fear of all things unknown to us. One sunny summer day I was playing outside on the grass when she came up to me and said, "Want to come to the attic?" We both knew that the answer to that question was always yes. We were frightened of the attic but also fascinated by its smells and sounds. Whenever one of us needed something, the other one would come along. Together we would fight the life-size spiders and battle through the numerous boxes until we found what we needed.

Over time, the visits to the attic became less scary. Eventually there came a time when we would go by ourselves, but my sister and I stayed as close as ever. When the time came for us to go to college, what better way than for us to go together? My parents were pleased because that way we could "keep an eye on each other" and of course report back on what the other one was up to. But now that our college days were over and I was off to a foreign country, all I had left were my memories.

The plane shook heavily, and the bag that I had shoved onto the seat next to me fell on the floor. My aspirin, hairbrush and a copy of the book I planned to read were spread on the floor. I bent over to gather them up when I saw an unfamiliar little book in the middle of my belongings. It was not until I picked it up that I realized that it was a diary. The key had been carefully placed in the lock, so I opened it.

Immediately I recognized my sister's handwriting. "Hi Sis, What a day it has been today. First you let me know that you are moving abroad, and then my boss . . ." Only then did I realize that my sister had been keeping a diary for the past month, and that she was now passing it on to me. She had been scheming to start the diary for the past year, but now the time seemed right. I was to write in it for the next couple of months, and then send it back to her.

I spent the rest of the flight reading about my sister's comings and goings. And even though a large ocean separated us, at some point it felt like she was actually there. It was only when I thought that I had lost my best friend that I realized that she was going to be around forever.

Martine Klaassen

Joined at the Heart

With one manicured hand
my sister can reach back into the past
and pull out memories
I haven't thought of in years.
Her brown eyes are mirrors,
reflecting me and my life in a way no one else can.

When we look at each other
we see all stages of ourselves simultaneously,
like buds unfolding into full bloom
speedup film.

Though she is unique,
recently one of her observations
on something entirely new to both of us
sounded exactly like our mother.
That alone would be reason enough
for me to treasure her company.

We go way back.
We remember Happy the dog
Eleanor the singing hen—
all sorts of crazy things.
Sisters, not twins
we are not joined at the hip
but at the heart.

Ruth Latta

Vital Chatter

Every Tuesday and Thursday, between 3:00 P.M. and 4:00 P.M., I picked up the phone and called my sister, Diane, who was slowly dying from the complications of diabetes. I didn't call on Mondays, Wednesdays or Fridays because those were her dialysis days, and she was always too drained and exhausted to talk. I also didn't call her on weekends because Saturdays and Sundays were designated as immediate-family and recovery days. I didn't mind about weekends since we had our own special time.

I was never sure if Diane's beauty parlor appointment was on Tuesday or Thursday at 2:00 P.M. since it changed from week to week. What didn't change is Diane never missed getting her hair done no matter how sick she was. And when she returned home, we'd have our precious time to visit with each other privately by telephone as we'd done for most of our adult lives.

The only times we didn't keep those phone dates was when she had a doctor's appointment or was in the ICU. We didn't let her numerous hospitalizations stop us. It surprised other members of our family that Diane and I seldom talked about how she was feeling, about the latest lab test or surgical procedure, or about how well her heart and lungs or kidneys were functioning. Right to the end, we carried on our typical conversations—sister to sister, friend to friend.

We spent most of our time on the phone gossiping. I left home when I was eighteen years old, and Diane was my anchor to the small Southern town where we were born and the close-knit Italian family I had left behind. She filled me in on whose husband was running around, on the latest family squabble, on who was sick and who had died. She announced the new additions to the family. Told me who got engaged, married, divorced or separated. She loved describing the weddings I missed. Also the funerals, especially if we didn't think too much of the person who had died.

Diane and I laughed a lot during those phone conversations, which often lasted an hour or so in the beginning. We consoled each other when one or the other was down.

We talked about everything from her beloved New Orleans Saints team to our favorite Danielle Steele novel to our favored "Barb" singers—she loved Mandrell while I preferred Streisand.

The last Thursday I talked with Diane she told me about a spat her husband and one of our other sisters had about her dialysis. She raved about the delicious hot tamales she'd eaten for dinner the night before. She told me about the progress yet another sister was making in her pursuit of a divorce. She asked about my kids and grandkids and told me about her daughter's latest love interest. Her voice was stronger than it had been in a long time, and I was encouraged that she would keep beating the odds.

The next Tuesday, I didn't get to talk with Diane because she was in the ICU. On Wednesday she was asleep when I called the hospital. Her husband said he'd have her call me from home after she was discharged later in the day. She never did. She died on Thursday, early in the morning.

And so, it's Tuesday again as I pick up the phone to call her and write this instead. What would we talk about today? What would I want to say to her? To hear her say? I know. We'd talk about her funeral.

I'd tell her how the whole town turned out because she was so well-loved. How everyone in the family, even those who'd been feuding for years, had made peace with each other. At least for the day. I'd tell her how really sad I was, but that as I looked at my new grandson sleeping peacefully in the pew beside me, I felt everything was okay with this new phase of her being.

I'd tell her about her daughter getting up and talking about all the things she had been taught by her mother. And how her husband even donned a suit for one of the few times in his life to stand in front of her friends and relatives and profess his undying love for her. I'd tell her how I didn't listen while her husband spoke of their special relationship because I was remembering our own special bonds. How she was a large part of my support system. My link to my past. My confidante. More than my sister. My dear friend.

I would tell Diane about the two priests who said kind things about her. And how glad I was when my two-year-old granddaughter decided to babble loudly while one priest was extolling her virtues and how that made me smile instead of cry.

I'd tell her that Mama was too heartbroken to attend her funeral, but everyone else was there. Her six siblings and our children and grandchildren. I'd say how much we all loved her and are going to miss her, and I'd try to make her laugh. I'd tell her about the strong incense that almost knocked me out as the priest sprinkled it around her coffin and my head. I'd mention the fact that all of her panic-attack-prone sisters and brothers who usually sit in the back of the church ended up right next to her in the front, and not one of us passed out.

I'd describe the beautiful flowers on the altar because toward the end of her life when she'd lost her vision, it bothered her that she could only smell the wonderful floral creations of our Lord. I would finally stop and wait for her to talk to me. *What would she tell me,* I wondered? And I knew.

She'd tell me she knew all that because she'd hung around to make sure everyone was okay. She'd tell me that she was there in the form of a butterfly when Mama visited her grave that afternoon. And that Mama smiled when she saw the butterfly because she knew what it meant. She'd tell me how she rang the disconnected doorbell of one of our sisters to help console her because she had a special love for this sister and wanted to reassure her of life after death. She'd tell me how when all the roses were gathered so rosaries could be made from them, she made sure one single yellow rose was left so that another sister would know by prearranged signal that she was still alive.

And then, just before we'd hang up for the last time, I'd tell her how much I love her and how much I was going to miss her presence, her bravery, her sweetness, her sense of humor. And she would say, "Yes, I'm going to miss you, too. But I need to start my journey." She'd say she needed to find Daddy and Grandma and about twenty or so other relatives and friends and she hoped they were in heaven 'cause that's where she was going.

And I would reluctantly say, "Okay. Bye, then. But every Tuesday and Thursday between 3:00 P.M. and 4:00 P.M., I'll be calling you up in my mind, and I will never, never forget how much you meant to me."

Leona Lipari Lee

Over the Years

A new baby comes to stay, peering into the crib we say,
"This is my sister"

Toys spread out on the floor, someone watching from
behind a door.
It is my sister

"Who broke my doll?" I scream. "Who was that in my
dream?"
It was my sister

Helping with our bath time, sing a song in rhyme,
Thank you, my sister

Boyfriends come, boyfriends go. Who was kissing? Don't
you know?
It was my sister

Talking late into the night, sharing secrets, "Turn off the
light."
You are my sister

Growing up, bodies changing, all the time, rearranging
Oh, my sweet sister

Getting married, we move out. "Oh how I miss you!" I shout
To my sister

Pregnancy, long-distance calls, before you know it, baby
  crawls
Talk to me, sister

Now adults and we shall stay, friends as always a special
  way
Because you are, my sister.

Michelle A. Tessaro

Sisters Under the Skin

If you don't understand how a woman could both love her sister dearly and want to wring her neck at the same time then you were probably an only child.

Linda Sunshine

Some families sort things out around the dinner table. At my grandmother's house—where I spent most summers—we resolved our problems on the front porch.

Grandmother always sat in the swing doing some bit of work or other—hulling peas or crocheting a throw. I sat beside her, when that place wasn't usurped by an older cousin, because I loved her and it was peaceful to be right next to her.

It seemed odd to me that we didn't confine our family difficulties to some indoor room, and when I was old enough to ask about that, my grandmother said, "Well, honey, it gives us some perspective, I think. We aren't the only people in the world with troubles after all. Just looky there at the street."

It was true that in this small Southern town there was

often a parade of misfortune right there before our eyes. On almost any day, you could see the high school boys get into a fight on their way home from school, or watch old Doc Carrickle's horse get away from him one more time, or hear Louise and Parnell Webb fighting a block before they came into view. In fact, you could see most any aspect of the human condition at its best and its worst. My family was always careful to be at its best in public if that was at all possible.

And that is the reason I was amazed by the fireworks between two of my aunts. They were my grandmother's daughters, but I never thought of them that way. For one thing, they were too old for daughters. Aunt Golda was thirty-two, and Aunt Willa, her elder, was thirty-four. They were women in their own right and often said so. Both were anxious to marry, although Willa was the only one engaged. She was the relentless individual of the two; Golda, the conservative, was beyond reproach, so everyone said.

On this particular day, I was sitting on the porch swing with my grandmother, who was shelling peas from her garden. My Aunt Golda was sitting in the green wicker rocker putting pins in very tidy concentric circles in a red felt pin cushion made to look like a tomato. The dog, DD (for dumb dog), was laying in a dust bowl he'd created near the petunias, panting in the heat. It all looked, I guess, very tranquil from the street.

We were all having a nice time, when suddenly Willa appeared on the walkway to the house. She sashayed along, swinging her hips a little. Just as she got to the steps she put her hand to her head. It is hard to say what it was that rested there in her dark red hair. It was purple and looked something like a turban from the movies.

I could feel tension on the front porch just like you can feel static electricity before a storm. DD got out of the petunia bed and came to the steps to watch.

My Aunt Willa plopped herself down in a wicker rocker and smoothed her linen skirt over her thighs. Golda stared at her with an expression that somehow conveyed both contempt and disbelief. She said, "Willa, what on earth have you got on your head?"

"Why, it's a hat," Willa said. "Do you like it?"

"It is not a hat. It is a piece of purple velvet just twined around." Golda made a little impatient circular motion with her hand. "It looks like a purple cow pie." By that she meant the stuff you don't want to step in.

"Well, you are in a bad mood. This hat just makes me feel wonderful. I was up in the attic the other day. Fooling around. You know dressing up like we used to do, Golda."

"Willa, you are a grown woman. This family is talked about enough without you walking around town with that thing on your head. Now take it off."

"I will do no such thing," Willa said, gently touching her creation with the very tips of her fingers. "It was lying in the light from that little window in the peak. Just so beautiful, I had to try it on. So I made this of it. I knew Mama wouldn't care."

My grandmother looked up from the peas but didn't say anything.

"I want you to take that thing off your head this minute," Golda said. "If you do not learn to moderate your behavior, people will begin talking about you in whispers!"

DD moved his front feet up and down in anticipation and I sat upright, ready, waiting and hoping for the battle that was sure to come. Shots had been fired; war was declared. It was going to be an exciting day.

"Honestly, Golda, you are getting to be a regular fashion Nazi."

And with that remark all kinds of things happened at once. My Aunt Golda leapt out of her chair and snatched the coiled piece of velvet from her sister's head. The dog began to bark. The tomato pin cushion fell to the floor. Willa picked it up and pulled every single pin out of it. Every one. My grandmother put down her bowl of peas. Willa then threw the pinless cushion into the yard. DD went after it and began to toss it into the air, then shake it with obvious pleasure. Golda, who'd spent a good bit of time arranging the pins, put her hands to her face, began to cry and then ran into the house, slamming the screen door.

My grandmother said, "Well, I never. What is the matter with you two?"

My Aunt Willa looked at us both serenely and said in a very quiet voice, "I knew she'd do that. Such a crybaby. Always was."

My grandmother told me to retrieve the tomato pin cushion from the dog. It was a soggy, ruined mess. After a few minutes, Willa excused herself and went into town to shop. I got a book about the Amazon River and climbed to the high fork in our maple tree where I liked to read.

On and off during the afternoon, I imagined that we were at the beginning of one of those family feuds that would go on for generations. I imagined Willa and Golda would grow old and cripple up without ever speaking to each other again.

Neither of them came to supper. "I don't know where those girls could have got to," my grandmother said as she put the biscuits on the table. I didn't want to say what I thought: that they'd killed each other in the barn. So I was mostly silent.

After I'd had my fill of the fried chicken, my grandmother sent me out to the garden to pick some mint for iced tea. When I rounded the corner of the house I saw an unimaginable sight. Willa and Golda were strolling down the flower-garden path arm in arm. Their heads were inclined slightly toward each other as they walked in their pale summer dresses past the tall multicolored phlox and the blooming tea roses. I was amazed.

I ran back into the kitchen without the mint I'd been sent to harvest and pulled my grandmother to the kitchen window.

"Just look," I said. "Mawmaw, just look. How can that be? I thought they were mortal enemies. They were really mad. Mortal enemies. Forever!"

My grandmother looked out the window and then down at me. She smiled ever so slightly and said, "Well, no darlin', they're sisters. Now go get me some mint. And call those sweet girls in for tea."

I thought there were some things I just never would understand. But I did what I was told, and to my ever-lasting amazement they both bent down and kissed me on the cheek. Then we went inside to have iced tea and play hearts around the kitchen table.

Walker Meade

Forty-Five Years and Six Thousand Miles Apart

Invisible threads are the strongest ties.

Friedrich Nietzsche

It was a time near the end of the American occupation of Japan that followed World War II. My mother, the oldest of three siblings, gave up a rare opportunity to go to college so that she could work two jobs and support her family after her father fell ill and couldn't work. Her mother had already died when she was only twelve years old. She was not only the sole source of income but also a sister and mother to two little girls. Amidst all of this hardship, she fell in love with an American soldier. With a mind filled with hope and determination, she left war-torn Japan for the bounty of America with the dreams of being better able to provide for her family and, in particular, a better life for her two little sisters.

Life in America didn't turn out so well for my mother. The man she married turned out to be a severe alcoholic. Her survival and determination to provide for her own children rivaled any challenge she could have faced in her homeland. With constant pressure, her dreams moved from hope to long days of labor. Years went by, and she never wrote home. More years passed, and she became afraid to write. She wouldn't be able to bear the news of anything bad happening to the two little sisters she left behind. She couldn't bear to tell them that anything less than good had become of her life.

I had always wondered about the relatives that I must have in Japan, and as my mother never spoke of them, it created an empty space in my life. I assumed it was painful for her to bring up the past so I respectfully thought it was better not to ask. It took a long time, but finally I had the chance to go to Japan for a three-month project. Would I be willing to open the Pandora's box sealed by my mother's silence? I told my story to a charming Japanese family that had befriended me. They sensed my need to know about the relatives who were missing from my life. My new friends took on the quest of finding my lost relatives for me, as it would be too difficult for me as a foreigner to do it alone.

My time in Japan was passing quickly without news, but the hope of meeting at least one of my relatives never faded away. Two days before I was to depart Japan, Yokiyo phoned me and exclaimed, "I've found them!" Of course I was thrilled but had to ask, "Were they happy about it?" My mother had feared that maybe they had buried their emotions for her and didn't need a wound reopened. Yokiyo explained to me how the first aunt she spoke to immediately broke into tears, unable to speak with the joy of knowing her lost sister was still alive. My aunts were on the bus from Tokyo the very next day to meet me. They hugged me and were moved by the few characteristics I bore of my mother. They told me a day hadn't passed that they didn't think of her. They had a strong need for closure, and I promised to bring their sister to them.

My sixty-eight-year-old mother, after having outlived her husband, became a reclusive little old lady. We both knew the trip would be difficult for her, but she told me she swore to her sisters over the phone that she would swim to Japan if she had to. I told my mother that I would take her in the spring, giving us six months to prepare and save up for the trip of a lifetime. Her heart started to fill with childhood memories, and she began to tell stories about her past. Both of her sisters started to call her every weekend to make sure the plans were on schedule. My mother was excited but nervous, as she emphasized it had been forty-five years without any contact with her sisters. In reality, these women were total strangers to her.

On the plane ride to Tokyo, Mom confessed it was exactly forty-five years to the month that she last saw Japan. As the sea of lights came into view, her face was pressed against the window. She remembered a sea of lights fading away forty-five years ago, thinking that would be her very last view of her homeland. I silently watched her fight back the tears.

In Narita Airport, my mother eyed her sisters in the crowd and snuck up on them in a jovial way. The sisters wanted to laugh at her prank but broke into tears at finally being united with their long-lost sister. Too emotional to speak, the three of them mostly looked at each other on the train ride to Tokyo. At Aiko's house, over cups of green tea, the women began to talk.

Our week in Tokyo passed quickly. The two women ushered us around like two mother hens, taking us sightseeing and feeding us every delicacy they could think of. It didn't take long until the three sisters acted like sisters again, teasing each other, laughing and talking late every night. The atmosphere filled up with a priceless joy that fed everyone's heart. You couldn't tell that they had spent the last forty-five years apart. I took lots of photographs of the three sisters sitting in the park, singing childhood songs, cooking together.

I witnessed how their love for each other erased the forty-five years they had lost. Every moment together was precious for them, as we all knew this could be the last time these sisters would be together. What was important was they were sisters again, sisters forever. They had proved that time or distance could not damage their sisterly bond.

L. J. Wardell

Together, Achieving
Our Olympic Dream

It didn't start out as an Olympic dream. Back in elementary school, we were a pair of overweight, uncoordinated twins. When teams were chosen, it didn't matter if the game was baseball or dodge ball, we were always last to be picked.

It was so bad, our gym teacher said to us one day, "Penny and Vicky, you have been chosen, along with four other kids, to miss music class and go to remedial gym." This was because neither of us could catch or throw a ball. We were totally mortified.

Although this humiliation whittled away at our self-esteem, we continued to try other sports and activities outside of school. At age eight we discovered synchronized swimming. It was as if the sport had chosen *us*; we found we had a natural talent for it, and we loved it. It was an ideal sport for identical twins: The goal was to swim like mirror images with perfect synchronization. We had an advantage since we were as strong as each other, had identical arm and leg angles and the same sense of timing. We looked so identical that in one photograph even we couldn't tell who was who. At one competition, a little girl said, "Look, Mommy, they're wearing the same face!"

As youngsters, we were inspired to follow in the footsteps of our role models, the National Duet champions— also twins. We passionately loved working with other swimmers and our coaches and we worked incredibly hard. As twins, we were on the same wavelength; we had shared values and implicit trust.

At our first Nationals, we placed 24th out of 28 competitors. There we saw how great the best swimmers were, so we set our sights higher and worked toward one common goal. We rose to 6th place the following year, and then to National Junior Champions the next. Subsequent victories allowed us to travel all over the world, and our dream to participate in the Olympics was born.

We achieved many of our goals, becoming seven-time Canadian Synchronized Swimming Duet champions, world champions in team, and the first duet in the world to ever receive a perfect mark of "10".

But to our great disappointment, the 1980 Olympic Games eluded us when they were boycotted by many countries, including Canada. And then in 1984, we didn't make the team. After fourteen years of training and striving, we had to accept that our Olympic dream would remain out of reach. We retired from swimming to finish our degrees at McGill University.

Then one day five years later, while watching a synchro competition, we both experienced an unexpected sensation. Penny leaned over and whispered: "What if we tried one more time? What do you think about shooting for '92?" My eyes opened wide as one eyebrow lifted slightly. We suddenly realized our Olympic dream was still alive, and we could no longer ignore it. On April Fool's Day 1990, we decided to make an unprecedented comeback and shoot for the 1992 Olympics. We were afraid to announce our plans in case we didn't make it, but in the end, we were more afraid of not trying and having to live with the thought of *What if*?

Everyone said it would be impossible, but our intense desire provided the energy we needed to persevere. We had only two years to get back in shape, only two years to become among the best in the world. No swimmer had ever come back after a five-year absence, especially not at the age of twenty-seven!

We weren't eligible for any funding, so we both maintained full-time jobs and trained five hours every day after work. We still had to support ourselves and fund all our travel to international competitions. For two full years we maintained that grueling schedule without ever knowing whether we'd make it.

Thankfully, we had four dedicated coaches who poured their souls into helping us achieve our dream. Though pushed to our physical limits during training (we had to make up for the five years off), we still loved it. Sometimes we laughed so hard with our head coach Julie, we ran out of air and ended up sinking to the bottom of the pool. Julie helped us to continue believing in ourselves.

When the day of the Olympic trials finally came, we were confident but nervous. We could hardly breathe as we waited after the finals to hear our marks. When they were announced, we jumped up and down, hugging each other: We had won by 0.04!

We could hardly contain our excitement as the '92 Olympic Team gathered in Toronto, en route to Barcelona. During the Opening Ceremonies, we were thrilled to walk into the packed stadium to thunderous applause. Our spirits received another tremendous lift during those last few stressful days of training, thanks to the Olympic Mailbag Program. After practice each day, we would rush to dig through the giant pile of bright yellow postcards sent to the Canadian Team, and pick out those to us, many addressed simply to "Penny and Vicky Vilagos— Barcelona." The messages came from old childhood friends, complete strangers and former athletes. Imagine how we felt when we read, "Dear Penny & Vicky: You are swimming my dream. I used to be able to swim two lengths of the pool in a single breath. I am now disabled, and can no longer swim at all. I am sending you my strength—May the sun shine on you." And the sun did shine on us in Barcelona.

When our big day finally came, and we stepped onto the pool deck and heard "Competitor #9 . . . Canada," our considerable stress turned to a sunburst pride. As the crowd cheered and waved their maple leaf flags, we ignored the temptation of the moment to reflect on the 30,000 hours of training it had taken to get there, and looked at the water, in order to fully focus on the job at hand.

Swimming that day was magical. Despite the stress, we enjoyed every moment. As the music ended and the applause began, we looked up at Julie, and her expression told us what we already felt—we had given the performance of our lives!

Finally, we marched around the pool for the medal ceremony. As we stepped on the podium to receive our silver medals, our joy was doubled as we shared the moment together. We hugged each other, as if to say, "Thanks for your commitment, support and encouragement."

We'll remember forever the electric atmosphere as everyone swayed back and forth and joined in singing "Amigos Para Siempre," or "Friends for Life." That's when it began to sink in: After twenty-one years, our Olympic dream had come true!

As one of the many celebrations after we returned from Barcelona, all five Quebec medalists were invited to throw the opening pitch at the Montreal Expos baseball game! Now a lot of things had changed since elementary school, but throwing a ball was not one of them. When we received the invitation, we immediately thought, "Oh no!" and for an instant we both felt like little kids again, as memories of "I don't want her on my team," came flooding back.

On game day, we drove to the stadium with a sinking feeling. We followed the organizer onto the field, along with the other Olympic medalists—Sylvie Fréchette, Guillaume Leblanc and Nicolas Gill. The baseballs felt unnatural in our hands; our single solace was knowing we would only have to throw them a short distance.

We watched uneasily as the organizer kept on walking . . . and walking . . . all the way to the pitcher's mound! Glancing sideways, we saw fear in each other's eyes . . . and tens of thousands of fans who were cheering loudly and doing the wave. Time for the opening pitch . . . five catchers lined up, ready to catch our five balls. . . . On cue, we wound up and threw. Penny's catcher leaped forward—but neither fast enough, nor nearly far enough. Her ball, falling short, hit the dirt with an embarrassing thud.

For a split second we froze, reliving that awful, elementary school feeling. We prepared ourselves for the laughter, but this time, everything was different. As we heard the roar and the applause, the sinking feeling evaporated and we smiled—at the crowd, at each other, at the memories—and we waved back.

Penny and Vicky Vilagos

I Wish for You

Carol and Helen didn't like the same foods, clothes, boys, books . . . you get the idea. But these sisters loved each other with a heavenly love. Throughout childhood, they played a silly game called "I wish for you." More often than not, good things did come their way.

Carol and Helen stayed close when graduation sent one of them away from home. Carol married and had children. Helen remained single and found fulfillment in the advertising world on Madison Avenue.

Years passed. One day, the day Carol found a lump, she instinctively ran to call "Sis." Through a long-distance line and many tears, the sisters comforted one another.

The doctor was very up front: cancer. Carol was stoic, even upbeat. In the still of the night, Carol curled up on the couch and called Helen. By the next afternoon, they were meeting at the airport.

Helen's visit became indefinite. As the weeks slipped by, so did Carol's hope. Oh, she'd try to be her old funny self. "Cancer Carol and Healthy Helen," she'd say. But the prognosis wasn't good. When the tears came, Helen learned that Carol was fearful only for her family.

On a crisp December morning Helen returned from a predawn walk. Carol grabbed her arm. "I'm scared," she admitted. Helen was very positive, strangely reassuring. She didn't even cry.

That evening, Helen suddenly announced she was going home. Carol blinked. *How could she leave now?* Carol assumed Helen had reached a point where she could no longer deal with a terminal sister.

At the airport, Helen embraced her sister and put a hand to her cheek. They said very little, just the usual good-byes.

Waiting for her doctor one day, Carol gazed at one of the office paintings. Two little girls walking hand-in-hand through a meadow. Carol closed her eyes and could almost smell the wildflowers.

"Carol," the doctor said as he eased into the room. "I'll just tell you right now that we can't find any cancer from these tests. It's gone, and I have no explanation. You're cancer-free."

Jumping up the front steps in one leap, Carol burst through the door. She had good news, she told her grim-faced husband. "But I have bad news, honey. It's Helen. She was in a car accident today, and I'm afraid . . ." His voice trailed off but Carol knew. And the rest of the evening, indeed, the rest of their lives, was bittersweet.

So, what is your speculation on this story? What do you think Helen did on her morning walk? I like to think she did a little bargaining with someone. Someone who had the power to grant wishes. Fervent wishes. Sister wishes.

Robert Strand

A Heart-to-Heart with Rosel

There can be no situation in life in which the conversation of my dear sister will not administer some comfort to me.

Lady Mary Wortley Montagu

Still under the mirage of sleep, I watched the long procession snake lazily down the winding lane through endless rows of graves. The clouds hung low and threatened to weep as the mourners scrambled from their cars and huddled around my sister Rosel's casket, and the waiting deep, dark hole. Neighbors cared for Karen, Rosel's baby, while we buried her mom. . . . It started to snow. Rosel's last words to me, "I'm not worried. You'll take good care of my baby . . . ," rose from the grave and competed with the song of the wind, that came and went again and again . . .

The cries of the crows awoke me with a start. "Karen," I shouted at the top of my lungs, while slipping into a new pair of slacks. I raced into her room and tickled her toes. "Get up," I urged. "We're late."

I felt my sister's presence. It had happened before. Whenever Karen created disorder in our otherwise docile life, she seemed to appear. And so I remonstrated, in a thought that is, *Why did you have to die?*

Karen pulled the blanket over her head and turned to the other side.

"Did you forget," I gasped pulling the covers all the way off her bed. "Today is the test for the scholarship."

"I don't want to go," she moaned. "I'm tired."

You see Rosel, that's what she puts me through every day, late to bed and late to rise.

"Come on now," I urged, my voice softening. "If you hurry we can still make it in time."

She has a good chance of getting that scholarship to the School of Visual Arts. That girl of mine, I mean yours, I mean our girl is very artistic. Maybe even gifted. And her high-school counselor says that it's a fine school and perfect for Karen.

Exhausted and weary, Karen slouched in her seat as I weaved in and out of the morning rush traffic. Approaching the George Washington Bridge, the traffic slowed to a crawl.

"We'll never make it in time," I sighed shaking my head from side to side.

We were waiting in one of at least ten lanes to pay the bridge toll. I jerked the car out of our lane, passed at least a hundred cars, and then boldly squeezed back into the lane just before the toll collector. The driver in back of us disapproved by keeping his hand on the horn.

"Oh, be quiet!"

Karen turned around, then grinned my way in admiration.

I sensed a strong displeasure from our phantom companion and quickly remarked, "I never do this . . . I hate when anyone does this . . . it's so rude."

I'm just trying to get her there on time, you know.

Rain began to pelt the bridge as we crossed the churning

Hudson below and slowed the traffic even more.

Nervously, Karen ran her hands through her hair. "Do you think I can take the test another time?"

"No-o-o . . . I don't think so. I don't think they make allowances for lateness." And after a long pause I added, "When we get there, you run inside. I'll go and park, okay? We'll find you later."

"We?"

"I mean I'll find you later. Look, we're here." We had arrived at the entrance of the School of Visual Arts, and I watched as Karen darted from the car. The wind, generated by her haste, disarrayed her long blonde hair. *Isn't she beautiful?* I smiled watching her vanish through the door together with a few other latecomers. *Maybe you could put in a good word for her. With four already in college, we could use some help you know.*

I parked the car in a nearby garage and hurried toward the school. It stopped raining but the morning remained as gray as the old weathered building that housed the classrooms of the famous school. *Does it rain where you are? No, I didn't think so.* The entrance hall was crowded with people milling about, chatting amicably. Karen was nowhere in sight.

"I have six children," a woman to my left was telling a middle-aged couple to her left, "but this one is impos-sible." This one, I gathered, was the creative one in her flock. The one she had brought here and was now some-where in this building, behind closed doors, competing with Karen and others for a scholarship. "I gave up on him a long time ago," she continued, a warm edge to her voice. "He marches to his own tune."

I felt a nudge. *Stop it . . . I'm not going to give up on our girl.*

I was never good at idle conversation, so I listened mostly. To my delight, I realized quickly that we all had something in common. We all had an impossible child, just like Karen.

"I know what you mean," a baritone voice from across the room overpowered my neighbor's conversation. "Up all night, but don't wake me in the morning."

I nodded in agreement, inching along a few paces, *just like Karen.*

"Tell them to do something," a woman in a black leather skirt, exclaimed to no one in particular, "and you'd think you started World War Three."

And so it went on and on. Everyone here had a complaint against his or her child. But there was a smile behind the mask of complaints. I could see it. I could feel it. And I felt a close bond to these strangers for I realized that, although we all learned to embrace the creative mind, we also learned to walk at the edge of the world and not fall off. *So, what do you think? Karen will fit right in . . . don't you agree?*

The day rolled along. We saw a movie, listened to several speakers, had lunch and studied with fascination the students' awesome works. At the end of the day, once more reunited with our kids, we stepped outside and said good-bye. It must have rained some more. Vapor steaming off the wet pavement in the late day's sun scented the air refreshingly. Any last-minute best wishes were silenced by the New York City sounds.

"Did you see the guy with the orange hair?" Karen asked as we crossed the George Washington Bridge on our way home.

"Which one?" I chuckled.

Karen threw her head back in exasperation. "There was only one with orange hair," she huffed. "Some had green hair . . . two guys had purple hair . . . but only one had orange hair."

See what this world is coming to? Green, orange, purple

hair . . . You didn't see that when you were still here.

"Did you say something?" Karen gave me a sideways puzzled glance. "Anyway, I think he'll get the scholarship . . . the guy with the orange hair. . . . You should have seen his portfolio."

"I hope his father isn't a rich doctor," I remarked not without irony.

"Tell me about it . . ." Karen grimaced in a half smile.

"Don't worry," I added on a more somber note. "You'll go to that school. Somehow we'll work it out." And then I made a silent vow: *She'll go to that school. I promise.*

Although my sister was no longer with us, we were never without her either. And so we drove home, the three of us that is, into the brilliant skylight of dusk.

Christa Holder Ocker

Right with Me

You are my sister, but more than that
You are my dear friend, too.
I appreciate so very much
The things you say and do.

When I am sad, you cheer me up
So my blues will go away,
Then we talk a little while
About our yesterdays.

Though life has brought much happiness,
Still, there's been sadness, too.
I am so grateful
That I spent those times with you.

Though no one knows the future,
My prayer will always be,
While I am traveling on life's road,
You'll be right there with me.

Alora M. Knight

Melody

"Melody asked me to do this for her, and I said I would because I want her to be remembered well. But this is very difficult for me. There were thirteen months between us; she is in my memories as far back as they go, and I don't know how to live in a world without Melody in it." With these heartbroken words, and in a voice hoarse from weeping, I began my sister's eulogy. For the next twenty minutes, shaking with tension and overwhelming grief, I tried to explain to those in attendance how wonderful, good and worthy of life my sister was, and give them a glimpse of the void her death caused.

By all understanding of the bond, we were good sisters. Until our marriages we slept together, sharing our secrets in whispers and giggles once the lights were out. We played often, fought sometimes and stuck together fiercely in school. We double-dated in high school, and she married first. We each had two sons and two daughters and poured ourselves into motherhood. Though our marriages forced us to live several states apart, we wrote often, and burned the phone lines between us with our calls because sometimes we just had to hear the other's voice.

I thought we knew all there was about being good sisters. Then she was diagnosed with cancer. Eleven months before she died she called and told me the dreadful news. The doctors gave her five years. She was scared, and I said I was, too, and we cried. We were not yet forty: How could we face separation in just five years? I still feel angry and cheated that we didn't get those other four years.

I determined to write her nearly every day and share every bit of the experience with her. I was with her often through the initial treatments, and there was a blissful three months in which no cancer could be found. Then suddenly the cancer returned with a vengeance, terrifying in its rapid growth. Her first reaction, when the doctor told her, was to run. She *did* flee—straight to me. We spent a week together—praying, talking, crying and laughing. With everything in my soul fighting against the reality of her prognosis, I decided to embrace this horror with her, feeling every emotion, encouraging her in every step. I held her when she cried, and we mourned for the dreams we would never fulfill, the places we would never see together, the weddings she would miss and the grandchildren she would never hold. I promised her everything she asked for. We planned her daughters' weddings and talked of gifts she wanted her children to have. She listed all her personal belongings, and entrusted their distribution to me. She told me her deepest fears, confessed her shames and regrets, and shared her earnest longing for more time with her kids. During the day, I calmly listened to her, respecting her thoughts, completely awed by her strength and dignity and faith. At night I wept bitterly.

I went to her home for two weeks after her visit, to help prepare for the harsh chemical therapy plan about to be launched against her disease. When the day came for me to leave, my emotions were raw, the emotional intensity of our time together gripping me strongly. I was so afraid she would die during the treatments, and I wasn't nearly ready for it.

Taking her now-thin face in my hands, I whispered, "I don't know what to say."

Quietly, gently, she whispered back, "There are no more words, Jenn. We've already said them all."

I held her gently, as long as she could bear the pain of the embrace, trying to memorize for all time what she felt like. I cried the long drive home.

Weeks later the doctors reluctantly told us there was nothing more to be done. Other family members held back the report from Melody, fearful of causing her more pain by taking away all hope.

In simple words, for the morphine had ravaged her senses, I explained it to her. My eyes were shining with tears, my throat closing on the words. Inexplicably, she said, "No tears." I choked them back, and we made plans for her to go home, where she most wanted to be. Plaintively, she told me she was afraid she would be alone at the final moment. I promised her I wouldn't let that happen.

Very early the next morning, I returned to the hospital, so we could be alone. Sitting as close to her as I could, holding her fragile hand, I asked her to please let me cry.

"Why?" she whispered.

"Because I'm going to miss you so much. I don't want you to die."

Laying my head down on her bed, I wept hot, anguished tears, while she stroked my hair and comforted me in my sorrow. It was an agonizing moment. Later, I again found the strength to walk through it with her, but that morning for those minutes, I leaned on *her*, and she stood strong for *me*.

I had to go home. My family needed me, and the inevitable end had no definite date. Our mother stayed with Mel the last few weeks but called me on the last day and said to hurry, that the hospice nurse was sure it would be within hours.

I dropped everything and made the trip as fast as I safely could, praying desperately that she could hang on till I got there. Mom told her I was coming, though she was doubtful Melody understood. Walking in the door of her room, I was weak with relief that I had made it in time. For ninety-eight minutes I talked to my sister, prayed over her, kissed her, sang to her and read aloud all her favorite scriptures. She never spoke, but I know she heard me. The nurse was amazed she hung on for so many hours with a 107-degree fever, only four respirations a minute and almost no blood pressure.

I will always believe she waited for me.

This is the part of sisterhood I'm still learning: going on after a sister is no longer there. The pain and loss are worse than I imagined, and time without her stretches before me in aching loneliness.

I'm at peace in knowing she is with Christ, but as our older sister said bitterly to a well-meaning friend who tried to comfort her at the funeral, "Heaven would have been just as beautiful thirty years from now."

My memories are indescribably precious. I have no regrets; we wasted no time, faced the dreadful future together, said all the right words, smiled and laughed and cried in complete unison, all the way up to the last moment possible. She was a perfect sister.

A few weeks ago her eighteen-year-old daughter, Melissa, called me, sobbing with grief. "Aunt Jenn, I'm afraid everyone is going to forget how wonderful Mama was." Weeping with her, I promised that wouldn't happen. I won't let her be forgotten.

Jennifer Koscheski

Light in the Window

It was the first night of Chanukah and the night before Ellie's last final. As a freshman, she was more than ready to go home for the first time since August. She'd packed everything she needed to take home except the books she was cramming with and her menorah, the eight-branch candelabra that's lit every night of Chanukah. Ellie had been so tempted to pack the menorah earlier that night. However, just as she was getting ready to justify to herself why it was okay to skip the first night's lighting—(A) she'd have to wait for the candles to burn out before she could leave for the library, and (B) she had no clue as to where her candles were hiding—her conscience (and common sense) kicked in. The voice coming from that special place in her body where "mother guilt" resides said, "You have the menorah out, so light it already." Never one to ignore her mother's advice, Ellie dug up the candles, lit them, said the blessings, placed the menorah on her windowsill and spent the rest of the evening in her room studying.

Ellie's first winter break was uneventful, and when she returned to her dorm on the day before classes started, she was surprised to find a small note taped to her door.

"Thank you," the note said. It was signed "Susan." It was dated the day that Ellie had left after finals. Ellie was totally perplexed. She didn't know a Susan. Convinced that the letter had been delivered to her by mistake, Ellie put the note on her desk and forgot about it.

About a half an hour before she was getting ready to head out for dinner there was a knock at Ellie's door. There, standing in the hall, was a woman Ellie didn't recognize. "I'm Susan," she said. "I wanted to thank you in person, but you'd already left before I finished my finals."

"Are you sure it's me you're looking for?" asked Ellie. Susan asked if she could come in and explain.

It seemed that Susan had been facing the same dilemma that Ellie had been that first night of Chanukah. She really didn't want to light her menorah either. Not because she was packing, or was heading home, couldn't find the candles or because she was busy studying, but because her older sister Hannah had been killed by a drunk driver ten months earlier, and this was the first year that she'd have to light the menorah candles alone. The sisters had always taken turns lighting the first candle, and this wasn't Susan's year. She just couldn't bring herself to take her sister's place. Susan said that whenever it was Hannah's turn to light the first candle, she'd always tease Susan that the candles she lit would burn longer and brighter than when Susan lit them. One year she even went so far as to get a timer out. It had always annoyed Susan that Hannah would say something so stupid, but still, it was part of the family tradition. Susan said that it was just too painful to even think about Chanukah without Hannah, and she had decided on skipping the entire holiday.

Susan said that she had just finished studying and was closing her drapes when she happened to glance across the courtyard of the quad and saw the candles shining in Ellie's window. "I saw that menorah in your window, and

I started to cry. It was as if Hannah had taken her turn and put the menorah in your window for me to see." Susan said that when she stopped crying she said the blessings, turned off the lights in her room and watched the candles across the quad until they burned out.

Susan told Ellie that it was as she was lying in bed that night thinking about how close she felt to Hannah when she saw the menorah, that it dawned on her that Hannah had been right. Hannah's last turn always would have candles that would burn longer and brighter than any of Susan's, because for Susan, Hannah's lights would never go out. They would always be there, in her heart for Susan to see when she needed to reconnect with Hannah.

All Susan had to do was close her eyes and remember the candles in the window, the ones that Hannah had lit the last time it was her turn.

Eileen Goltz

$\overline{3}$
SIBLING
REVELRY

Sisters are probably the most competitive relationship within the family, but once the sisters are grown, it becomes the strongest relationship.

Margaret Mead

Stone Soup®

An Untraditional Holiday Tale

More than Santa Claus, your sister knows when you've been bad or good.

Linda Sunshine

As kids, my sister and I were enemies. Three years my junior, Wendy would borrow my clothes and leave them scattered on the floor. We'd fight about who got to use the bathroom first and how much hot water was left. At times, we'd be locked in hair-pulling brawls.

As we grew up, dislike turned into tolerance, acceptance and then friendship. Today, she's not only my best friend but also my partner in crime as we try to undo the nutty traditions my parents won't give up. There's one in particular we've tried to buck; each year we're unsuccessful.

For more years than I can remember, Wendy and I have read *The Night Before Christmas* aloud to our family on Christmas Eve. The routine repeats itself each year.

After midnight church service on Christmas Eve, Wendy and I are instructed to go upstairs, where we find new pajamas. Then, clad in our new duds, we scamper downstairs for a late-night snack of homemade cookies and wine, sit on the fireplace, and read from the book that belonged to my grandmother.

Wendy's twenty-seven; I'm three years older. We're still reading the story. In fact, we're still receiving new pajamas, although Victoria's Secret has replaced the OshKosh.

Every year, we vow to quit reading. When we tell my parents we're too old for this, they laugh. "Santa Claus won't come tonight if there's no reading," my mom says. She's not kidding.

Santa still leaves us presents in exchange for milk and cookies, although the milk's long since been replaced by beer. In fact, the Easter Bunny still hides our baskets, but that's another story.

Admittedly, Wendy and I have sunk so low as to make our reading obnoxious, hoping this would force us out of this yearly duty. One year, we read in country twang. The next year, we read one word at a time, slowly. Another year, we read as fast as we could. Our family calls the variety cute and won't consider ending the tradition.

So Wendy and I decided to get even. Seven years ago, we planned our first revenge.

We were giving my parents a grill, and rather than just give it to them, we wanted them to work for it, punishment for those years of reading.

When my parents opened their present that year, they found a riddle. Solve the riddle and they'd find another clue leading them closer to their present. Thirty minutes later, after running around the house, they located the grill on the porch.

We still had to read the next year. So we got meaner.

We filled a box the size of a mattress with Styrofoam peanuts. Inside three peanuts, we stuck a rolled-up message that directed my parents to their present. Luck struck, unfortunately, for after fifteen minutes of searching, my dad located a coded peanut.

A year later, we employed intellect for our payback scheme.

The box my parents opened contained a booby-trapped Twister board. To find their present, my parents had to make it to one corner of the board. Getting there required successfully passing through a maze of challenges. After completing each challenge, my parents could move to the next spot.

Wendy and I spent a day putting the maze together, but it was worth it. On Christmas morning, my parents sang "Jingle Bells" with their noses plugged, kissed our two cats (which you couldn't have paid them enough to do ordinarily), stood on their heads, and yes, read *The Night Before Christmas.*

We weren't excused from our duty.

Wendy and I have since made my parents play our version of "Let's Make a Deal." They traded away everything except a bag of kitty litter. Two hours later, when Santa called to say there'd been a technical error, my parents found a new television.

The next Christmas, we put together a huge jigsaw puzzle, scribbled their present on the back (a trip to San Francisco), disbanded the puzzle, and then watched them spend the next several hours putting it together. The following year, they had to complete a list of crazy activities before they received a map, which directed them to their presents. In our pajamas, we piled into the car and drove to a friend's house where we'd stashed their gifts.

Last year, they played our version of *Who Wants to Win Their Christmas Present,* modeled after *Who Wants to Be a Millionaire.* Our rules were different, though: Goof up and they had to perform certain activities before they could play again. So they ran around the outside of the house in their bathrobes, clenched my dog's pig-ear treat between their teeth, and did twenty push-ups on the floor.

Our plan for revenge has obviously backfired. My parents enjoy their payback so much—they even look forward to it—that our goofy way of giving gifts has now become a tradition of its own.

That means Wendy and I will be stuck reading *The Night Before Christmas* forever. If only the story would change. But it doesn't, and maybe that's the point. As much as I hate to admit it, I would never trade the reading for the hours I spend with my sister planning new, zany ways to give my parents their Christmas present.

At least Wendy and I will never have to shop for pj's again.

Karen Asp

Sundae Confessions:
Breaking the Ice Cream Rule

I worry about scientists discovering that lettuce has been fattening all along.

Erma Bombeck

As the hottest days of the year approach, my thoughts turn to ice cream. For me, ice cream holds the fascination of illicit sex.

My mother, a zealous nutritionist, held all refined sugars in the category of unmitigated evil. When I was a child, she would call the hostess before I arrived at friends' birthday parties. "My daughter isn't allowed any cake or candy," she would warn sternly. I would sit alone at the end of the table while the other girls gobbled their goopy treats. When the hostess offered me an apple, I tried to look happy and avoid unwanted sympathy. I didn't want to cry.

My mother's goal was to raise pure, untainted children. Avoiding sugar—and the resulting flab and tooth decay—was more important than life itself. She would prophesize with morbid glee: "When you're lying in your grave, you won't have a single cavity in your mouth."

For my sister, Lisa, and me, breaking the rules was the superglue that held us together. When we weren't fighting for scraps of parental attention, we were scheming to sneak candy and ice cream.

On Halloween, our mother allowed us to harvest trick-or-trick candy if we handed over all the contraband upon arriving home. Always practical, she would give it back out to the goblins and astronauts who came to our door. One year, Lisa and I contrived to hide half our hoard under our beds. At night, we gorged ourselves on Reese's Peanut Butter Cups and miniature Snickers bars.

Even as teenagers, sugary treats held more allure than drugs or sex. Ice cream sundaes, the most evil of confections, offered a sensual pleasure without the risks of intimacy or pregnancy. I first learned the dangers of sex from my mother. In sixth grade, on a long walk, she told me about all the rubbery and plastic forms of birth control and the importance of using them when "with" a man to prevent pregnancy. As a prepubescent girl, with no whisper of breasts or sexual urges, I was terrified.

Although we are both happily married, Lisa and I still take great joy in breaking the rules and indulging in the sensual depravity of ice cream sundaes. On a summer visit to our parents' house, we decide to sneak away to Friendly's. At the counter, with the sinful delight of the deceitful, Lisa and I contemplate our sundaes.

"I'm considering hot butterscotch and fudge with Swiss almond crunch and butterscotch ice cream," I tell Lisa. She is lost in thought, staring up at the selection of ice creams. I suspect she is trying to decide between chocolate chip mint ice cream with hot fudge, or vanilla with caramel sauce and chocolate jimmies.

The waiter, a bored high school student, brings the glossy sundae menus. The bright scoops slathered with sauces reel before my eyes. "Are you ready to order?" he asks. He is looking toward the entrance, perhaps expecting his girlfriend or his gang. He could care less about our high moment. He is tall and thin with brown hair falling over his pimply forehead.

"Let me ask a few questions," I say in a feigned voice of calm. "Does this sundae have two scoops or three?" I hold back an urge to order the super-duper five-scooper. My mouth is watering, my hands are cold, my speech is high-pitched and wavering.

The waiter slowly gets into the spirit of the thing as I press him with questions about the temperature of the hot fudge and the saltiness of nuts in the Swiss almond fudge. Lisa wants to know if the mint ice cream is very minty or mildly minty. Our taste buds are whipped into frenzy.

The waiter leans over us jotting notes on his pad. He carefully explains the types of sauces and options for whipped cream, leaving to check on supplies in the kitchen. After finalizing our orders, he asks: "How about if I just go wild on these sundaes?" We agree.

We fidget until our sundaes finally arrive: pure bliss. With my long spoon, I plunge through the frilly whipped cream and the hot sauce covering the frozen scoops nestled below. It's sweet, cold, hot, all at once. We trade tastes, making sure we scoop equal amounts of ice cream and sauce on each spoon. We gorge ourselves until our spoons clink on the bottom of the thick glass dishes. I see the waiter looking over at us. We sigh contented. No need for cigarettes.

Andrea D'Asaro

CLOSE TO HOME　JOHN McPHERSON

10-31

"Look, why don't we save ourselves a lot of time
and trouble. You give us all of your candy,
turn out your lights and go to bed, and
we'll be honor-bound not to go to any other homes."

My Sister, the Star

When she was eighteen, my older sister Elizabeth was cast as Timothy Hutton's girlfriend in *Ordinary People*. A year later in 1981, her picture was on the cover of *Newsweek*, and she had dropped out of the acting program at Juilliard to make two more movies. By the time she was twenty she had been nominated for an Oscar for her performance in *Ragtime*.

I distinctly remember my own life at that time. I was eighteen; I worked as a supermarket cashier and wore a polyester smock that I never once washed. On my fifteen-minute breaks, I read magazine interviews in which my sister, who is two years older than I, talked about the "grounding influence" I had on her life.

For my sister, becoming famous at such a young age was an overwhelming and often isolating experience. It meant embarking on an adult life at the same time most of her friends were partying their way through college. It also meant being under constant scrutiny: in grocery stores, in restaurants, on the subway.

As my sister was adjusting to and resisting her own stardom, I was loving every minute of it. My first year in college, I decorated my room with lobby-size posters of movies she was starring in. Everyone at school knew who she was and many of my conversations had to do with what it was like to be a movie star's sister. I never grew tired of this; in fact, I was grateful. It meant trotting out stories no one else had, even making some up. Had I been on sets? Did I know famous people? In truth, not really, but in the moment, you bet. In some inexplicable way, I believed that I did know them, that these were the people I should be friends with. So much so, that when I graduated from college, I rushed to New York with no job or career ambitions other than parking myself solidly in the shadow of my sister's fame.

Now that I look back on it, I have to wonder what I was thinking. Part of the explanation had to do with my relationship with my sister. I'd stood in her shadow ever since I could remember. When we were young, she was the brave one and I was the homebody, the scaredy-cat. I spent my childhood with her in my sights, trying to keep up. My desire to be with her was insatiable. I actually gave her my allowance to get her to sleep in my room at night.

She seemed to love my adulation until she got to high school. By that time, she had discovered acting and the crowd that came with it—intense, handsome guys; beautiful, enigmatic girls. We lived in Los Angeles, and many of her friends were already professional actors. I hated all of them, hated that she was growing up without me, hated that I wasn't included in her life.

Then, in her senior year of high school, everything changed again. Success tapped my sister and none of her friends, most of whom disappeared within a few months of her making *Ordinary People*. That year was probably the loneliest of my sister's life. She was living by herself in New York. Suddenly, she was calling me all the time, suggesting trips together, begging me to visit her. I would feign hesitation for a while, and then, because some part of me will always be the younger sister who paid good money for her time, I'd agree to whatever she suggested. It has to be said: most of the reason I loved her fame was that it ended the battle for her attention and brought her full-square back to me.

For five years after I graduated from college, our lives were completely enmeshed. I visited her on every movie set, flying to France, England, Italy, New Orleans and Toronto. "My sister has to come," she'd say, stipulating in her contracts that an airline ticket be provided for me. To this day, I'm not sure why we both thought it was so important that I keep her company. Practically speaking, no star on a set has a chance to get lonely; she isn't left alone long enough.

In retrospect, I suppose I was there to register it all; the enormous hotel suites, the gigantic fruit baskets, the trailers stocked with candy. How can you savor that kind of luxury without a piece of your past standing there with you, screaming with amazement and reminding you that you're still the girl who grew up in a one-car family? And reminding you, empathetically, that you deserve none of this?

Over time, I became good at being on sets. I no longer had to make up stories about famous people because I started getting to know some. I'd hang out in make-up trailers and tell beautiful women how beautiful they looked in new and original ways, as if it were my job. I gained a reputation for being easy to talk to. Once, I sat with Susan Sarandon while she showed me a stack of pictures of her baby. Afterward, she hugged me and told me how "amazingly together" I was. For what? For not having a real job or life? For never accepting work I wasn't willing to quit to hang out on a set? I never questioned such compliments.

Instead I loved easily surpassing the world's low expectations of someone like me—a hanger-on, a star's sister. If I mentioned a book, no one could get over how intelligent I was. If I ventured a joke, everyone would tell me I should be a stand-up comic. What wasn't to love about a world that sang my praises for doing nothing more than making conversation?

Eventually though, I realized something was wrong. I remember Alec Baldwin asking me one day if I wanted to be an actress. "Oh, God, no," I said. It wasn't such a far-fetched question. This was on the set of the one movie I acted in, *She's Having a Baby*, in which I played my sister's sister. Sitting there in full costume and makeup, I was embarrassed that anyone would think I was trying to make a career out of the same thing my sister did. "So what do you do?" he asked.

It was a simple question, but it caught me off guard. "I work as an administrative assistant," I said, referring to one of the temp jobs that made up my career. An awkward silence hung in the air until my sister looked up and spoke. "Really, she writes," she said.

I wanted to kill her—I felt she had humiliated me in front of Alec Baldwin. I had always wanted to be a writer, but that was my secret. Instead, I told people I wanted to teach, study marine biology, anything to masquerade my real desire. But Elizabeth knew the truth. She knew I'd spent my childhood filling up diaries and writing terrible stories, all romance about handicapped people falling in love. She knew about my first book (a collection immodestly titled *Cammie*) that had been the center of a childhood fight: She twice vandalized the shirt cardboard cover—once to write I HATE above the title, the second time to write I LOVE. In that moment of silence with Alec Baldwin, Elizabeth announced my most private fantasy and, in so doing, very gently insisted that we start thinking about me instead.

Later that week, we had what I still think of as the worst fight of our lives. I told her I thought she was dismissive of the crew and spoiled; that I was tired of people fluttering around her, coddling her. "You take everyone for granted," I yelled, meaning the production assistants—but of course, I really meant me. The fight was teary and emotional and went on for hours, filled with accusations that dated from years back. But, by the end, I understood: Maybe the state of my life wasn't exactly her fault.

For years, I thought not having a job or accomplishments was okay if I appeared "together" to the famous people and hairdressers I was at my best around. As Elizabeth was trying to build a life despite her stardom, I was tugging at that fame, stretching it to see if I could wear it, too. It fit neither of us very well. I think I wanted my life to be about her in those days so that it wouldn't have to be about me. If I was never called upon to rise to my own challenges, I'd never be put on the spot and fall.

When we returned from the set of *She's Having a Baby*, Elizabeth helped me form my first writing group. Even though she didn't write, she came to all of our meetings and told people she just liked to listen. "I'm a fan," she'd say.

To this day, I suspect I became a writer because my sister believed I could and should be. I also think she was tired of being the center of attention and wanted to sit in the audience for awhile. In the beginning, she was far more ambitious for me than I was for myself. She gave my first play to her agent, who helped set up a reading, and she called all of her friends to get a crowd to show up for it. I distinctly remember listening to her on the telephone, telling them, "This play is so good. It is better than Arthur Miller."

It wasn't; trust me. And when I look back to that reading, what stands out is not the play but an image of my sister at the end, when it was my turn to stand up and, for the first time in my life, take a bow. I was embarrassed and thrilled, and I turned to her beside me. To my surprise, her face was red and puffy with tears.

I don't know if it was painful for her to watch me shift from being an appendage of her life to having a life of my own. Probably she felt a little sad and also relieved, just as becoming less famous has been sad and also a relief to her. In the end, we both realized that her being famous was neither sustaining nor interesting for either of us.

Now Elizabeth lives in London, is married to a British director and has two daughters, and is acting in plays and movies there.

I'm in Massachusetts with my husband and son, working on a novel. Our lives are very separate these days. Her last five movies were all shot without me perched on the set, working my magic. Although we talk on the phone regularly, we see each other once a year, at most. Sometimes this scares me. She has been such a constant presence in my life, a figure on my horizon. If we aren't hovering like magpies in the backgrounds of each other's lives, then who are we, exactly?

Last Christmas, my mother kept remarking on how much I sounded like Elizabeth when I talked to my baby; this, I confess, irritated me. I'm still a child about this. I may have spent five years following her everywhere, but, please, I wasn't trying to imitate her.

Then, it occurred to me: My mother was right. I do sound like Elizabeth, for the simple reason that I love the way she is as a mother, and I do imitate that. Even far apart, it seems, we are still inside each other. Perhaps, after all these years, the tables have turned and she has become the grounding influence for me.

Cammie McGovern

"What's-her-name-here claims she's always lost in
Renee Elizabeth Alexandria's shadow."

Reprinted with permission of Jonny Hawkins.

Sisters

Though they have so much in common,
They are different.

Though they love each other,
They often throw punches.

Sometimes they feel hatred toward one another.
Then they embrace with hugs and kisses.

While they never really get angry with one another,
They can constantly fight.

They are the same and the opposite.
They are sisters.

They are best friends.
They are reflections of one another.

Hope Fillingim
Age eleven

The Importance of Conscience

When there's a sibling there's a quibbling.

Selma Saskin

I was faced with a decision. While delivering laundry into the appropriate bedrooms, I stumbled upon my thirteen-year-old sister's diary, a modern-day Pandora's box, suffused with temptation. What was I to do? I had always been jealous of my little sister. Her charming smile, endearing personality and many talents threatened my place as leading lady. I competed with her tacitly and grew to resent her natural abilities. I felt it necessary to shatter her shadow with achievements of my own. As a result, we seldom spoke. I sought opportunities to criticize her and relished surpassing her achievements. Her diary lay at my feet, and I didn't think of the result of opening it. I considered not her privacy, the morality of my actions, nor her consequential pain. I merely savored the possibility of digging up enough dirt to soil my competitor's spotless record. I reasoned my iniquity as sisterly duty. It was my responsibility to keep a check on her activities. It would be wrong of me not to.

I tentatively plucked the book from the floor and opened it, fanning through the pages, searching for my name, convinced that I would discover scheming and slander. As I read, the blood ran from my face. It was worse than I suspected. I felt faint and slouched to the floor. There was neither conspiracy nor defamation. There was a succinct description of herself, her goals and her dreams followed by a short portrayal of the person who has inspired her most. I started to cry.

I was her hero. She admired me for my personality, my achievements and, ironically, my integrity. She wanted to be like me. She had been watching me for years, quietly marveling over my choices and actions. I ceased reading, struck with the crime I had committed. I had expended so much energy into pushing her away that I had missed out on her.

I had wasted years resenting someone capable of magic—and now I had violated her trust. It was I who had lost something beautiful, and it was I who would never allow myself to do such a thing again.

Reading the earnest words my sister had written seemed to melt an icy barrier around my heart, and I longed to know her again. I was finally able to put aside the petty insecurity that kept me from her. On that fateful afternoon, as I put aside the laundry and rose to my feet, I decided to go to her—this time to experience instead of to judge, to embrace instead of to fight. After all, she was my sister.

Elisha M. Webster

Of Yellow-Haired Dolls and Ugly Clay Bowls

A few months before my wedding, my mother and I were breezing through all the details that go along with planning a large wedding. My fiancé, on the other hand, was happily making our honeymoon arrangements. Dennis and I saw each other only on weekends, and we were looking forward to our two-week wedding trip. About three weeks before our wedding, my parents moved into their newly built log home, where I shared a room with my younger sister. I spent what weeknights I could rooting through the boxes we'd moved from the old farmhouse, deciding what was my sister's and what I should move to our new apartment. Twenty-three years of nostalgia awaited me each evening. I opened box after box filled with high school yearbooks, 4-H ribbons, kites made from construction paper, paper-plate seed-shakers and crayon drawings. And at the bottom of one box, I'd discovered a homely brown clay bowl that only a child could have fashioned and only a mother could have loved. I couldn't remember making the bowl, so I assumed it was my sister's.

When my sister entered the room, I held up the lumpy clump and confidently announced, "Here, Sharon, this is yours." She grimaced and denied ever seeing the clay vagrant. But I was sure it was hers. So after she left the room, I slipped it under her pillow, a subtle way of saying, *This really is yours!*

She grinned the next morning at the practical joke, and I headed off to work—only to find the bowl in my purse at lunch. That night, I put it in her high school backpack where I hoped she would be forced to pull it out in front of all her friends. We spent the next week trying to outwit each other until last-minute wedding details took my attention.

A few days before the wedding, my sister approached me, towing a child's doll along by the foot. The doll stood about two-feet high and had straw-yellow hair. I'd never seen it before. She simply said, "Here, Gail, this is yours." I told her it didn't belong to me, and even if it did, I'd have no use for it now and certainly wouldn't care to hand it down to a daughter if and when that time came. In other words, she could keep it. She walked away, and I completely missed seeing the mischievous twinkle in her eyes.

Our wedding day dawned bright and beautifully warm for early April. The church was full, my sister stood beside me as a bridesmaid, and we danced our hearts out at the reception. As the last few guests said their good-byes, I went from table to table with my mother gathering the fresh flowers for her and me. Dennis and I stopped back at my parents' home, changed clothes, loaded the car, and gave hugs and good-byes all around.

Our three-hour drive to the Poconos gave us a chance to relax and wallow in the pleasure of finally escaping together. We pulled into the resort, signed the register, found our cottage and unloaded the car. I hauled my suitcase up onto the heart-shaped bed and flipped open the lid as my new husband came up behind me. He slipped his arms around my waist and then froze. There, inside my suitcase, atop all the clothing, was a yellow-haired doll looking up at me with outstretched arms. My husband's face turned to utter horror as he thought I'd brought my baby doll along with me on our honeymoon. I laughed so hard that it took a few minutes before I could explain that my little sister really got me good this time.

Gail E. Strock

Snisters

A sister is the cure for swollen heads and ego trips. One may be a star, a chief executive— famous and rich and beautiful. But one's sister has the family photo album, and a long, long memory and a tendency to wink at one on top occasions.

Pam Brown

Laugh, and the world laughs with you. Snore, and you sleep alone.

My two sisters and I recently slept four-in-a-room with our mother during a mother-daughters weekend at the Greenbrier in White Sulpher Springs, West Virginia. If you know the place, you understand why we decided to bunk together. It's not your average Motel 6. We tried to economize so we could afford a few postcards from the gift shop. Besides, it was togetherness we wanted, so why not?

The slumber party lasted exactly one night.

One very long night.

Mother said it wasn't her. My older sister, Mary, said, "Don't look at me!" Anne said she never snores and it certainly wasn't yours truly. I am a very quiet sleeper; besides that, I was awake the whole night. How can you sleep when the room is vibrating and the windows are rattling?

At one point Mary took the cushions off the chair and moved to the tub. I tried to filter the noise through the pillows I stole from under other people's heads, making a kind of foursquare sound barrier around my face. Anne spent a lot of time flipping through the channels with the "mute" button on, and Mother says she lay awake all night counting her blessings, which did not include daughters with normal nasal passages.

So who was doing all the snoring?

Nobody is admitting to anything, but I personally KNOW it was all three of them.

"It's nothing to be ashamed of," I told them as we lined up at the hotel desk to rearrange our sleeping accommodations. "Some of us snore, and some of us do not. . . . Me, for example."

"Do too," they said.

"Do not."

"Do too."

"Girls, girls," Mother sang in the same tone of voice when we used to argue over who was kicking whom under the table. "You all snore. It's something you inherited from your father."

Having been raised in a nice family, we did not sass. We just rolled our eyes way back in our heads and said, "Sure, Mom."

What's so bad about snoring? Not that I have any kind of confession to make. Snoring is no reflection on a person's morals or intelligence. In fact, it's a sign of personality. People who snore are just expressing themselves, even as they sleep, right?

My sister, Anne, is a medical doctor, always concerned

about others—and very frugal. All this comes through (loud and clear) while she sleeps. She saves each snore up, sort of like she's reluctant to bother with it. She goes along quietly for a few minutes, then all of a sudden, "SNNNNNNNGGGGGRRRRRGGGG!" A hand grenade goes off in the bed next to you. Mary—the one who slept in the tub—is dependable, deliberate and straightforward: Hhunnnnn . . . shhhhhh . . . Hhunnnn . . . shhhhhhh. All night long, she never missed a hunnnnn-shhhhhh.

Mother is the most ladylike, mannerly person I know. Her snores are polite, dainty whispers. Most of the time. Every once in a while, she gets a little out of character, but just yell "MAMA!" with authority, and she stops. For a while.

I read somewhere that the body requires eight quarts of air per minute when lying down, which means, in the room that night—if my math is right—my sisters and I took in and let out 14,960 quarts of air between us, give or take a few thousand coming from the tub. Researchers at the Stanford University Sleep Disorder Clinic say sixty percent of all men between the ages of forty and sixty-four "snore heavily." They don't give the figures for women. But I can tell you this: only one out of four in my immediate family of origin does not, and I am the DOES NOT.

I looked up the word "snore" in the dictionary, and there on the "sn" page were all those noisy-nose words: snarl, sneer, sniff, snicker, snivel, snoot . . . but there was one missing:

Snisters.

Ina Hughs

Little Sisters

Little sisters are brats
They're just like rats
They think they are so cool
But really they drool
When your friends are over
They act like Grover
Crawling, barking on the floor
Banging on your bedroom door
They leave toys in your room
So you hit them with the broom
They run to their mother and cry
As you scream at the top of your lungs, "Bye!"

Destiny McIntosh
Age ten

Truly Blessed

It is best to be with those in time we hope to be with in eternity.

Sir Thomas Fuller

Some gifts in life come wrapped in bright red bows, and some gifts share your bedroom, your Elvis records and the late-night giggles.

We call that kind of gift a sister.

When you're a child, a sister is a wonderful playmate, sharing bride dolls, chicken pox, matching plaid jumpers and a Crisco can filled with pennies to help Mommy and Daddy "buy" a baby brother.

As little girls, sisters cry over the paddle mom swings with gusto, argue over who gets the rich deposit money from the lucrative pop bottles a favorite aunt and uncle save for them, and scheme over plans to sell their storybooks so they can buy a special anniversary gift for Mom and Dad.

When the teen years approach, sisters share one thing in common and that is fighting. Fights over bathroom time, who's to do the dishes, telephone calls, who told Mom and Dad "who" was in a parked car smooching with "you know who," the angora sweater they both want to wear the same night to the dance out at St. Sabina, and just about everything from A to Z.

As pimples give way to engagement rings, sisters share a late-night soda and their dreams, the dividing of the lingerie drawer, the solemnity of the wedding march and the good-bye tears to a chapter of life that has ended.

When buggies and basketballs begin to fill their lives, sisters exchange recipes for 101 ways to cook ground beef. They swap maternity clothes, cuddle nieces and nephews, weep over children's mistakes, travel over mountains and mosquito-laden lakes to vacation together, and hold each other close when happiness is overwhelming or grief overpowering.

Sisters can be aunts, wives, mothers or grandmothers, but if your life has been truly blessed, a sister can be your friend.

I know, for my sister, Jo, is my friend.

Alice Collins

My Life: The Sitcom

I have determined that I am living in a television situa-
tional comedy. Most people who already know me would
say that this is no great revelation, but it's news to me. It
started back in November when my wife's sister and husband sold their house. They're building a nice new home
in Avon for their budding family, and construction was
slated to be finished sometime in late February. By a
stroke of fortune (good or bad—who can say?) they
quickly sold their former house, thus relieving much of
the stress of the move. Of course, this meant they would
be without a home for nearly three months. This led them
to instant nightmares about living with either set of in-
laws or renting a short-term apartment. In a pure gesture
of Christian fellowship and family love, my wife offered to
let them move in with us for a few months. (I don't recall
endorsing the idea, but I'm firmly assured that I did.)

Thus, my wife's sister and her husband became our
houseguests. Of course, most of my guy friends predicted doom from the outset, but I was cheerfully confident. I adore my wife's sister, her laid-back husband and
their daughters, who are cute as proverbial buttons. We
all get along swimmingly, and my wife and her sister

have always been best friends. But that's when my life became a sitcom with the sheer chaos that goes with having eight people and an insolent house cat living under one roof.

Let's start with the increase of noise and activity level. My house used to be a fairly quiet place. It was nice to come home after a hectic day at work, take my shoes off and enjoy a relaxing dinner with the family. Now it's a combination day-care center/amusement park. As soon as I enter the home it's as if I've wandered into a Chuck E. Cheese on a Saturday afternoon. We parents now call the period between 8 P.M. and 9 P.M., when the kids get bedded down for the night, "Happy Hour."

My kitchen has been transformed into a twenty-four-hour diner. With four adults, two youngsters, two babies and the aforementioned cat, there are always dirty dishes in the sink and something cooking on the stove. Sometimes we all throw in for one large dinner together when our schedules allow. Other times, my guests may serve one dinner, me another when I get home, and my wife a third dinner when she arrives home. By the time the third dinner of the evening is served, it's time to prepare bedtime snacks. (We go through enough milk that I'm considering buying a small cow.) You would think that with all this cooking going on, I'd be able to score a decent breakfast in the morning. I go through the kitchen and say "two eggs, sunny side, on a shingle, coffee black." Then either my wife or sister-in-law will put a hand on her hip and hand me a Pop Tart. The basic rule is, "If you don't help cook it, you don't help eat it." Pop Tarts will do fine for me.

Just like in a real sitcom, my wife and I usually end the day giggling about the hijinks that occur during a "normal" day. Like naked babies chasing the cat through the kitchen. Or a naked cat chasing babies through the kitchen. I've never had a sister, but I can honestly now say that my wife's sister is mine.

Chadd A. Wheat

CLOSE TO HOME   JOHN McPHERSON

THE RELATIVES OF ED + SUE VOSBURG TOTALLY UNANNOUNCED TOUR

My Sister, the Martian

Mrs. Pendergast's peppermint carnations magnetically drew my sister Marsha and me into Mz. P.'s backyard. Steam shot from the taut silver buns old Mrs. Pendergast wore above each ear; she snorted and charged at us with her broom, yelling profanities in German, the day we picked her prize carnations. We ran home at near light speed!

So when it came time for the annual Girl Scout cookie sales, my sister and I debated whether or not to stop at the Pendergasts' house. We got brave but didn't stray from the front entry, and we made sure that we walked far from the flowers. Mr. and Mrs. Pendergast were both hard of hearing and slow to respond to the doorbell and our shouts. After some fussing, Mz. P. bought five boxes of cookies!

A few weeks earlier, Marsha broke her right wrist playing basketball at a neighbor boy's house. I was her four-year-old sidekick. Sporting Shirley Temple curls, I tagged along to help my sister carry the carton of cookies that weighed about as much as I did. It took both of us to tote the cookies from house to house and lug them up and down the neighbors' front steps. In 1961, Girl Scouts delivered the goods on the spot, as they sold cookies door-to-door for fifty cents a box. Mz. P. and all the neighbors took pity on Marsha, who was nine years old and a fourth-grader at Henderson Elementary School. They all said that she seemed to manage so well—broken wrist and all. The neighbors bought extra boxes out of sympathy. In fact, people bought so many more boxes that year that Marsha won the award for top sales out of the entire Girl Scout troop—and we didn't tell anybody that she was left-handed! My silence was bought with a box of mint cookies.

We moved from the house in 1964. I was seven years old, and Marsha had just turned thirteen. In our new house, we each had our own bedroom. My sister traded her bobby socks for pantyhose. We didn't do much together anymore. Secretly, I wondered if Marsha hailed from a distant galaxy. She was so different with her blonde hair (mine's brown) and amber-colored eyes (mine are blue), and Marsha's behavior seemed light years beyond the sister who used to parachute off housetops holding mom's clean bedsheets.

Marsha made a new friend named Susan, and Susan hung out at our house all the time. They fancied their hair, applied buckets of makeup, sang Beatles' songs and talked to boys on the phone. When I pestered them, they shooed me away.

"Old Mz. P. was nicer to me than you are!" I stuck my tongue out. "I'm gonna tell Mom."

Marsha grabbed my chin with both hands. "Be careful what you tell Momma."

"You're weird," I retorted.

"That's because I'm really *not* your sister. I'm an alien from Mars. That's why I'm called Marsha. If you tattle, I'll just have to telephone my spaceship and then I'll go back to Mars and you'll never see me again!"

"That's right!" Susan chimed in. "You just better be quiet, kid. Scram."

I ran to my room sobbing. Several weeks passed. Marsha and Susan kept up the tales of aliens and space travel. I was baited into believing the whole charade. Finally, I couldn't hold the secret inside any longer. I told Mom. "If your sister is an alien, then I'm an alien, and you're an alien. Let's all go to Mars!" she belly-laughed.

"But I don't wanna leave. I like my new school!" I cried.

I was a gullible kind of kid, and Mom realized I was duped into believing the whole Martian story. Mom made Marsha apologize for leading me on. Marsha admitted that she fabricated the story so I'd leave her alone. "I'm sorry I laughed, Stephanie," Momma said. "You shouldn't play games with secrets, Marsha. Confidences are for keeping," she reprimanded. My sister wasn't sorry that she tricked me, but she was sorry that I had taken it so hard.

When Marsha turned fifteen, she got her learner's permit. Mom and Dad left a spare set of keys to the old Chevy Nova station wagon hanging on a hook in the cupboard.

Marsha said, "It won't hurt if we just drive around the block before they get home."

"I'm not going . . . I don't want to get in trouble," I replied.

"You have to go. I can't leave you home alone. Get in the back seat," she commanded. We didn't make it out the driveway. Marsha backed straight into the ditch.

"Where's your spaceship now?" I asked sarcastically. "What are you gonna tell Dad?"

"He won't find out unless you tell him. Promise me you won't tell."

"I won't tell."

We pooled our piggy-bank money to pay a tow truck when all our efforts using old boards to leverage the car out of the mud failed. Mom arrived home from work just as the tow truck left our driveway. My sister confessed to driving without permission.

"Wait until your father gets home. You have to tell him!" Mom said sharply. Mom, Marsha and I waited anxiously for Dad to return home. "You'll wish you lived on Mars when Daddy gets through with you!" I ribbed.

Instead of being angry, Daddy laughed when he saw the ruts in the ditch. "Temptation too strong, huh? You're grounded, my little Martian. Next time you try to take off on an adventure around the block, make sure you leave the driveway with a parent in the car." Marsha was humiliated. I did my best to console her after I finished teasing her. Marsha was too embarrassed to go inside right away. Two weeks of grounding seemed like an eternity. We sat on the porch swing until dark, counted the stars and talked.

In time, I grew into a teenager and depended upon my sister's advice concerning foreign matters like grammar and boys. I would call her at college, and we'd talk for hours. Sharing secrets was the best part of sisterhood.

Thirty years passed. The Martian story had long been forgotten and replaced by stories of our own children. I smiled as I wrapped my sister's Christmas gift in preparation for mailing it to her home a thousand miles away. It was an electronic flying saucer with an enclosed card that read "I still think that, as a sister, you're out of this world!"

Stephanie Wyndance

A Year Behind Sister and Forty

Don't get you knickers in a knot. Nothing is solved and it just makes you walk funny.
Kathryn Carpenter

This spring is my sister's fortieth birthday. More to the point, that means *my* fortieth birthday can't be far behind. Since my sister is only eighteen months older than I am, I followed a year behind her goody two-shoes all the way through school.

By second grade, I was already dreading the moment when Mrs. Stevens took roll for the first time. I knew that a beatific glow would transform her careworn face as she noted my last name. "Is your sister *Vicki* Christian?" she eagerly asked.

I squirmed uneasily in my chair and admitted that I was, indeed, the lesser sibling of Vicki the virtuous. St. Vicki, that is, of the immaculate anklet and continually upstretched hand. St. Vicki of the highest reading group and lovely manners, always appointed monitor when Mrs. Stevens was summoned to the office. St. Vicki, the tattle-tale and bossy cow, ever her sister's keeper when it came to matters of deportment and conscience.

I wish I had a nickel for every time I saw Vicki peer at me over the top of her bat-wing style, rhinestone-studded, blue eyeglass frames (which Mrs. Stevens thought were "very becoming") and sniff, "I don't think Mama and Daddy would like that very well."

A family legend was made the first time I had an opportunity to follow my own base instincts instead of her pure ones. One day after school, she and her best friend Cindy were recounting to my mother the incident in which the school's most loathsome boy, Edward, dropped his drawers to his ankles on the blacktop at recess, and bellowed, "Lookie here!"

"What did you do?" my scandalized mother asked.

Vicki and Cindy replied that they had closed their eyes and run down the hill, holding hands, in the opposite direction from Edward. "And what did *you* do?" my mother asked me.

Being only in first grade and not having the wits to dissemble, I replied that I was on the jungle gym at the time and had climbed to the top of it to get a better look.

As the years went by, the eighteen-month gulf separating us closed. Vicki was a voracious and indiscriminate reader. What she read set the scene for our dolls. Our mother wouldn't let us play with Barbies. "Their bosoms are too bodacious," she declared.

So we had Tiny Tears dolls instead. Vicki's was Tina; mine was Betsy. We also had a homely, rubber-faced doll we called Brother Deanie. Depending on what Vicki was reading, Tina and Betsy would rescue the hapless Brother Deanie from a prairie fire (our four-poster bed was the stagecoach), change his diaper at Plymouth Rock or present him to King Arthur's Court. It was wearying to play dolls with other girls, who didn't get it and had to be taught how to talk like a Quaker or an Arabian princess.

"Now we can play!" we'd exclaim when they went home.

When we packed our dolls away we shared boyfriends, makeup, accessories and clothes. The boyfriends we were generous with, but we got pretty vicious over the rest. Our most memorable battles were reserved for a black velvet choker, a mink hair bow, a pearlized snood and a tube of Bonne Belle white-white. White-white was weird stuff, like typewriter correction fluid, that we dotted around our eyes to achieve the wide-eyed, sexy yet innocent look of Twiggy and Mia Farrow. I guess you had to be a skeletal blonde to pull it off.

Looking back at photographs, our generous applications of white-white made us look as if we were either recuperating from tuberculosis or else incredibly surprised. Why it never occurred to us to buy duplicates of such coveted items—none of which were expensive—I don't know.

My sister has become my dearest friend, and today I am ashamed of the names I called her and the fits I pitched. If they still sold white-white, I'd buy her a lifetime supply. All the same, I can't help gloating that she'll be forty before I will.

If we should live so long, I'll give her a mink hair bow for her eightieth birthday—right before reminding her that I'm still a mere girl of seventy-nine.

Rebecca Christian

How to Torture Your Sister

Wander into the room when she calls a friend on the telephone. Pick up a book and sit down on the couch. Pretend to read, then mimic her as she begins her telephone conversation.

Hi, how are you? *Hi, how are you?* Wha'd you do today? *Wha'd you do today?* What? Wait a minute, my sister's driving me crazy. Would you cut it out? *Would you cut it out?*

You dirty creep. *You dirty creep.* Stop repeating me! *Stop repeating me!* I said STOP! *I said STOP!* STOP IT! *STOP IT!*

Put book down and run.

SHE is eating peanuts. Whisper in her ear, "You can turn into an elephant if you eat too many peanuts. I read it in the *World Book.*"

FOLLOW her everywhere.

IMITATE her best friend talking. Say that her best friend is fat.

TALK to your mother while your sister is listening: "Do you remember Christmas when I was three years old and you gave me that stuffed animal? That was so much fun." Turn to your sister. "You weren't alive."

Delia Ephron

For Better or For Worse®

by Lynn Johnston

4

OVERCOMING OBSTACLES

So closely interwoven have been our lives, our purposes, and experiences that, separated we have a feeling of incompleteness—united, such strength of self-assertion that no ordinary obstacles, differences, or dangers ever appear to us insurmountable.

Elizabeth Cady Stanton

A Promise to Keep

Last night Margot and I were lying side by side in my bed. It was incredibly cramped, but that's what made it fun.

Anne Frank of her sister

I have a story to tell you about my sister. While my account is surely full of sisterly love, it's not necessarily about anything soft, sweet or womanly. Really, it's the story of how a bond not known to many developed between my sister and me, under some pretty raw but honest conditions in our little brick house in Fort Worth, Texas.

My sister and I weren't just sisters to each other, we were mothers, too. My mother committed suicide when I was five, and my sister and her twin brother were six. Mama wasn't living with us at the time, as she had suffered some pretty serious mental illness that eventually split up my parents, and she had moved in with one of my half-sisters in another state.

Dad has never stopped loving my mother and would marry her again today if he could. After her death, things were hard for Dad, not that they were ever easy before. Dad was doing his best with work and getting the three of us to school every day, and the house around us suffered. With just Dad to raise us, I think we figured early on that it would fall to us to do a little of our own parenting.

Besides the house being neglected, we couldn't afford a lot of things. I remember many winters being without heat or even hot water, and there were many years that we lived without a refrigerator and stove.

One winter when we were nine and ten, my sister and I decided we needed to be bathing more regularly. At the time we didn't have a hot water heater, but Dad would boil water about once a week and we would take a "splash bath" in the sink. After an embarrassing trip to the doctor, my sister and I concluded this wasn't enough.

One day the school nurse had taken us off campus to see the doctor, and it turned out we had scabies, which is a kind of skin lice. I guess our teachers noticed we had a weird skin condition and alerted the nurse. In any case, when we went to see the doctor and had to undress, we were ashamed for him to see the dirt rings around our ankles and wrists.

That night, we made a pledge that we would bathe every day. I remember it being a cold night in winter, and the air was plenty chilly in our old house that had just a gas heater in one of the bedrooms. To make good on our promise, my sister and I drew a tub full of COLD water up to our ankles, and both stood in it shivering. Following was some sort of discourse about who would be first to plunge into the water and suds up. I think my sister decided to be the courageous one and down she went into the icy water.

It was pure torture and the air didn't offer any relief, but we bravely took our turn at soaping up and then rinsing off. I remember how we felt for a few moments falsely warm as the cold air burned our wet skin.

As we promised each other, the bath ritual turned into a nightly routine. Something that we would never have done on our own, we had the discipline and willingness to do because we were doing it together.

There were plenty of other experiences in which we drew together the same way: like when we contracted head lice the year before and had to painstakingly comb each strand of the other's hair in a dark cold room in front of the fireplace.

I also remember the summer nights without air conditioning when we would open the windows and sleep head to toes, inviting the cats to sit on our stomach. Those nights we would sing every song we had ever learned. What magic we created, just the two of us!

There were plenty of worries those days and lots of reasons to feel insecure, but we created a temporary haven from all of it in the little cocoon of our bedroom.

Later in life, we would both go on to be academically and professionally successful. Others would never guess our origins—in fact, they often assumed we had come from a family of privilege. And indeed we had.

When I think back to those nights in the tub, I understand now where we both got our ability to face the hard things in life. My sister and I, without knowing it at the time, were teaching each other how to find solutions to tough situations, seek promise in situations that didn't seem to offer any, and mostly to have bravery of spirit.

Although certainly an ice cold bath is not the harshest experience a person can endure, I realize that what we overcame was mostly mental rather than physical. It was believing in ourselves enough to give ourselves our own comfort when Dad was asleep and the house was falling down. The hard part was not the bath but that we had to be adults for ourselves, and to learn a little early to be able to right our own situation rather than be defeated by them.

No one ever modeled this for us, yet somehow between the two of us we figured it out. What we didn't realize at the time is that the way we handled our bath problem would be the foundation for the way we attacked all problems later. It's the reason we have both been able to rebound when tough things happen.

When times arise that I don't feel immediately equipped to endure, I think back to our wintertime cold baths and feel such a sense for who I am. I remember the girls who made a game of it and didn't think of their own discomfort, but tried to make it more fun for the other. And then I am filled with the extreme knowingness that through my sisters love, I am still able to accomplish everything.

Phoebe Elizabeth Sisk

No Matter What

No matter the distance between us—physical or emotional—there will always be one in the world who knew me in my innocence, and knows the heart of me in a way that no other can. And should I ever know real trouble in my life, she will suddenly appear beside me, to hold my hand in hers.

Anthony Brandt

I remember my sister, Linda, always sticking up for me when we were kids. She's four years older than I am, and out of five children in our family, we were the peacemakers. We promised to be there for each other—no matter what!

Whenever I did something wrong, I was sent to my room with the sentence of "Wait until your father gets home." We sat quietly together on the edge of the bed holding hands, knowing what was in store when Dad arrived. She helped me put every pair of underwear on that I owned and layered pajamas and shorts under my nightgown in an attempt to pad my behind.

One day, after my oldest sister forced me to swallow a

penny, Linda and I silently waited for the copper coin to rip out my insides, thinking it would kill me. She tried everything to get me to throw up and rubbed my aching belly for an hour. When old Mr. Lincoln came out the other end, we laughed so hard we almost peed our pants.

Both of us shared a private world of happiness and sanctuary to which we escaped from the rest of the family. Late-night popcorn, tea parties, giggling under the covers in our beds and sharing dreams of future happiness were the most peaceful times in my childhood.

Punishment sometimes included pulling weeds from the yard. One day, we decided to bend thorns off the prickly rose bushes. We licked the base and stuck them on the end of our noses. We became rhinoceroses in the wild of Africa, chasing each other throughout the yard.

Our grandmother told us stories of life in Sweden and about a beautiful young princess. Whenever I had a bad day or felt plain ugly, Linda let me dress up in her clothes, painted my face with makeup, and made believe I was that princess.

As we grew into adults, we both chased our individual dreams. Although we had husbands, careers and children of our own, we were never far from each other's heart or mind. Linda named her youngest daughter after me, and I named my little girl after the princess we pretended to be.

I knew I could always count on her for anything, anytime, anywhere. When my son committed suicide after suffering brain damage from a car accident, Linda took the first plane out to support me.

Words were of little comfort, but she held me close and we cried together, as though it was her own loss. She helped make the funeral arrangements and graciously dealt with visitors, opening up her heart to strangers.

I'll never forget how I stood so broken in front of the casket as she held me tightly so I wouldn't fall faint. Once again, she brushed my hair, made tea and held my hand in silence. Linda promised to always be there and would never let me suffer alone, no matter what!

Other family members and friends shunned me over the situation because of their own ignorance. "Let's just sweep this under the rug," they would say. Linda always gave me unconditional love, never judged or blamed me, and continues to offer me strength.

She seemed to understand the agony and insanity I was living with and waits patiently while I continue to heal. Linda taught me how to release some of my guilt and love myself again. Our late-night talks on the telephone gave me courage and hope to live again. I owe my life to her for standing beside me, giving me hope.

When I feel raw and my heart aches inside, we cry together on the telephone. I'm reminded of the stubble on my son's face as he lay in his eternal peace and the small mole located on his neck. I always tripped on the size-fourteen tennis shoes he left in the walkway and realized it would be one of the many things I missed. We reminisce about the smile he wore so proudly and his blue eyes that I can see in the mirror when I squint just right. The greatest gift I taught him was to love unconditionally, and Linda reminds me of the tenderness and affection he displayed for his mom.

Every month, my daughter receives a special treasure of love from her favorite aunt. A small toy, a homemade craft, a picture or a simple postcard ensuring my child is still a special little sister. I have learned to love my own princess more deeply because of a terrific role model.

On anniversary dates, the pain of my loss is unbearable. I receive calls and special tokens of friendship. An angel rests on the marker at the cemetery, keeping watch on the young nephew who is deeply missed.

Life was much simpler when I think of the laughter we

shared as children traveling through the desert. We hung our legs over the tailgate of the family station wagon watching the world go by. The hot sun warmed our legs as the breeze kissed our toes with delight. Together we devoured a bag of cherries meant for the whole family. Free of any cares in the world, we sat side by side, spitting the seeds into the wind. The cars receiving these pits were not appreciative of our talents. My father never understood why the parade of cars behind would honk and wave their fists in anger.

I miss those days of innocence from our youth and feel blessed to share my soul with Linda. I am so thankful for having her beside me through good and bad times. I honor her with unconditional love and hope I've made a positive contribution to her life. We will remain best friends forever and will accept each other for who we are no matter what!

Judy Lynne Lucia

Hidden Treasure

Is solace anywhere more comforting than in the arms of a sister?

Alice Walker

Several years ago, a blunt, and as it fortunately turned out, brilliant doctor removed a suspicious mole from my back. Two weeks later he called me at home on a Friday night to announce, "You have malignant melanoma. You're lucky we found it this early. Six months from now, you might have been dead. Come in Monday for more surgery."

My hard-earned independence dissolved as I hung up and began dialing my sister's number automatically. I hadn't even realized I knew it. I got her machine and managed, in what I thought was a calm voice, to choke out, "Give me a call." Then I sat on the floor, wondering through a haze of terror, why I'd called Lori. It was instinctive and yet . . .

We had been very close as children. Almost three years old, I decided to be her guardian starting on her first night home from the hospital when I woke my exhausted parents because I heard her whimper in her crib.

"My little sister's crying. Go get her," I commanded imperiously, glaring into their sleep-deprived faces. I then followed them doggedly down the hall to her little bedroom. Just to make sure.

It was just the start. By the time she was two, she was climbing out of her crib every night, scampering down the dark hallway and leaping into my "big girl's bed" to spend the long nights snuggled by my side. My beleaguered parents finally disassembled the crib and gave her a little bed next to mine. Sometimes, we fell asleep holding hands. Every Christmas Eve, she squirmed into my bed so Santa wouldn't scare her should he look in on us.

Because Lori rejected every teen in the cavalcade of baby-sitters my parents desperately paraded through our home, I began baby-sitting at an early age. It was the only way my parents could transform her from a shrieking pint-sized tyrant, catapulting up and down on the couch by the window so they wouldn't miss her furious, red face as they drove away, to a happy toddler, hand-in-hand with me, calmly waving good-bye.

By the time we were old enough to have kids over to play, we were a team. We could beat any group at just about any game we chose, from tag football to "capture the flag." My father was proud that his girls could beat any boy in the neighborhood. The pattern continued when I enrolled in St. John's School. My mother was an aide there before Lori was old enough to attend. She would accompany Mom, clinging to her until recess when she would emerge long enough to find me. One day as we played near my mother, Lori suddenly fled again to the safety of Mom's skirts. I turned to see the meanest of the nuns bearing down on us. I brashly blocked her way with my seven-year-old self and said, pointing to Lori, "That's my sister, and she's afraid of you, so you better leave her alone!" Both the nun and Mom were dumbfounded, but Lori was delighted. I never got punished for that little incident.

In high school, our relationship changed. I had a few good friends, an obsession for books and a rebellious attitude. This was the seventies, and I was determined to question every authority in my life, every chance I got. Lori became a basketball star who was popular, bright and pleasantly conventional. We grew farther apart during college. I still attended her basketball games, but I didn't think she really noticed. She disapproved of my vehement need for independence, and I was disconcerted by her disinterest in anything outside her world. How had we become so different?

I started a career as a writer in a city an hour away. Lori began teaching first-graders in our hometown. She visited my parents almost daily. If I stopped by on major holidays, family members had to hide their surprise. She married her college sweetheart when they graduated. I stayed single and spent the winters writing in Key West.

I missed my sister, but I mourned more for the relationship between the children we'd been than the adults we'd become. We were polite and pleasant, superficially courteous when we met, but there just didn't seem to be any common ground. I was convinced she didn't care about me, even remarking once to my mother, "If something happens to you and Dad, I bet we won't even have holidays together."

My mother looked devastated, and I realized the rift had hurt her as well. "I'd hope the two of you would do something about this before it comes to that," she said. But I wasn't sure exactly what, and I knew I wouldn't like her answer if I asked. So I didn't.

Yet the first thing I'd done after the doctor hung up was to call Lori.

Startled out of my memories, I grabbed the phone halfway through the first ring, but before I could speak, Lori's calm voice came through.

"I know."

"How?" I asked her, "How could you know?"

"I knew from your voice on the machine."

She wasn't crying. She'd become the strong sister. Surprised that she even recognized my voice on the machine, I sobbed out my fears. She listened. And listened. I finally blurted out, "You know, I could die."

"No," she answered stolidly. Then after a few moments, "You won't die, Marci. You're like God's personal Internet, and he wants you here." She went on to talk about the important things I was doing in my life, how many people I was touching.

I was stunned. How did she know anything about my life or work? How did she know I belonged to a parish and facilitated a discussion group? How did she know about my work with a nonprofit group that helped people with AIDS? How did she know that people read my work and depended upon me for honesty?

Probably the same way I knew about the important events in her life—Mom. Always hoping we would reconcile, she'd made sure each of us knew about the other's achievements and frustrations. But as vital as they had been, Mom's ministrations had not led to this conversation—and the many that followed.

Cancer had unlocked this door and already light was streaming through the crack.

It continued to shine. My regular doctor's appointments have become Lori's and my time. The doctor's office is near her school, so I often stop by her classroom after the children have gone home and before my appointment. We sit in teeny-tiny first-grader chairs and talk about everything, not needing to focus on what's coming for me in the next few hours. When I've been late and had to go directly to the medical offices, she's been waiting outside my doctor's suite. There, she hugs me softly because we both know that hard hugs after biopsies are not a good idea. She waits with me, though we are quieter than in her classroom. If I have a biopsy, when I walk out of the surgery room, somewhat unsteadily, she's still there, having gathered my coat and book and other accoutrements. "Don't forget this stuff," she tells me, very much the organized teacher.

Am I grateful for cancer? No. Have I learned there are hidden treasures to be mined from its dark, scary depths? Yes. And that treasure has untold value when my sister puts her arm in mine and leads me to the car.

Marci Alborghetti

The Miracle of My Sister's Laughing

There can never be enough said of the virtues, the dangers, the power of a shared laugh.

Françoise Sagan

Some of the lowest days of my life came shortly after my husband's death. While still grieving, I came face to face with the reality of raising our four children alone. The funeral was over, friends and family gone. It was the kids and I, each of us grieving as our ages and personalities allowed. One son angry, the other quiet; one daughter demanding, the other mothering. And somehow I was supposed to deal with it all. I was supposed to give the sole direction, the lone understanding and single wise responses.

While at the bottom of this inadequacy well, my sister arrived. She'd planned it that way, saving her visit until everyone else had left. Within hours, the closeness we had shared in the past came flooding back. She let me talk and cry but also helped me begin doing things. We got my kids returned to school, and then started tackling projects. We started with my closet since its half emptiness constantly reminded me of my now-gone husband. We decided to install a closet organizer, so I could add my sweaters and other clothes to fill it up.

Things didn't go well. While she held one end, I'd try to install and hammer the other. Nothing fit. As we improvised, things got worse. Then in the midst of our frustration, I noticed the picture on the organizer's box. A two-dimensional woman smiled back from it while she single-handedly installed what my sister and I were failing to do. While still holding up my end, I said, "Hey Jeanne, look at that picture. I wish!"

She took one look at the woman and said, "Yeah, right. She's even wearing a dress." That's when it happened. Somehow the whole situation turned into a joke.

Every fumble we made, every board that slipped, every screw that refused to twist brought us back to the perfect lady on the box and made us laugh. We laughed until the tears came. We laughed until we had to drop the organizer and run for the bathroom.

It was the first time I'd laughed in weeks.

That laughter happened fifteen years ago, yet I remember it as if it happened yesterday. It changed nothing, yet it changed everything. My kids were still grieving. I was still hurting, overwhelmed and inadequate. But when I hugged my sister good-bye, I knew God had used her to give me a miracle. For in the hard months following her departure, on my worst days, I inevitably opened my closet and spotted my slightly tilting organizer. No matter how I felt, I just couldn't help smiling.

Deborah Hedstrom-Page

My Special Sister

There are two ways of spreading light, to be the candle or the mirror that reflects it.

Edith Wharton

I'm running late as I pull into the circular drive in front of the apartment building. My sister is waiting for me as I knew she would be.

"Hi, Sis," she says, wriggling into the seat.

"Hi. How are you today?"

"The people in my building are trying to get me in trouble," she grumbles.

"Oh? What are they doing?"

"They're still trying to break John and me up."

That routine exchange out of her system, we pull away from her building. "Where we goin'?" she asks.

"I'm taking you to my acting class. We'll go shopping afterwards."

I sensed the wheels turning in her head, and I knew what was coming next. "What floor is it on?" she asks. Now in her fifth decade, she's more and more unsteady on her feet, and stairs fill her with trepidation.

"It's on the third floor, but they're easy stairs to climb, and I'll help you," I say in what I hope is a reassuring tone. She's quiet as we head into the city.

At the first stoplight, she breaks the silence. "Guess what, Sis."

"What?"

"I made two dollars." (She lifts two fingers.) "Two dollars," she repeats, louder.

"At Pizza Hut? They must really like you there."

"Yes, they do," she says, matter-of-factly. "I have lots of friends there."

As I weave my way through traffic, I'm having second thoughts about bringing her. If I hadn't detoured off my usual route, I'd be on time for my class. Heavy traffic and signal lights seem to conspire against me. I strike the steering wheel in exasperation as a city bus swerves in front of us, then immediately slows down to pick up passengers on the next block.

What was I thinking? I had figured I could save time and give my sister an interesting experience in the bargain. I knew that once we got to the studio, she would sit quietly through the class, waiting with infinite patience nurtured through years of depending on the goodwill of others. But now she represents an impediment to getting to class on time.

We continue to crawl down Lake Street. I would have been there long ago if I had taken the expressway. At 9:00 A.M., when the class is beginning, I'm still ten to fifteen minutes away.

But finally, we're there. I take my sister's hand and guide her along the cracked sidewalk to the front entry. She's nervous, partly because the building itself is unsettling. The block had housed an upscale department store in the 1930s. Once-prosperous storefront windows are now boarded up and covered with graffiti.

It's not a neighborhood she's used to being in.

The old brick building had once echoed with the sounds of swing music and dancing from the third-floor ballroom. But now, paint on the well-trodden wooden staircase is flaking. The place is dark and musty-smelling. The stairs above look as if they disappear into a second-floor cavern. My sister is shaking, distressed about this dismal building, afraid of the stairs. I take her hand firmly in mine, and trusting me, she begins to ascend the stairs slowly. Very slowly.

Finally, clearing the third flight of stairs, we enter the dingy foyer that decades ago served as an entry to the once-elegant ballroom. The studio is off to the right. My teacher has just finished passing out the day's assignments. As we enter, he sees right away that my sister is "special," and to his credit, he welcomes her warmly.

But the bad news is that the students have paired up to act out scenes for this, our last day. I'm the "odd man out." The teacher says to wait until one of the teams has presented a scene, then I can pair up with one of them for another assignment. A few minutes pass, and he comes back to me.

"I have a couple of scenarios here that I think you could act out with your sister," he suggests. I stare at him incredulously. He's got to be kidding. She can't read. She can't learn lines.

"Why don't you give it a try?" he persists.

I look at the scenarios and select one. It's better to be doing something than sitting and waiting. My sister and I cross the foyer into the old ballroom to work on the impossible. In the scene, one person is trying to persuade the other to take a plane trip.

Until recently, my sister traveled alone by plane each year to see relatives. But along with her general unsteadiness, she now refuses to fly. I decide to just talk to her and let her respond naturally. She will have nothing to memorize.

I begin with, "Why don't you take the plane to see Wally." She tenses up and huffily responds, "No way." I continue to feed her lines to react to. I repeat questions and entreaties to her several times and get her consistent responses. We return to the studio for our presentation.

Finally, it's our turn. "Lights! Camera! Action!"

I lead my sister onto the stage and begin. "Lelia Mae, the fastest way to get to New York is to fly."

"I *won't* fly!"

"But, Lelia Mae, you know you look forward to seeing Wally every year. And he wants to see you." She tenses and glares at me, hands on hips.

"No! I want *you* to drive."

"But I don't have *time* to drive," I plead with her.

"I won't go if I have to fly." She stomps her foot and turns away from me. I turn her back toward me.

"We've been over this and over this. I don't have time to drive."

She keeps resisting, pushing me away.

Finally, I put my arm around her shoulders. "It'll be okay. I'll be sitting in the seat right beside you."

She folds into me and begins to whimper softly. "Are you sure?"

And the scene is over.

I look sheepishly into the lights, waiting for a reaction, when my teacher erupts with applause. "Bravo! Bravo!"

I think it's nice of him to make my sister feel good. But it slowly dawns on me that he's sincere. He explains to the group that what they have seen is a perfect example of what he has been trying to teach us for the last five sessions. "Acting is simply tapping into the natural emotions that we all have. This was wonderful!" My classmates applaud, and everyone pats my sister on the back. "Great job. Great job."

We negotiate the stairs back down to the street.

Yet once again, my "special sister" had demonstrated her love for me, her trust in me and her eagerness to please me. I also realized how mutual that love is and how important it is for me to go out of my way to do what I can to please her.

Betty McMahon

If the World Could See with My Sister's Eyes

And be my sister blessed in every spot
In every station and in every lot
Long may she live with sweet contentment here
For ever cherished and for ever dear.

Elizabeth Barrett Browning

I was six years old and my brother, Hud, was three when my sister, Mintie, was born. That day we were staying at our great-grandparents', and Daddy came home to tell us we had a new baby sister. I remember I grabbed Hud's hands to jump around but he didn't feel like jumping; he'd wanted a brother. On the way to the hospital to see Mom and our new baby sister, Daddy told us that Mintie was sick when she was born with a very high fever and something called "jaundice," so she would be in a special place at the hospital. Well, that was okay. I was just excited about seeing the new baby.

After we saw Mom, we went down the hall to meet our sister. Right from the start, our sister was different. We looked into the nursery through the huge window. Most of the babies were near the window, but Daddy showed us "our" baby at the back of the nursery. She was in a kind of clear box with a bright light inside. She was very small, red and wrinkled, with crazy black hair and a black mask over her eyes. Daddy said it was to fix the jaundice. Hud and I seemed to decide right then and there that we were the big brother and big sister, and if our sister was small and sick we'd just have to take care of her!

Because she had been so sick, Mintie didn't get to come home when Mom did, but when she did come home I was ready to be the big sister. Mintie was so quiet you could barely hear her cry, and she was so small! Not premature small, but petite and delicate small, like a porcelain doll. The crazy black hair was replaced with the traditional Athey baby-blonde. Except for being so quiet, Mintie seemed to be growing and developing just like any other baby I knew. She was as pleasant as could be, and Hud and I thought we had a real live doll because she'd let us dress her up in crazy costumes without any fuss. When she should have started talking, however, she just didn't. The doctors told us that parts of her brain had been damaged from the fever she had when she was born. She would never learn to speak more than a few words, and she would always be tiny and fragile. The family was going to have to learn sign language to communicate with her. So we enrolled in sign language classes. Hud and I were going to have a big job taking care of this little sister.

Mintie had been experiencing several medical difficulties. She was in and out of Children's Hospital in Pittsburgh for treatments and operations. She was always in pain, and we learned she always had been. In fact, when the doctors pinched her and asked her if it hurt, she shook her head no; they said she didn't know what it was not to hurt. Everybody at the hospital loved Mintie, both children and adults. One evening while we were visiting, a little boy with leukemia, with whom Mintie had played often, died. The nurses made everyone close their doors as the doctors tried to revive him and then wheeled him down the hall. Mintie was five.

Due to the combination of language deficit and medical problems, it was recommended that Mintie reside at the Rehabilitation Institute in Pittsburgh for six months to monitor her medical progress and receive intensive language therapy. She would only come home on weekends. So every Friday we made the two-hour trip into Pittsburgh to pick her up, and every Sunday we did the same to take her back. As at Children's Hospital, everyone at the Institute loved Mintie. She was always in a good mood, sweet and loving. My favorite memory from the Institute days is of Mintie's special buddy, one of the nurses, a very large, very dark ex-NFL player, walking across the parking lot holding the hand of our very small, very pale sister. The contrast was so great we just had to laugh. I've never seen such a large man be so gentle.

Throughout our experience with our special little sister, our family relied heavily on our faith and friends in the church. After serious thought, discussion and lots of prayer, the elders of the church performed a laying on of hands ceremony to pray for Mintie's healing. No miracles happened that evening; she didn't jump up and shout and spout full sentences. But that evening things started to change. Mintie's next operation was her last. She started saying more words until she was speaking in sentences. We joke that today we can't get her to shut up! And the only signs I remember are for "cookie" and "play" because she used them so much.

This was not the end of the obstacles, however. Mintie had several learning exceptionalities. She was placed in special education classes in school, and we were told she would never learn on grade level. I remember sitting with her for literally six hours a night working on homework assignments that took the other kids only an hour or so. By seventh grade, however, she had been mainstreamed into the regular classroom for all subjects. When it was time to go to the high school, however, we had concerns. The high school program would be a step back for Mintie, involving resource classrooms and little or no mainstreaming. We decided to homeschool her and joined a Christian homeschool group through which Mintie could earn a technical diploma in child care. She began working at a local preschool, learning practical skills in all areas of child care and management.

All of Mintie's academic accomplishments despite the obstacles she faced are not what make her so special; it's Mintie herself. She is an innocent, and her love is unconditional. She always finds the good in people and never notices the bad. Put a crying baby in Mintie's arms, and it is calmed. All those around her are soothed. Some people have pitied her innocence, but prejudice and cruelty have never touched her. When kids made fun of her, Mintie simply didn't understand or even realize their cruelty. She would come home and ask, "Why did they do that?" or "Why did they say that?" She doesn't understand because there is no cruelty in her, and what is not in her simply does not exist in her eyes. The needs and wants of others always come first. Anyone whose life has touched hers has come away better. She has never been angry. She is never in a bad mood. She has cried only out of frustration or when she sees others hurt or fighting. Neither Hud nor I have ever had a fight with her, and believe me we fought with each other! She is peaceful and a lover of peace.

On May 23, 1997 at 7:30 P.M., Mintie graduated from high school. And she was no longer our fragile little sister; she is taller than I and broader than Hud. The ceremony was small, only the other members of the homeschool group, a few family friends and immediate family. Several people were asked to speak, including me. As each speaker addressed the gathering, silent tears fell. I struggled through my own tears as I stood behind the podium. I was not crying because she is my sister and graduation is an emotional event. I was crying because Mintie is what humankind has striven to be. In so many ways, instead of Hud and I taking care of her, she takes care of us. When our faith is weak, hers is always strong. When we are hurt or angry, she is soothing and calm. When we expect the worst in people, she sees the best. As the Chinese proverb states:

> If there is light in the soul,
> There will be beauty in the person.
> If there is beauty in the person,
> There will be harmony in the house.
> If there is harmony in the house,
> There will be order in the nation.
> If there is order in the nation,
> There will be peace in the world.

You see, Mintie has light in her soul. She is the most beautiful person I know. She brings harmony to the lives of all those around her. She sees good and order where many see none. If the world could see with my sister's eyes, there would be peace in the world.

Amanda Athey Swain

The Perfect Garden

It was over dinner, thirty years ago, that Dad first told me I had a younger sister. I was twelve. I thought he was joking, until I looked across the table at Mother. Her face was rigid, her gray eyes unfocused, and I could sense the magnitude of what she was holding back.

Stunned, I nodded silently while Dad told me about Annie. He kept his voice calm, as if to reassure me that my world was still intact. He said that she lived in a good hospital with other mentally handicapped children, but I imagined her tucked away in a shoe box in some dark corner of a closet. I thought our parents had filed her away in their minds and expected me to do the same. "That's how it's done," they seemed to say.

Though I never saw my sister while I was growing up, I sometimes wondered about her. *Was she as thin as I? Did she braid her hair, too?* I remembered Mother had said something about water on the brain. Years later, Dad told me that the doctors believed Annie would die shortly after birth. He and Mother debated whether to bring her home. Finally, they decided she'd be better off living "with her own kind."

Perhaps they were right. Ours was a polished world, rooted in self-restraint. Our house felt like a museum. The furniture was dark with age and laden with family history. Flower arrangements came from the florist, and a stiffness in the air discouraged easy conversation. Outside, the elegant garden was immaculate. Tidy clusters of iris stood in a sea of yellow daylilies. Peony blossoms were held aloft on stakes, and vines of flowering clematis clung neatly to a pair of arched trellises. Unblemished by weeds or fallen leaves, it was a model garden.

There was no niche for Annie at home. She'd have stood out like a weed in a proper English garden.

In 1993, I finally went to meet her. I was thirty-nine. She was thirty-six. I went knowing little about her likes and dislikes, except for tidbits I had gleaned over the phone from a social worker: her favorite color, red; her dress size, ten.

I found her home in a line of brick row houses not far from where I'd grown up. The curtains in the windows were closed. The tiny porch was shedding its paint; the child-size garden bed out front was a barren patch of soil.

I sat in the car for a moment, feeling uncertain. Then I started across the road carrying a shopping bag full of presents. Earrings, chocolates, a red pocketbook, sweatpants, red tennis shoes. My heels tapped along the pavement, then up the three front steps to her house. Lanky men smoking cigarettes on a porch next door followed my movements with dull eyes.

The social worker ushered me into a dimly lit room. A TV blared from the corner. Several young women approached me at the same time. There were four of them. They peered up at me, jostling each other for a better view. I scanned each face, confused. "Annie?" I said to them all.

The women became silent. Then one of them grabbed my hand, and there she was, looking as startled as I felt. There was something familiar about her face. We had the same brown hair and green eyes, though her complexion was pasty and she was shorter than me. I handed her the bag of presents.

Annie looked right into my eyes. "I've missed you," she said loudly, her voice husky as a schoolboy's.

"Annie, open your presents," the social worker said. "See what your sister has brought you."

Annie tore the wrapping paper off each present eagerly. She hugged the pocketbook to her chest. She asked me to put the earrings on her and then admired herself in the mirror. She pulled the sweatpants on under her skirt and danced around the room. When we went upstairs to her room, she chattered to me as if she'd stored up words for years. She gave me a pad of paper and asked me over and over to write down my name, the date and the exact time I would call her the following week.

Five years have passed. Seeing her often, I've become used to Annie. I've learned to hear her say "I've missed you" without cringing at the emotion in her voice. I've been delighted when she announces, "I'll see you next month, don't you worry." And when she leans over and sniffs me, announcing loudly, "You smell good today," I no longer stiffen with embarrassment.

Today, as I drove her to my house, I said we'd plant some flowers. She said, "I'll watch you." But when we arrived, she said, "Okay, buddy, I'll help you out. Yes, I will." She'd already spotted the marigolds waiting beside my bedraggled garden.

When she moved the little plants into the holes I had dug, I flinched. She gripped the stems with her fist and ground the roots into the dirt until I put my hand over hers. She relaxed her fist, looked straight into my face and said, "Am I doing good?"

"You're doing great!" I said quickly, padding dirt around the flower. My words sounded shrill to me. I was afraid I'd offended her. But she had already grabbed another plant.

She cupped the flowers in her hands and thrust her nose into the tiny polished petals and wisps of green. She breathed them in as if she were breathing in the fragrance of the world. "This flower smells good," she said. Her face lit with pleasure. Then, stepping closer and holding the plant out like a gift, she pressed it against my nose and lips. I sniffed the flower in her hand. Breathing in the marigold scent, I could almost taste its briny bitterness sliding down my throat. But the delight Annie took in presenting it to me was disarming. Something seemed to lift, softening the barriers raised by years of separation. For a moment, the flower resting in the cup of her hands was all that mattered.

Now, after taking Annie home, I pause to admire our marigolds. Only a few of the tufted yellow heads hang from their stems. I hardly notice that some of the tiny blossoms are crushed. Most of the flowers will surely survive. For there is a whiff of Annie's presence all around, a vitality and a bittersweet bite to the air. No doubt our parents would think this bed of marigolds an eyesore. But to me, it's perfect.

Molly Bruce Jacobs
As appeared in Chicken Soup for the Gardener's Soul

For Better or For Worse®

FOR BETTER OR FOR WORSE. ©*United Feature Syndicate.*

The Seed Jar

Look around for a place to sow a few seeds.

Henry Van Dyke

Being the youngest of four girls, I usually saw to Grandma Lou's needs at family gatherings. Lucinda Mae Hamish—Grandma Lou for short—was a tall twig of a woman, with a long gray braid and sharp features. She was the undisputed Master Gardener in our family, for she had come of age in the Depression, where she learned to use every old thing twice. And when it was worn out, she'd use it again—in her garden.

When Grandma Lou visited, she brought packets of her own seeds, folded in scraps of envelopes and labeled with instructions. Her handwriting was precise and square. She gave each of us a particular plant; usually tomatoes and carrots and marigolds for my sisters—foolproof sorts of seeds, for my sisters were impatient and neglectful gardeners. But for me, she saved the more fragile varieties.

At the time of my next oldest sister's wedding, Grandma Lou was eighty-four and living alone, still weeding her large beds herself. And as she had for my older sisters' weddings, Grandma Lou gave Jenny a Mason jar layered with seeds from her garden.

Round and round the colorful spiral of seeds curled in the fat-mouthed jar. Heavy beans in rich, deep earth tones held the bottom steady. Next came corn kernels, polished in cheesecloth until they gleamed like gold. Flat seeds of cucumber, squash and watermelon filled the upper reaches, interspersed with the feathery dots of marigolds. At the very top, separated with cheesecloth, were the finer herb seeds of mint and basil. The jar was crowned with a gleaming brass lid and a cheerful ribbon. There was a lifetime supply of seeds pressed into the jar; a whole garden's worth of food for the new couple.

Two years later, Grandma Lou suffered a stroke, which forced her into an assisted-living apartment. And though she was unable to attend my own wedding that year, I was delighted to see a Mason jar among the brightly wrapped gifts at my reception.

But unlike its predecessors, my jar held no graceful pattern of seeds. Instead, it was a haphazard blend, as if all the seeds had been dumped into a pillowcase and then poured into the jar. Even the lid seemed like an afterthought, for it was rusty and well used. But considering Grandma Lou's state of health, I felt blessed that she remembered the gentle tradition at all.

My groom, Mark, found work in the city, and we moved into a small apartment. A garden was all but impossible, so I consoled myself by placing the seed jar in our living room. There it stood as a promise to return to the garden.

Grandma Lou died the year our twins were born. By the time our sons were toddlers, I had moved the seed jar to the top of the refrigerator, where their curious little hands couldn't tip over my treasure.

Eventually we moved to a house, but there still wasn't

enough sun in our yard to plant a proper garden. Struggling yet courageous fescue grass vied for what little space there was between the dandelions, and it was all I could do to keep it mowed and occasionally watered.

The boys grew up overnight, much like the weeds I continuously pulled. Soon they were out on their own, and Mark was looking at retirement. We spent our quiet evenings planning for a little place in the country, where Mark could fish and I could have a proper garden.

A year later, Mark was hit by a drunk driver, paralyzing him from the neck down. Our savings went to physical therapy, and Mark gained some weak mobility in his arms and hands. But the simple day-to-day necessities still required a nurse.

Between the hospital visits and the financial worries, I was exhausted. Soon Mark would be released to my care, and at half his size, I knew I wouldn't even be able to lift him into our bed. I didn't know what I would do. We couldn't afford a day nurse, let alone full-time help, and assisted-care apartments were way out of our range.

Left to myself, I was so tired I wouldn't even bother to eat. But Jenny, my sister who lived nearby, visited me daily, forcing me to take a few bites of this or that. One night she arrived with a pan of lasagna, and she chatted cheerfully as we set our places. When she asked about Mark, I broke down in tears, explaining how he'd be home soon and how tight our money was running. She offered her own modest savings—even offered to move in and help take care of him—but I knew Mark's pride wouldn't allow it.

I stared down at my plate, my appetite all but gone. In the quiet that fell between us, despair settled down to dinner like an old friend. Finally I pulled myself together and asked her to help me with the dishes. Jenny nodded and rose to put the leftover lasagna away. As the refrigerator door flopped to a close, the seed jar on top rattled against the wall. Jenny turned at the sound. "What's this?" she asked, and reached for the jar.

Looking up from the sink, I said, "Oh, that's just Grandma Lou's seed jar. We each got one for a wedding present, remember?" Jenny looked at me, then studied the jar.

"You mean you never opened it?" she asked.

"Never had a patch of soil good enough for a garden, I guess."

Jenny tucked the jar in one arm and grabbed my sudsy hand in her other. "Come on!" she said excitedly.

Half dragging me, she went back to the dinner table. It took three tries, but she finally got the lid loose and overturned the jar upon the table. Seeds went bouncing everywhere! "What are you doing?!" I cried, scrambling to catch them. A pile of faded brown and tan seeds slid out around an old, yellow envelope. Jenny plucked it from the pile and handed it to me.

"Open it," she said, with a smile. Inside I found five stock certificates, each for one hundred shares. Reading the company names, our eyes widened in recognition. "Do you have any idea what these are worth by now?" she asked.

I gathered a handful of seeds to my lips and said a silent prayer of thanks to Grandma Lou. She had been tending a garden for me all these years and had pressed a lifetime supply of love into that old Mason jar.

Dee Berry

My Sister's Shadow

Love lets the past die. It moves people to a new beginning without settling the past. Love prefers to tuck the loose ends of past rights and wrongs in the bosom of forgiveness and pushes us to a new start.

Author Unknown

"Can we send her back? I'd rather have a kitten."

Instinctively I knew, even at five, that this little bundle everyone cooed over would profoundly impact my life.

From the moment she could walk, she became my second shadow. Wherever I went I had to take "her" with me. But it wasn't long before I discovered I was the one in the shadows.

My bedroom became "our" room. My things were constantly in the "share with your sister" pile. She "borrowed" everything of mine. Nothing was sacred or off-limits.

"Mom!" I yelled down the stairwell. "She's wearing my underwear! But Mom . . . not my underwear. Isn't any - thing just mine?"

My sister had soft blonde curls. My hair was mousy brown. She was homecoming queen. My prom date was nicknamed "Drippy Dreps." She won the lead in the school play. I was too afraid to audition. She was bubbly, funny and fickle. I was serious and sensible. She made people laugh out loud, drawing them to her like a moth to a flame.

As much as I resented being in her shadow . . . never feeling I was pretty enough or funny enough . . . I, too, basked in the warmth of her love for life. And my days were sunnier, more interesting and more enjoyable for each day I shared with her.

As adults, we were the best of friends. Our rivalry became more subtle. She bought a bigger house, a newer car. The rivalry was nothing more than an occasional annoyance.

The final competition . . . the one I couldn't overlook . . . involved a man—my man! Nursing her emotional wounds after a second divorce, my sister moved in with us. Six months later, my husband, my house, my *world* belonged to her. I took my two sons, filed for divorce, and tried to survive what I felt had been a terminal blow. To me, it was the final straw—the ultimate betrayal—she was my sister . . . my best friend . . . my enemy.

I went on with my life, raised my children, remarried and graduated from college at the age of forty-five. Meanwhile, I made sure my sister and I never crossed paths, carefully avoiding family gatherings she attended. And every time my inner self reminded me of how I missed her, how my life had lost some of its sunshine, I would silence it.

News of my sister would come through the family pipeline. Her life was one of pain and heartache. Her relationship with my ex didn't last. She ended up in jobs she hated and with men she hated more. Now word reached me that marriage number four was on the skids.

"Hello?" I asked, breathless as I caught the phone on the fifth ring. I thought I had missed the caller, but I heard someone breathing. "Is anybody there?"

"It's me."

I froze in disbelief as I recognized my sister's voice.

"Please don't hang up. I need to talk to you. Please."

My mind exploded with thoughts and emotions I couldn't voice. *How dare you call me. Are you crying? Good, I'm glad you're hurting. No, I'm not. It's been so long since we've talked, but that's not my fault, is it? I've missed you. Did you ever miss me? How could you do what you did? Why did you?*

"I'm getting a divorce . . . again," she said with a wry laugh. "I . . . I need your help. I know I don't deserve it, and I won't blame you if you say no. But I have nowhere else to turn."

Her pain was almost palpable and yet I couldn't find it in myself to make it any easier for her . . . all the hurt, tears and resentment of the past bubbled to the surface.

"I was wondering if I could come and stay with you for a few weeks." Her voice was barely a whisper. "Just until I find a place and can get on my feet."

I can't believe it. The nerve. She can just call up out of the blue and ask to move in with me . . . like what happened before never happened . . . is she crazy?

"Please."

Finally, I found my voice. "Let me think about it," I replied. "I'll call you back."

Our first days together were awkward. Forgiveness didn't come easily. It didn't come at all—until I faced two painful truths.

My sister didn't break up my marriage. A good marriage, one of strong character and united strength, would never have been threatened. The relationship I had with my husband had been nothing more than a straw house built on sand, incapable of weathering life's storms. For years, I couldn't admit my marriage was a fairy-tale illusion, and when the happily-ever-after didn't happen, it was easy to point blame outward and too painful to acknowledge my own mistakes.

Second, I wanted revenge for her betrayal. When the line in the sand was drawn between my husband and myself, she had to make a choice. I was her flesh and blood, her sister, her best friend—and she had picked him.

I found that once I was able to honestly access the past—and forgive myself—I was no longer a victim. I understood that anger and hatred was a choice—and I chose to let it go. I was free. It was an exhilarating feeling. Happiness at having the opportunity to have my sister back in my life became my priority. Weeks turned into months, and the bond between us grew.

One evening, as we sat before a fire, clinking wine glasses and toasting her new house, new job and the first day of her new life, her eyes filled with tears.

"I feel like such a failure," she whispered. "When I think of all the mistakes I have made . . . the people I love but have hurt . . . the bad choices . . . I can barely look at myself in the mirror. I want it to be different this time. I want to do things right. I *have* to do things right. I won't survive another wrong turn."

Attempting to comfort her, I said, "We've all made mistakes, done things we wished we could take back." I grinned. "Even me."

The ghost of a smile touched her mouth.

Laying my hand on hers, I whispered, "It's going to be okay."

Suddenly I realized the truth in my own words. All our lives, we had both seen things in each other we admired yet envied. I loved her personality, her ability to make people feel good just being around her.

For her, I was a safe haven. She trusted me to listen and

give advice even when it wasn't what she wanted to hear. And she knew I would always be there for her, even when I hadn't known it myself, because of my strong commitment to family.

We were sisters, not shadows of one another, nor competitors, nor rivals. We were threads of the same cloth. Our differences, as well as our similarities, had colored our lives in unique ways. But when blended together it turned into the most beautiful of fabrics. Strong. Resilient. A magnificent tapestry.

Diane Burke

Midnight Black

If your sister is in a tearing hurry to go out and cannot catch your eye, she's wearing your best sweater.

Pam Brown

As kids, we divided our bedroom down the middle with sticky masking tape and dental floss. Naturally, that didn't keep us from fighting for very long. Everything between Karen and I turned into a major competition which we eagerly played out with balled up fists, kicking legs and name-calling. With a little brother and a third bedroom to vie for, Karen gave her warning. "If I am forced to share this room with you any longer, the walls will go from this sickening pink to midnight black. And you know I make good on my threats." She loomed over me as a predator. I shivered in her presence. So that is how Russ and I ended up as roommates for a few years. (He never once complained about my favorite color but now as a grown man in his forties he has an uncanny passion for cotton candy.) She accused me of stealing her Cinderella glass slipper while I tried to right the wrong of it being addressed to the incorrect sister at Christmas. For a science experiment, she made me eat caterpillars.

Teenage years did not prove easier; I announced she was a good example of what not to be and she stole my boyfriend. As young adults we revered being dissimilar. Karen became "Miss Manners" and lived her life by etiquette books. I gave them as gag gifts.

Years later, you would think we divided up the interstate much the same as we had our bedroom years earlier. "I'll stay on the east side of I-35 and you can have the west side." Three hundred miles apart, we were worlds away from each other. It was not just our lifestyles that were diverse; she lived in the country surrounded by animals, while I lived in the suburbs and taught, but it is our life philosophy as well. Somewhere in the interim of our last tumultuous visit I have grown older and mellowed, even making friendships of people with viewpoints that are quite different than mine. Could Karen and I take an adult stance and bridge the gap to become friends?

Wistfully sighing, I watched sisters shopping together, sharing undisclosed childhood secrets that they carried into womanhood, making them closer. I envied their holidays spent together with gift exchanges. With us, birthdays went unnoticed. Dreams never shared, heartbreaks never carried. Karen had not seen my daughter since Kim was a baby. She was about to graduate from college. I had not seen her son since he drove his matchbox car through his peanut butter and jelly sandwich on the silver tray of his high chair. Today Ben stands over six feet tall and sings in a country western band.

Pondering the issues of everything that went wrong in our relationship, I decided to go for expert counseling; my sixteen-year-old son, Matthew was available.

"So tell me your secret. How come you and your sister never fight?"

"Easy. We accept each other as individuals. I do not try to change her and she doesn't try to change me. We just love each other." What a new idea! Total acceptance. It may just work.

Karen and I were stuck on opposite sides of our pink room still back in childhood, surrounded by sticky tape and dental floss. It is a grief that reaches deep inside my soul. I decided to erase the invisible line that we drew between us, separating us, dividing us. It was time. I deserved a sister.

Sitting cross-legged on the carpeted floor, I turned page after page of old scrapbooks. Happy faces of another life smiled up at me. I remembered useful things Karen taught me, like how to mash up peas and put them on the back of my ears then cover with hair, so Mom thought I ate them. We watched Roy Rogers on TV and became cowgirls together, riding our broomsticks into the sunset.

I yearned to return for just one day to straighten out our misunderstandings, tell her I loved her and say how grateful I was to have her as my sister. Laying down my battle weapons of competition and pettiness, I was left with raw honesty. Deep affection remained. Since our parent's death, I yearned for part of a family I no longer knew. Could we leapfrog over the past? Would she tell me the secret ingredient in her delicious apple pie? Maybe we could ride her horses together and feel the wind of renewal in our faces as we rode side by side into the sunset of life.

It was time to see Karen and build a relationship from rubble. A time of new beginnings. At long last I would have my sister to confide in, to send frilly grocery store cards that read: "I am so glad that you are my sister."

Driving to her house unannounced, I saw rounded cheeks in the rearview mirror. I was alone in the car so I knew they had to be mine. Once I had gloated over being the thinner sister. Now that couldn't be further from the truth. Time dropped my chest squarely onto my waist, making me thankful to have a large stomach to keep them from journeying down to my knees. I felt embarrassed, apprehensive. Would she receive me?

Arriving at her little country house, I saw Karen stooped over digging with a spade in her garden. Hearing the approach of the car, she stopped and cupped her hand to shade her eyes from the bright summer sun. I could tell when she realized it was I, for her hand dropped to her side and the spade fell to the ground. Yes, a slow smile burned its way across her face. Her hair was gray and she was trim and fit looking. Time had been good to her. She came closer to me as I walked quickly to meet her. We giggled.

Karen patted my fanny. She thought she had won the weight competition.

"Did you know being overweight is in vogue now?" Karen asked to my amazement.

"Really," I replied pulling my blouse down to help hide bulges.

"I just read an article about it." Karen opened the door to me.

"No kidding."

I smelled apple pie . . .

Robin Janson-Shope

Footsteps

My sisters knew I loved them, but I was very closemouthed about it. I didn't say it enough, because it was hard for me. But let me tell you, if you have sisters still living, you'd better hug them. You'll regret it if they go and you didn't get a chance to express that feeling. And they'd probably have been waiting for it. I know my sisters were waiting for me.

Patti LaBelle
of her three sisters

My family lived in one of those old Florida houses that was raised up on stilts so the water does not rush into the house during high tide. You could hear the footsteps of anyone walking around the house because there was nothing beneath the floor, and you learned to recognize the walker by the sound of his or her footsteps. It was not until I reached adulthood that I realized I never heard the sound of my sister's footsteps.

My sister and I shared a father (ours), a mother (mine) and a younger full brother. We did not grow up in an idyllic household. Our father was an active alcoholic until the day he died five years ago, and my mother took out a lot of her rage against my father on his daughter, my sister. There were times when I put myself in front of Mom during one of her rages to deflect some of her anger, but I always got shoved aside. So my sister learned to be quiet, to not be a bother, to stay out of the way. She learned how to walk without making any noise.

She left home early, at age sixteen. I remember coming home from school that day and immediately sensing something was wrong. When I checked our bedroom, her clothes were gone. An empty space was on the dresser where before had been her perfume bottles, her hair barrettes, her Bible. She had moved out with no warning, no celebration, no good-bye.

We lost touch after that as we both moved into adulthood. Occasionally there were the awkward phone calls or luncheons that left us feeling further apart rather than closer together. Our differences were acute, worn like badges around our necks. These differences had been emphasized so much in childhood—I was our parents' full child, she only a half. She was always made to feel less than whole because of that, a burden and a shame to the family. She was forced to carry the weight of our parents' feelings of inadequacy. Now something that neither of us had control over controlled us.

She moved to South Florida, got married and had children. I moved in the opposite direction, to Atlanta, got married and later divorced. We did not see or speak to each other for months at a time, yet the sticky past I was forced to confront in therapy kept bumping me into the feeling that I had lost something important when I lost my sister. I also realized with tremendous sadness that I had not really lost her because I had never found her to begin with. We had grown up in the same house together, but we were total strangers.

Last summer, at age thirty-seven, I decided to step through the past and reach out to her. I made a phone call—I was coming to Florida on a business trip, did she want to get together? Our voices arched over the hundreds of miles bridged by a telephone line—the tension was audible. We had not seen each other in almost ten years.

Finally she said yes, her voice high with nervousness. We made plans to meet at the airport. She would bring the children. I had met her oldest when he was an infant. Two more had followed who were only names on birth announcements to me.

I got off a plane in Tampa two months later, my stomach knotted with anticipation. Looking around, I discovered that my sister was not at the gate. I checked with a flight attendant to make sure the gate number had not been changed. No, she assured me, it had not. I was at the correct place. I sat on a cement planter and waited. *Had she forgotten? Had she decided not to come after all?*

Suddenly, a familiar face bobbed through the wall of people who were moving toward baggage claim. The face belonged to my sister, and right behind her, the small round eyes of a child peeked shyly from behind her. Her face looked exactly the same as I remembered, and when she saw me, she smiled. It was a smile I rarely saw in childhood.

My heart broke with relief and something else I could not name as I watched her approach, fast and anxious. She was sorry she was late, she said. She got caught in traffic. We hugged an awkward hug. I wanted to throw myself at her, squeeze her and scream that I was sorry for how my mother treated her when we were kids. But something inside me held back, afraid to show too much emotion.

As we waited at baggage claim for my luggage, I thought

about all she had been through in her life and how far she had come. The realization that the simple act of forgiveness can give a person the strength to put the past aside and build their life anew lit me up inside. She was nervous and I was, too. But suddenly it did not matter. What did matter was that we had finally connected. We both stepped out on to that shaky limb and were holding on for dear life. At her home, we grilled shrimp, and I got to know her children. We talked about our parents as if they were just two people we both happened to know. Her husband, whom I had met only once before, treated me like family. And that's what we were for that one night, a real family.

We have not been able to see each other since that time. Responsibilities and obligations in different states tend to interfere. But the connection has been made, and it will never again be severed. The bond of sisterhood persevered. It is a bond that is stronger than the damage done to it by our father's alcoholism or our mother's rage. It is a bond that was formed and sealed when, as little girls, we lay side by side in our beds, listening to the fighting going on outside our bedroom door, each of us secretly praying for the night to end. I remember one time we saw the light from under the door reflected in the window pane above the bed. My sister said it was the staff of God, and it meant he was protecting us. And protect us he did, but with more vision and compassion than either of us could have realized at the time. And as my sister walked through her Florida home that night preparing our dinner, I sat back and listened for the first time to the sound of her footsteps.

Kelly L. Stone

It's All Relative

Other things may change us, but we start and end with our family.

Anthony Brandt

If someone were to ask me what I would do if I "had it to do all over again," my answer would be this: I would love my friends and relations so well that no matter what, they would love me back in the same way. No reservations, no quid pro quos. No angst, no sibling rivalry, no holds barred. Maybe then I wouldn't be wondering now what it is that gets in the way of relationships between people whose connection to one another is so profound that nothing ought to be able to harm it.

I started thinking about this because of the extraordinary and painful rifts that seem to be tearing through the bonds of sisters I know. Has it always been there, I wonder, this awful, almost inevitable hurting of each other's souls? Are we just now owning it, or has something fundamental gone out of our relational lives, making space for the hot acid of recrimination that appears to creep so readily into the crevices of our hearts? Much has been made of the complex mother-daughter dyad in recent times, but almost no one, it seems, has explored the delicate territory of sisterhood, or friendship for that matter. If not altogether unmapped, those are tough topographies worthy of further exploration.

I became convinced of that when a friend told me with great sadness recently about the falling-out she'd had with her sister shortly before the sister's death. This was followed by a tearful conversation with one of my favorite cousins whose relationship with her beloved sister had become so fragile that she feared they would never repair the damage done. Shortly afterwards, another cousin, and then another, told similar stories. "She's not there for me when I need her," they told me. "She did this or didn't do that." "She just doesn't understand me." "I love her dearly, but we can't seem to talk." "She doesn't know where I'm coming from." "There's too much competition between us." All of it was familiar to me. I, too, had suffered the emotional split from a much-loved sister and had grieved the change in our relationship for years. It is an experience of loss that only those who have gone through it can know.

In each case, I gave them the same advice. "No matter what your issues are," I said, "find your way back to what binds you. No matter what it takes: hours of talking together, weeping, screaming, whatever—have it out until you get back in touch with the love, the loyalty, the special relationship you once had. Reclaim your sister before it's too late. If you don't, you may live to regret it." I could say this with quiet authority: I lost my sister, my only, much-loved older sister, before I could reclaim her, and it was too late. Each of them understood me, I think, but none has been able yet to act.

This scenario, while perhaps more dramatic between siblings, isn't confined just to family. Friendship and other meaningful relationships are destroyed every day over mundane as well as profound issues. One friend of mine, a lifelong friend on my short list of people I could count on, told me recently that an offhand remark of mine had offended her so much that she could not accept my invitation to an annual holiday dinner. I was stunned. Even if I had been unintentionally tactless, was that a reason to virtually end all contact? *If I stopped talking to everyone I love who had ever offended me,* I thought, *life would be a pretty lonely affair.*

When did relationships become this cheap, this dispensable? When did we begin to give up on "working things out"? When did we start junk-piling the important connections in our lives and stop stockpiling the reservoirs of forgiveness and tolerance that made family and friendship work in spite of themselves?

I've talked to my cousins and my friends about this a lot lately. And every time, a familiar ache roots itself in my chest, and I wonder what would have happened had my sister lived. Would we have done our screaming, weeping and talking until we were able to hug our way back to sisterhood and the bond of sibling connection?

Will her daughters, with whom I struggle so heartily now to forge family ties, ever understand why my heart breaks when they keep me at arm's length because of the baggage they insist on bearing? Will my cousins reclaim their own sisters before it's too late?

With all my heart, I hope so. Because they are the lucky ones. They can do it all over again. And that is an opportunity just too good to pass up in this time of fragile friendships, remote relatives and hungry hearts yearning for simple connection.

Elayne Clift

5

OH
BROTHER!

Brothers and sisters are as close as hands and feet.

Vietnamese Proverb

The Intruder

Our house is very often visited by relatives who come from out of town and spend two or three weeks with us. Most of them are very nice but it is still an inconvenience to have all of these extra people in your house. Recently, we had a relative come to our house late one evening. It was a young lady. She came about three and a half months ago and is still with us. We are very much inconvenienced with this young lady as her habits are very different from ours. She likes to sleep during the day and at night she keeps us awake to amuse her. We must always keep her in good humor as she becomes cross at the slightest irritation. She has her meals regularly enough but they are not at the same time as ours and this is a big problem. She also doesn't eat what we eat. She has her own special foods. She smiles when in good humor with such a broad and pleasant smile we can't help but smile back at her even though she has disrupted our lives completely. In spite of all of these things, we hope that she never leaves for we love our baby sister very much.

Joseph Brandes, twelve years old,
three months after the birth of his baby sister

Falling in Love with Molly

A gorgeous example of denial is the story about the little girl who was notified that a baby . . . sister was on the way. She listened in thoughtful silence, then raised her gaze from her mother's belly to her eyes and said, "Yes, but who will be the new baby's mommy?"

Judith Viorst

My son Joe knew about Molly even before I did.

He was fourteen years old and had just walked through the open door of the bathroom, where I was standing at the sink. "Just need to grab my hair gel," he said, reaching up to the shelf above my head. I was startled and turned slightly away from him. But it was too late. He had already noticed that I was holding something in my hand.

"What's that?" he asked.

For a moment, I didn't answer him. *Just mumble something,* I said to myself. *He doesn't listen to most of what you say anyway.* But there was something about the depth of his voice behind me, something about the fact that it was coming from a good five inches above me, that made me turn and tell him the truth.

"It's a pregnancy test," I said, looking down at the little white wand. "I . . . I don't really think I'm . . . you know . . . it's just a possibility . . . a remote possibility . . . your Dad said I should try one of these kits . . ."

I looked up at Joe as my voice trailed off. His face had gone white. He didn't look so grown up after all.

"How do you know if it's . . . positive?" he asked.

"Well," I said, reaching for the instruction leaflet, "it says here that a little red line would appear."

Just then, the phone rang. I had been waiting to hear from my husband all day—I didn't want to miss his call. "Hold this for a minute," I said, handing the wand to Joe. "Don't tip it. I'll be right back."

It wasn't my husband. "Okay," I said, heading back into the bathroom. "Sorry about all this, Joe, the time's up anyway. I'll just throw that thing in the—" I stopped. The wand was lying in the sink. Joe was staring down at it. Slowly, he raised his head, turned, and looked straight at me.

"There's a line," he said. "A little red line." His eyes narrowed. "A gross, disgusting, little . . . red . . . line."

And then he walked past me, out of the bathroom, down the stairs, out the side door, and as much as was possible for the next nine months, out of our lives.

By the time our daughter Molly was due to be born, I had grown accustomed to my eldest son's embarrassment and animosity. I had grown accustomed to a lot of things, not the least of which was having an unexpected child at the age of thirty-nine, long after we thought our family of two boys was complete. My husband, to his eternal credit, was delighted. Our younger son, eleven-year-old Shea, pored over the baby books with me, keenly following the week-by-week progress of his little sister's *in utero* development. Throughout it all, Joe rarely spoke to me, except to say, "You don't have to come to my school," and—after a marathon baby-naming conference—"Molly is Ron's dog's name."

When Molly finally arrived—tiny, quiet and perfect—six family arms were there to draw her close. But Joe's remained tightly crossed over his chest, on the far side of the hospital room. It was an effort to step outside my bliss, to call to him, to beckon him into our circle of adoration. Shaking his head just slightly, he backed up farther into the corridor. I could see him standing there, arms still folded, staring straight ahead.

Joe arranged to be at a friend's cottage when Molly and I came home from the hospital. He was still gone ten days later when I took our daughter for her first check-up. He arrived home just as I was coming back, tears streaming down my face. "The doctor thinks she might have a hearing problem," I sobbed. "She's too quiet, she's not responding like she should. We have to have her tested."

As my husband soothed me, downplaying my worry, I noticed that Joe had stopped beside the baby, sound asleep in her car seat. He reached out to her, shifting her slightly away from a bump in the carpet. "She's okay," he said, looking down at her. "There's nothing wrong with her. She's just little."

He looked up at us. I stopped crying. I held my breath. "I'm going in-line skating," he said. "I'll put my stuff away when I get back."

Three months later, as I walked the floor at 4:00 A.M. with a fretful, inconsolable (and otherwise perfectly healthy) baby in my arms, I stumbled into Joe's room and nudged him awake. "Joe, could you take her? Just for a few minutes? I can't settle her down, Dad's at work, I just really need a break."

Saying nothing, but throwing off his covers, Joe took his

little sister from me. He laid her briefly on his bed, tightly
rewrapping her blanket. Putting her over his shoulder, he
patted her back, spoke to her softly, slowly walked her up
and down the hall outside his room. It wasn't his first
night with Molly, and it wouldn't be his last.

In the months before Molly was born, a lot of people
told us about the pleasures of a baby who comes late. "A
do-it-yourself grandchild," said one old gentleman. "We
had one of those, the best thing that ever happened to us."
"A change-of-life child," said another. "What a blessing." "A
caboose baby," said an aunt. "They're always the sweetest." They assured us that we would cherish this unexpected detour in our lives.

They were right. But they didn't mention the bonus.
They didn't tell us about the sight of a baby stroller
parked perilously close to a backyard basketball net, a
mop-haired one-year-old shrieking in delight as lanky
teenagers tore back and forth in front of her. They didn't
talk about a chubby toddler, dressed in a size-large
hockey jersey, scooping up the puck that always slid
directly into her oversized glove. They didn't describe a
two-year-old, sitting high atop a stack of cushions at the
kitchen table, "helping" earnestly with grade-eleven
math. Or the four-year-old wrapped tightly around the
legs of the smiling graduate, in each and every photo.

No one ever predicted the first family visit to a college
dorm, where sixteen drawings of the same two stick figures competed on the wall with air-brushed, leggy calendar girls. They didn't portray newly muscled arms
holding up a struggling swimmer, a shaky skater, a first-
time skier. They failed to account for an impish little face
hanging out the window of a rusty, rumbling car, or prepare me to be bypassed on the platform for tiny outstretched arms. Certainly, no one ever warned me that I
would have to will my heart to stay intact one Christmas

Eve, when a seven-year-old with a brother on the other side of the world asked if she could trade all the presents under the tree for "our Joey at the door."

No one ever told me about the joy of seeing your own little girl perched on the shoulders of your own grown-up son, her arms reaching down toward him, his grinning, handsome face turned up toward her laughter. They couldn't tell me. Because they couldn't describe it.

Liz Mayer

Joe and Molly out for a day of skating.

Change of Heart

We acquire friends and we make enemies, but our sisters come with the territory.

Evelyn Loeb

When our youngest sister was born sixty years ago, my little brother was six and I was eight. I had always been the "big sister" and he had always been "the baby."

Our sister's arrival was a complete surprise to both of us. In those days no one worried much about sibling rivalry, and no "experts" told us how to deal with another child in the house. We had wise and loving grandparents, however.

I was thrilled about the baby and loved to hold her and help care for her. My brother's feelings were quite different! He looked at her briefly and left, preferring to spend the evening in his room. When I went to his room to talk to him and try to get him to play games with me, he just looked away.

"Why did they have to go and get that old baby?"

Later that night, Grandpa came over to see the new baby. As he held her, he said to my brother, "You know, she's a lot like that lamb I'm raising on the bottle. I have to take care of her and feed her often, just the way your Mama does with the baby."

My brother said, "I'd rather have the lamb" under his breath, but just loud enough for Grandpa to hear.

Even though Grandpa seemed pretty old to me (at least fifty, I figured), he could hear very well, and he heard my brother's muttered comment.

"Well," said Grandpa, "if you'd rather have a lamb, maybe we could trade. I'll give you a day to think it over, and if you still want to trade tomorrow, we'll do it."

I thought I saw him wink at Mama, but I knew I must have been mistaken because Grandpa never winked at anyone.

After Grandpa left, Mama asked my brother if he wanted her to read to him. He cuddled up beside her, and she read to him for a long while.

He kept looking at the baby, and Mama asked him to hold his little sister while she went to get a diaper. When Mama came back, my brother was gently touching the baby's smooth black hair, and as he held her hand, she grasped his finger.

"Mama, look! She's holding my hand!"

"Sure, she knows you're her big brother," Mama smiled. He held the baby for a few more minutes, and he seemed much happier at bedtime. Grandpa came back the next evening as he had promised and called my brother to talk to him.

"Well, are you ready to trade the baby for a lamb?"

My brother looked surprised that Grandpa had remembered the bargain.

"She's worth two lambs now."

Grandpa seemed to be taken aback at this breach of contract. He said that he'd have to think it over and would be back the next night to talk about it.

The next day was a Saturday, and my brother and I

spent much of the day indoors watching the baby have her bath, watching her sleep and holding her. My brother held her three more times that day. He looked worried when Grandpa came to see us that evening and called him over to talk.

"You know, I've thought about that baby-and-lamb trade all day, and you really do drive a hard bargain. I've decided, though, that the baby is probably worth two lambs. I think we can do business."

My brother hesitated very briefly before answering Grandpa. "She's a whole day older now, and I think she's worth five lambs."

Grandpa looked shocked, and he slowly shook his head.

"I don't know. I'll have to go home and give your offer some serious thought. Maybe I'll have to talk it over with my banker."

Grandpa left soon after, and my brother seemed worried. I tried to get him to play some games with me, but he went to Mama's room and held the baby for a long time.

The next day, Sunday, Grandpa came to visit us in the early afternoon. He told my brother he had come early because if he had to round up five lambs and get a room ready for the baby, he'd need an early start.

My brother took a deep breath, looked Grandpa squarely in the eye and made an announcement: "The baby is worth fifty lambs now!"

Grandpa looked at him in disbelief and shook his head.

"I'm afraid the deal's off. I can't afford fifty lambs for one little baby. I guess you'll have to keep her and help your parents take care of her."

My brother turned away with a little smile he didn't know I saw, and this time I really did see Grandpa wink at Mama.

Muriel J. Bussman
As appeared in Chicken Soup for the Golden Soul

Sugar River

It was the last day of our family camping trip in Wisconsin. We had been driving for nearly three hours. It was a really hot day, and I thought I couldn't stand another minute in the car. My younger brother and sister were squirming and fighting, and I had to sit between them, so, of course, I was getting the worst of it from both sides. I'm three years older than Aaron, and five years older than Emily, so my parents expected me to be more mature and try to keep the younger kids apart.

I was trying really hard to ignore them and just read my book, but then Aaron reached over and pinched my arm. I couldn't take it anymore. "Cut it out!" I screamed at him, grabbing both of his hands in anger.

"Ow, you're hurting me! Let go!" he cried.

My mother turned around and gave me a stern look. "Leave him alone! You know you have to be patient with him!" I let go of his hands with a sigh. My parents were always telling me to be more patient with him, but it really wasn't fair. Just because he had learning disabilities, just because he was a "special" kid, he shouldn't be allowed to get away with stuff like that. But he knew he could, and that I couldn't pinch him back. He grinned at me. I glared back at him. He was such a pain.

Finally we rounded the last turn on the dusty country road, and the sign came into view: "Sugar River Tubing". My brother and sister were out of the car almost before it stopped moving and raced toward the ticket booth.

I followed them more slowly, but I was pretty excited to be there, too. We would be provided with large inner tubes, driven several miles upstream in a van, and then would spend the afternoon lazily floating back down the river.

From the clearing where the shack stood, we couldn't see the river, since the trees were thick with leaves. We followed the attendant over to a beat-up old van and climbed inside. After about ten minutes, we reached the drop-off point a few miles upstream.

As we got out of the van, the driver went around to the back and pulled out our inner tubes.

"Just walk down that path to the river," he instructed us.

My mother gestured toward the inside of the van, where several life jackets lay tangled in a heap. "What about the life jackets?" she asked.

"Well, we're required by law to have those," he said, "but you won't need them. The water's really shallow. In some places you might even need to stand up and carry the tubes because they'll scrape the bottom."

We were already heading down the path, so despite her misgivings, my mother agreed to forgo the life jackets. She probably decided it wasn't worth the arguments she would get from us if she tried to make us wear them. After all, I wasn't a baby! I was fourteen, and I'd known how to swim since I was five. Emily knew how keep her head above water for a long time, and even though Aaron was "disabled," he was a natural athlete and was a better swimmer than I was. As I followed my brother and sister down to the river, I heard the tires skidding on the loose gravel as the van turned around and disappeared down the road.

When I caught up with the kids, they were standing silently on the riverbank, surveying the water. Instead of a shallow stream, we saw a wide, quickly flowing river. My father stepped closer to the edge and studied the water for a moment.

"I think it looks okay," he said. "I can see the bottom; it doesn't look too deep. Just let me get in first, then I can help the kids get on their tubes."

He stepped off the riverbank with a splash; the water was up to his chest—and apparently colder than he had expected.

"Jeez Louise, that's cold!" he exclaimed, and then grinned at us. "Okay, who's first?"

Within a few minutes, the rest of us had managed to climb onto our inner tubes, and we started floating downstream. I quickly realized that this was not going to be quite as much fun as I had thought. The water was flowing so fast that it was difficult to steer the tubes. The current kept pushing us to the sides of the river, where we found ourselves constantly having to paddle and push off the riverbanks in order to avoid being scratched by the branches overhanging the water.

As we made our way down the river, our tubes began to drift away from each other. Whenever there was a bend in the river, we would lose sight of at least one of the others, and my mother began to get nervous.

"Can you see Aaron?" she asked me at one point, as we rounded a bend. She was always checking up on Aaron.

As we came around the bend, I spotted him. He was pretty far ahead of us, which wasn't surprising. He always insisted on being first, no matter what it was. Whenever we went somewhere in the car, he would push me and

Emily out of the way to get in first, even though we all sat in the backseat anyway. And when my mother put a platter of food on the table, he would grab to take his piece first, as if there wasn't a whole refrigerator full of food. It was really annoying, but everyone was always making excuses for him because of his learning disability. I knew that I was really getting too old to care about things like that, but I couldn't help it.

Aaron was still pretty far ahead of us on his tube, and I could tell that it was even making my father nervous. Since I was by now much closer to him than either of my parents, my father told me to try and catch up with him. I started kicking and paddling, and gradually began closing the distance between us.

As the river straightened out, I saw that there was a fallen tree extending nearly all the way across. Aaron was heading straight for it.

"Aaron, watch out!" my father yelled to him. "Try to paddle over to the right!"

Either Aaron was too far away to hear him, or he was just ignoring him, but he didn't even look up.

Suddenly I got scared. The current was pulling Aaron's tube really fast, and I could see that it would only be a matter of seconds before the tube would slam into the log. He was moving fast enough that he could be badly hurt. I kicked and paddled as hard as I could, and I had almost caught up to him. I screamed, "Grab my hand!" But just as I reached out for him, his tube smacked into the tree. The force of the impact caught him by surprise, and he was catapulted off the tube into the river. Instantly he disappeared under the water. I immediately jumped off my tube—and was shocked to realize that I couldn't touch the bottom. I grabbed onto the tree for support. The current was so strong that I was nearly sucked underneath. Frantically I looked for him—the tree's branches formed a dense thicket under the water, and I knew that if he were caught in there he would be trapped.

Suddenly I saw them—his two little hands sticking up out of the water, desperately grasping at the slippery trunk. With one hand hanging on to the tree, I grabbed his wrist with the other hand. With every ounce of my strength, I fought to pull him above the water.

He came up gasping and choking; he threw his arms around my neck and we hung there, sobbing with fear and relief. He had lost his glasses; his face and arms were scratched from the branches; but he was safe. A moment later my father was there. He helped us up onto our tubes.

I still couldn't stop crying, and I couldn't let go of Aaron's hand. After making sure that neither of us was hurt, my father said, "Let's get out of here. Maybe we can climb up out of the water and walk back the rest of the way."

I reluctantly released my grip on the trunk, and the three of us worked our way around the end of the tree and back into the current. My mother and Emily were huddling under the branches of a small bush overhanging the water, where the current had dragged them. I could see the fear in my mother's face, and I was at that moment very thankful that she had not seen how close we had come to losing Aaron.

We surveyed the riverbank, but it was too steep to climb. We had no choice but to continue downstream on the tubes. We linked hands to form a chain and pushed off from the riverbank. The fifteen minutes it took to reach the dock seemed like an eternity. The young man who had dropped us off leaned over to help us off our tubes and out of the water.

"How was it?" he asked brightly.

My father just glared at him. The rest of us headed off to the car, leaving my father to fill him in on exactly "how it was." When he came to the car, he said simply, "He said they had a lot of rain last night and they didn't know the water was so deep. They're closing down for the rest of the day."

We set out toward the nearest city, in search of a mall that might have an optometrist, where my parents hoped to replace Aaron's glasses. Emily sat up front between my parents, and Aaron fell asleep with his head in my lap. For once, it wasn't annoying to have him leaning on me. It felt good. His hair was still damp and his face was streaked with mud, but he actually looked kind of cute.

As we drove into the mall parking lot, Aaron stirred. Gradually he sat up, his face flushed from the heat. He squinted in the late afternoon sun. I had never seen anything so beautiful.

"Are we there yet?" he asked.

I just smiled. "Yes," I said, "we're there."

"Can we get ice cream?"

"You bet," said my father, glancing at him with a grin.

One evening a few weeks later, my parents went to a movie, and I had to stay home and baby-sit. I was in Aaron's room, looking for his new glasses, which had flown off his face while he was doing back flips on his bed. After we found the glasses under the dresser, he put them on and adjusted the slightly bent frames. Then he looked up at me. "You saved my life," he said seriously. I was so surprised, I couldn't speak. Aaron rarely said anything nice to me, and he hadn't said anything at all about the incident. I didn't think it had made any impression on him at all. But before I could think of what to say, the moment was over, and Aaron resumed doing flips. I don't think he noticed the tears in my eyes.

Maybe it's just that I'm getting older and I can see things in a more mature way.

Now that I thought about it, Aaron hadn't been nearly

so annoying lately. Not that his behavior was any different. He's still the same kid he always was. He still pushes me out of the way to get through the door first, and he still makes a big scene if he doesn't get to pick which TV show we watch. And my parents still give into him. But lately I really don't mind.

Even though there are still some times when I can't stand him, it's a little easier for me to be patient with him. I can even see why my friends think he's cute and funny. In a way, I'm actually glad that he's my little brother.

Aaron knows what I did for him that day on the river. He knows that I saved his life. But I'm sure that he doesn't know what he did for me that day. Aaron showed me that I did have it in me, after all, to be the kind of big sister my parents wanted me to be, the kind of big sister I always knew I should be. Aaron helped me bring out my best that day, when I grabbed onto his slippery little hands in the water and held on as tightly as I possibly could. He needed me—and I needed him, too. I held on to him then as if both of our lives depended on it. And I'll never let go. That's what being a big sister means. Our lives depend on each other, and that's always and forever.

Phyllis Nutkis

Aaron's thoughts about the river that day.

Where's My Little Sister?

Ten-year-old Bobby was given the assignment to write an essay in as few words as possible on two of life's greatest problems. He wrote, "Twin sisters."

Author Unknown

For months, we looked forward to the new baby sister. Even though we were not positive that she was a little girl, in all of our hearts, there was no doubt. My husband Roy, twin sons Brad and Chad, and I prepared a pink room filled with dolls and lace. Because the boys were at the ripe old age of four, they were able to help out a great deal. We made her future arrival a family affair, filled with fantasies of a precious little angel who would make our home complete.

The day finally arrived. My husband rushed me to the hospital, while my in-laws got the boys ready to go meet their little sister, the newest member of our family. The labor went quickly, and before I knew it, my husband and I were in the delivery room.

With the piercing of a scream, Becky came into the world. She was just as beautiful as we had imagined. After the nurse cleaned her up, she placed her in my arms. Her crying turned into a cooing hum, as her little eyes met mine. Tears flowed down my husband's face as he welcomed her into the world.

"Go get the boys," I shouted. "They are a part of this, too." With that, my husband rushed out the delivery room door, while the nurse pushed Becky and me into the hallway. In a few brief moments, the doors from the waiting room swung open. Roy came back in carrying a twin in each arm. I saw the perfect picture of my three men with huge smiles on their faces.

"Brad and Chad, this is Becky," Roy proudly announced, while the nurse watched.

"Hi Becky," Brad said, as he reached down toward his little sister.

I noticed Chad as he began wiping tears away from his eyes, looking all around.

"What's wrong, Chad?" I asked.

With his little lip quivering he asked, "Where's my little sister?"

"Becky is your sister too, Chad," I replied.

"Becky is Brad's sister. Candy was supposed to be mine," Chad said to the nurse. "We both wanted a sister."

After a few minutes of trying to console him, my in-laws took the boys back home. As they left, Chad continued to look around for his missing baby.

For several months their bedtime prayers ended in this manner: "Jesus, thank you for our little sister. Please give us another little sister."

Becky was a colicky baby and spent almost every night up screaming at the top of her lungs. After about three months of sleepless nights, I heard the boys as their prayer slightly changed. In unison they said, "Jesus, thank you for our little sister, but we don't need another one."

Nancy B. Gibbs

CLOSE TO HOME   JOHN McPHERSON

"It's designed specifically for colicky babies."

Precious in My Eyes

I long to accomplish great and noble tasks, but it is my chief duty to accomplish small tasks as if they were great and noble.

Helen Keller

At the age of sixteen, my sister, Cynthia, began working at a small local hospital as a summer volunteer. I would occasionally stop by the hospital and walk her home after her few hours of service.

One day, I arrived at the hospital earlier than usual, so I wandered around until I finally found her in one of the patient's rooms. As I stood in the open doorway, I saw her sitting on a chair near the bed of one young patient, staring out of the first-floor window.

The young boy, about seven years old, lay flat on his back, both eyes heavily bandaged. I heard my sister describing what she saw from his window. "The sky is clear blue, David. Just below the window is a small garden with clusters of tiny yellow, pink and red flowers and beautifully shaped leafy green shrubs."

The boy was silent. His facial expressions changed with

interest as my sister continued to illustrate the outdoor scene to him. It was as though he could see the world through her eyes.

Suddenly, Cynthia stood up and moved closer to the window to get a better look. She smiled and said with excitement, "A little brown and white spotted terrier just jumped into the garden. He's sniffing around a bit with his little licorice-colored nose."

Although I couldn't see the dog from my vantage point at the doorway, I closed my eyes as Cynthia described the scene. As I listened, I could envision everything.

As she continued her narration, I pictured her words in my own mind. "Now the little dog is running around in circles, stopping at every bush to dig holes. He's having such fun, David."

Only once, I opened my eyes to see the expression on the boy's face when I heard him laugh out loud. Wearing an ear-to-ear grin, his face lit up with excitement underneath the bandage. I smiled, too. Closing my eyes again, I continued to listen.

"Oh, oh," Cynthia said, "looks like the fun is over. One of the staff just came out and chased our little friend off. He scurried away with a yellow flower clenched tightly between his teeth."

As the small, spotted thief retreated, I knew my sister was finishing her observation, so I opened my eyes. I took one last look at the happy boy before backing quietly out of the doorway, leaving them alone once more.

When I joined that young boy in seeing the world through my sister's eyes I found myself looking into her heart.

I waited patiently for my sister at the nurse's station. She arrived soon after, happy as always. When I asked her how her day was, she gave her standard response,

"Good," while maintaining her smile. I smiled back as we began our walk home.

I said nothing to my sister about what I had witnessed, but she made me see there was much more to her than I realized—she was more precious in my eyes. I know, that with the many small acts of kindness she performed as a volunteer that summer, the hospital had found some of the best medicine for its patients.

Robert C. Fuentes

It's Not What You Think

There's something about teenagers—they love to be together. Robert and our son, Calvin, had been best friends all throughout high school and it seemed quite natural that he should become part of our family. In our small town of Delburne, Alberta, a well-to-do German couple had adopted him when he was an infant, but Robert didn't want to be "well-to-do." He wanted with all his heart to be a mechanic. He felt more comfortable in a pair of greasy coveralls than he ever would be in a three-piece suit.

His mother didn't consider this vocation suitable to his status, and this caused a lot of friction. Calvin approached us with the idea of taking Robert into our home. And after talking to his parents and getting their consent, this is exactly what happened. Robert was a sweet lad with a mischievous mind, full of tricks and life, just like our own son. That meant there was never a dull moment in our home.

The rest of the youth group began hanging out at our place, usually Sunday evening after the service while my husband John, the pastor and I were still at the church. And, as is usual with teenagers, they started pairing off. Robert already had a sweetheart. Debbie was a lovely young lady away studying at Bible College in another province. When he started paying attention to Cindy, a newcomer to the group, we became a bit concerned. We reminded him of Debbie, who was trusting him to remain faithful to her. But, to everyone's dismay, Robert continued to spend more and more time with Cindy. In a small community like ours, it's pretty hard to hide something like that.

Calvin hated to see his best friend being a cheat so he went to Robert's room one night and said, "Either you stop seeing Cindy or I'm phoning Debbie! How can you hurt her like this? She is bound to find out!"

Robert said nothing and just shrugged his shoulders. Meanwhile I had taken Cindy aside into our bedroom and told her more or less the same thing. She hugged me and cried, "Oh, but you don't understand! It's not what you think. Robert is like a brother I never had. We have so much in common we just have to talk to each other. I wish you could see it our way."

Then came the day we all dreaded. Robert had taken time off work and Cindy skipped college for the day. They headed for Calgary, a four-hour drive away. We were all disappointed and felt we had failed them along the way.

It was evening before they finally arrived home. Robert jumped out of his truck, ran around to the other side and hugged Cindy as she got out. They were both radiant as they came up the walk, hand in hand. As we watched through the dining room window our hearts sank. *Here it comes*, we thought.

At least you could have been a little more discreet about it, I thought to myself. But I said nothing. Robert spoke first. "Mom and Dad [that's what he started to call us right after he arrived], can we have all the family together? We have some very important news to share with you." Our hearts sank. After Calvin and our two daughters came into the room, Robert began to speak.

"You know Cindy and I have been seeing a great deal of each other lately, and we know you don't approve. But honestly, we had to do it."

We sat silent, waiting for whatever type of excuse would come next. He went on, "The more we saw each other the more we realized how much we had in common. Cindy really seemed to draw me. We discovered that we were both of Russian ancestry, liked the same foods and even disliked the same things. The more we talked the more apparent it became. So we went to the provincial courthouse in Calgary today."

We gasped, "Oh no, you didn't go and get married?"

Then Cindy said, "We searched old records for hours until we finally found Robert's birth certificate." Then, with a huge grin on her face she announced: "Robert is my brother!"

There was a stunned silence as the words hit our ears.

"All these years, I've known that I had an older brother who was given up for adoption at birth. But I never thought I'd ever find him. And here he had been living less than thirty miles away all that time. We got suspicious when we found out we were both Russian, and bit by bit things fell into place. But we didn't want to tell anybody until we had proof and knew for sure."

We all gasped as we heard the story—first in disbelief—and then with great joy! Lots of hugging and crying followed! We were all apologizing to one another for our critical and judgmental attitudes and then rejoicing again. It was all too incredible. It was the wee hours of the morning before we finally went to bed. None of us got much sleep that night.

In the years that followed, Robert became a journeyman mechanic—fulfilling his own vision for his life. And oh yes, he and Debbie did get married after all—with his sister Cindy there to catch the bouquet!

Greta Zwaan

$\overline{6}$

SISTERS BY HEART

It seems we just connected
Right from the start,
Meant to be—naturally,
Sisters by heart.

And though we don't share parents
As real sisters do,
Growing in my family tree
Is a special branch for you.

A time-tested kinship
In which God plays a part,
Through talks and laughter, sorrow and
  dreams
Of sisters by heart.

Darla Perkins

A Little White Lie

When my friend, Sadie, was taken to the emergency room at a local hospital, I rushed over to be with her as soon as I received the news.

Sadie was both surprised and pleased to see me. "How did you get them to let you in?" she asked, knowing visitors were not usually allowed in the emergency room.

I, too, had been concerned about that on the drive over. However, I knew Sadie needed a friend to comfort her. In desperation, I had decided if worse came to worst, I would be forced to tell a lie and say I was Sadie's sister. I hoped I wouldn't have to resort to that.

After I explained all this to Sadie, she threw back her head in hearty laughter. While I was trying to figure out why Sadie was laughing, I glanced down at our clasped hands—my very white one held gently between her two black ones.

June Cerza Kolf

Lipshtick

*Laugh and the world laughs with you.
Cry and you cry with your girlfriends.*

Laurie Kuslansky

A girl would be one lost soul without her girlfriends. An astronaut severed from the mother ship, yin without yang, an Oreo without the middle. Girlfriends are the elevated, the wise, the Good Humor truck on a hot summer day. We are bonded together like protons and electrons— nothing short of a nuclear blast could split us apart. We are together, we are one, we are *sistahs*.

Your girlfriend is your priest, your sounding board and your fashion consultant all in one. She is almighty and all forgiving. She will watch you drown in a gallon of Rocky Road and happily grab a spoon. In the harsh reality of the morning light, she'll know just where to take you shopping for clothes without seams. At 50 percent off, no less. She is your mother without the guilt, your sister without the competition, your therapist without the bill. She is sustenance itself, and without her, life is a vast pool of emptiness.

I heard a story the other day that exemplifies this

perfectly—everything there is to know about girls and girlfriends in one telling anecdote. It involves a man who was coaching his eight-year-old daughter's Little League team. His team was in the field when the batter hit a ground ball right to the shortstop. She scooped it up, beaming with pride at her accomplishment. Then she promptly threw it to the center fielder.

After the game, the group went out for ice cream, and the coach did the unisex politically correct thing. He congratulated them all on playing so well, told them how great they were, and talked a lot about teamwork and how important it is. Then he pulled the shortstop aside and said, "That was a great pick up you made on that grounder, you did a terrific job, but I know that *you* know that the ball should have been thrown to the first baseman. So tell me, how come you threw it to the center fielder?"

The shortstop just looked at him incredulously and said, "She's my best friend."

And there you have it. Girlfriends rule.

The heart of a girl is a sweet and complex morass. There is no telling what lies there until you pull on your boots and clomp around for a while, pick in hand. Sometimes you have to hack away at it for years and sometimes things come gushing out in a torrent. And it is like having the winning lottery ticket to have a pass to a girl's heart and what lies within—a rare privilege indeed, for she invites in only those who have proved themselves worthy (by slaying a dragon, pulling a sword from a stone, or maybe just cleaning out the coffee pot once in a while like he's been asked time and time again).

I know that you are just that kind of a person. You have worthy written all over you. You are a pillar of worthiness, a human testament to worth (or, maybe I'm not so picky). And that is why I extend an invitation to you to trample away. My heart is your heart. Bring on your flashlight, your chisel, your TNT. It's a jungle in there. Think of me as your own personal cadaver to cut open and explore. Maybe you will learn something, or maybe you'll just puke your guts out.

The following musings are an open confessional—Come right in, I say, plunk yourself down, get comfy and let's chaw, tawk, kibitz, confess.

I have chin hair.

There, I've said it. Now you know it. We can move on. You take a turn, then I'll take a turn, and when we are done, we'll be forever bound. Then you can see what is close to your heart is close to the heart of the girl sitting next to you. I guarantee that it will be, and then you are on your way. The two of you have a beautiful future together. You can talk over the most minute event in excruciating detail over coffee. Or coffee cake. Or, since one of you is dieting, fresh fruit. And then the circle is complete. Girlfriends beget girlfriends and the world keeps turning. They are the ones who will be there for the psychological dysentery that can hit after you drink from the wellspring of life. You will never be wanting for an ear, a shoulder, or a safety pin. In the great baseball game of life, you'll be playing shortstop, and before you know it, you'll be fielding grounders.

Gwen Macsai

CLOSE TO HOME　　JOHN McPHERSON

"Buying that mirror from that fun house was
the smartest thing we ever did."

Friendly Reminder

I refuse to think of them as chin hairs. I think of them as stray eyebrows.

Janette Barber

Friendships are a must for women. If it weren't for friends, women would have to go to the ladies' room alone. And who would offer a truthful assessment about whether an outfit makes your hips look big?

I have a Mustache Pact with my closest friends. If any one of us goes into a coma, the others are bound by our pact to come and wax the mustache of the comatose friend. We women love to share those special moments.

I shared another special moment with friends recently. Several of us were hurrying to a surprise baby shower. We were hurrying because it's tough to surprise the guest of honor when she gets to the party before the guests.

We had pooled our resources to buy "the stroller to end all strollers." It was a collapsible stroller that would stroll the baby, carry the baby, swing the baby—maybe even change the baby—I'm not sure. I thought I heard someone say it sliced, diced and julienned. It was Stroller-ama!

I told the others to run into the house while I got Super Stroller from the trunk. I jerked it into position and started sprinting. Unfortunately, about mid-driveway, Stroller-zilla realized I hadn't fully locked it into place (emphasis on the aforementioned collapsible feature). It collapsed neatly into storage mode.

I probably don't need to give you a science lesson on "momentum," but let me mention that I had a lot of it working for me. The fact that The Stroller-nator stopped on a dime didn't mean much to my little sprinting body, which was immediately airborne.

Please picture a graceful triple axle over the top of the stroller with sort of a one-point, back-end kind of a landing. I finished it off with a lovely flat-on-the-back pose, staring up at the sky for effect. I'd give it a 6.9.

Thankfully, I had my wonderful friends there to rush over and make sure I was okay. Of course, they couldn't actually *ask* me if I was alright since they were laughing so hard they were about to damage some internal organs! One of them couldn't even stay. She made a bee-line for the house. You know what can happen to laughing women.

That's another thing we love to share: laughter.

This is a little reminder. If it's been awhile since you've made time for friends, take the time and share a laugh with a sister. Both are a gift from God. We need each other—there are certain matters that only women understand. Two of those are "mauve" and "taupe." Another is, of course, other women.

Call up your special bud today. While you have her on the line, you might also want to take care of that coma-mustache-pact thing.

Rhonda Rhea

Loving Kelly

"I really like her," my brother told me over the phone.

"Well, tell me all about her," I said. Then I asked all those nosy questions only a sister can get away with asking. What's she like? Where did you meet? Is she "the one"?

I could hear the smile in his voice as he told me about her, and in my mind, I could see that familiar glint in his eyes. For the next twenty minutes, Steve told me all about his new girlfriend. As I continued to listen, I began to know something was not quite right. Then I realized he had not yet told me her name.

"What's her name?" I finally asked, trying to sound lighthearted.

Seconds of silence stretched into an eternity before he quietly, hesitantly, said, "Kelly."

Suddenly, the phone seemed to grow hot in my trembling hand, and I could not speak. Finally, with some effort, I said, "Oh." Then, "I gotta go. I'll call you soon." I sat there for a long time, staring at the phone, remembering another Kelly.

I still remember the first time I saw her. I was seven. I came crashing into the house after school only to be met by the shushing sound escaping around my mother's index finger held firmly against her pursed lips. "Quiet. The baby's sleeping," she whispered.

"Can I see her?" I whispered back, stepping up onto my tiptoes.

"When she wakes up," Mom said firmly.

I looked at Dad. I knew he would help me.

He winked and motioned me over. Ignoring Mom's warning, we sneaked into my bedroom where Kelly, wearing a tiny cornflower-blue gown, lay sleeping. I pressed my face against the rails of her crib. I reached between the bars and touched her cheek. Dad knelt beside me and gently woke her. Kelly opened her blue eyes and looked right into mine.

"My sister, my baby sister," I said in a proud sigh. I loved her from that moment on.

As we grew older and more aware of life, we giggled about boys, and clothes and hairstyles. I answered her questions about periods and love and falling stars. We crossed our hearts and hoped to die should we ever not be best friends.

At night, as we lay in bed with our backs pressed against each other, we shared all our secrets and all our dreams and carefully planned our old age. We would live together and travel the world. We would be "fun old ladies" like the Baldwin Sisters from Walton's Mountain.

When the day came for me to leave for college, Kelly and I clung to each other, and we sobbed into each other's necks for a long time. With Kelly still weeping softly, Mom finally pulled her away and assured me she would be okay. I wasn't sure I would be, though.

When I was twenty-five and Kelly was eighteen, my doctor diagnosed me with a serious illness that left me unable to bear children. Kelly came to me and offered herself as a surrogate to carry a baby for me and my husband, Jeff.

I thought about her offer for a long time. I was more

touched than words can say, but not at all surprised. In the end, I decided against it. I loved Kelly so much. I could not, would not, ask her to carry a baby in my stead then give it up to me, even though I knew she would. If only I could have known then what lay ahead just a year later.

Funny, isn't it, how you know when the phone rings it's bad news. It was January 26, 1986, Sunday afternoon, Super Bowl Sunday. We had hamburgers for lunch.

"Yes. When? I see," Jeff said into the phone.

There was no hiding it. I saw the shadow in his eyes. "It's bad, isn't it?" I asked as Jeff slowly replaced the receiver in its cradle.

He held me tightly and gently broke the news. "It's Kelly. She's dead. It seems that carbon monoxide seeped through a crack in an old heater in the hotel room where she was staying last night. She died in her sleep."

My sister, my baby sister. Gone! I couldn't believe it. We had so many plans. It just couldn't be true. It just couldn't.

Three years after Kelly's death, I still found it difficult to talk about her. I could not even speak her name without tears filling my eyes. The thought of Steve dating and possibly marrying someone named Kelly was almost unbearable.

Steve did marry "his Kelly," and I found myriad ways to speak of her without actually saying her name. To Steve—How's your wife? How's she doing? To Mom and Dad—Have you heard from Steve and his wife—from them—from her?

With Steve and Kelly living in Washington, D.C., Jeff and I by then in Alaska, and the lack of travel funds, I did not meet Steve's Kelly until six years after she married him. I did talk with her occasionally on the phone.

She seemed nice, and my brother was certainly happy. I began to look forward to her phone calls but still found myself holding back.

Then one Christmas everything changed. Steve and Kelly and Jeff and I met at my parents' home in Texas. Kelly and I spent a lot of time talking and really getting to know each other. In spite of my reticence, I found myself liking her more and more. We laughed and giggled and shared secrets, almost like sisters.

"I've always wondered something," Kelly said as we walked through my parents' neighborhood one afternoon.

"What's that?" I asked.

"I wonder if your Kelly would have liked me."

Surprising myself, I answered immediately without hesitating. "Oh, I know she would. She would have scrutinized you closely, but she definitely would have liked you," I said knowingly. "You are beautiful, sweet, adventurous and fun. You like cats. And, most of all, you make her brother happy. And she would have loved your name."

On Christmas Eve, with tears dancing in her eyes, Kelly handed me a small beige and dark green box tied with twine. I pulled the free end of the string and lifted the lid. I gently removed the top layer of cotton. Underneath was a small magnet. Pink and purple pansies surrounded carefully chosen words: "Sisters By Marriage, Friends By Heart."

Tears escaped my control and wetted my cheeks. "Thank you, Kelly," I whispered. Then, I hugged her. "I love you."

Several Christmases have come and gone since that one. Kelly has become one of my very best friends, and another sister whom I love very much. The magnet she gave me still hangs on my refrigerator so that I will see it every day and be reminded of the love we share, that I almost never knew.

Pamela Haskin

Long-Distance Sister

A true sister is a friend who listens with her heart.

Anonymous

Vickie's arrival was well-timed.

My husband had returned to our home in Colorado to pick up the pieces of our lives, resume his job and parent our youngest son. Now, I would continue the bedside vigil of our twenty-three-year-old who lay comatose, wasting away in a Los Angeles trauma unit.

I was all alone, alone with Kyle.

Offers to help flooded in via phone calls, letters and e-mail. Caring friends and loving family. But there was only one person I wanted, one person I needed: my friend Vickie.

A deep-seated desire for her support during this experience overrode my reluctance to impose on her. More importantly, it transcended my dread of dealing with the freshness of her shock and emotions at seeing Kyle in his vegetative state. I loved her with all my heart for her sacrifice and willingness to come.

Oh, I understood her silent fears; as a small-town Kansan, she was even less travel-wise than I. This trek to California meant her first flight—alone. It required a complicated layover and plane change in Dallas. And she would be met by a stranger at the Los Angeles airport.

For me, Vickie would cancel her piano students. For me, she would postpone her church and community obligations. For me, she would set aside her husband and five children.

For me.

For me and Kyle.

And I was too selfish to turn her away. I needed her.

Our thriving twenty-four-year friendship was cemented by a history of combined convictions, confidences and confessions. State lines had separated us. Crowded schedules had fragmented us. Bustling baby years had isolated us. But we never let that interfere. Instead, we nourished our relationship long distance, treasuring late-night phone calls, stolen weekend visits and sporadic letters.

"What if," Vickie once laughed, "we had lived next door to each other all these years? With squabbling toddlers, barking dogs and competing athletes, we might never have stayed friends."

But we both doubted it.

A deep sisterhood bound us; a mutual love and respect connected us. Irrevocably.

Vickie was the kind of friend who didn't notice the dust on the table but instead remarked on the daisies in the vase. I craved her vision, her enthusiasm and her optimism.

Vickie would be helpful and hopeful.

I needed both.

Only to her could I expose Kyle in his fragility. In fact, it was important to me that she—who had known and loved him since birth—share this stage, see him like this. Then, come what may, she would know how far he had traveled.

Come what may.

In the darkest hours of night, thoughts and fears swept over me. After all, we were dealing with traumatic brain injuries, collapsed lungs, pneumonia and shattered bones. Images of the future staggered me.

What if . . . ?

What if . . . ?

What if . . . ?

I couldn't even spell out my worries and imaginings because what if that made them come true? Such a juvenile, superstitious thought. I knew it, but I couldn't seem to help it.

Yes, I needed someone to rely on, someone to share my load, someone to understand my mother-fears. I needed a female friend.

I needed Vickie.

Suddenly, I felt a deep kinship with the pioneer I once read about who found herself, at the end of her trek, on the Great Plains—pregnant, heartsick and isolated.

Alone.

My plea joined hers as she cried into her diary, "I don't want a doctor. I want a woman."

Carol McAdoo Rehme

At Every Turn

I was an only child, hungry for siblings. I confess that I harbored envy toward my cousins. They had sisters, built-in playmates. I had none. I kept asking my parents for a sister. Even a baby brother would do. But they never listened. Okay. So I'd have to find my own sister. I could do that.

My first sister was my imaginary playmate. Punky urged me to act on my fantasies. We wandered the fields and climbed the leafy cottonwoods along the irrigation ditches. Late at night we held whispered conferences about the day. Punky encouraged me to resist parental control and share my adventuring exclusively with her. We never told about the kittens we rescued from the bottom of the out-house. My father never understood why the sheep ran from me when I entered their pens. *Who would've thought sheep could remember who chased them?* And my mother asked, but neither Punky nor I ever answered her questions about the sudden decline in egg production. Watching hens flutter in fright from their nests was so entertaining. Punky and I were inseparable. But then the yellow school bus stopped for me. And Punky was left behind.

At school, I discovered hanging from the monkey bars and swinging across the rocky ground. Susie brushed me off when I fell from those bars and led me to the nurse's office for repairs. From then on, we were inseparable. We ate lunch together. We fended off marauding cowboys who rode up to us on stick horses. Clutching *Dick and Jane* to our bony chests, we ached for a kitten as cute as Puff or a dog as lively as Spot. We ate our first tacos and watched crawdads lay eggs and reproduce in the class aquarium. Life was rich.

In high school, my circle of sisterhood widened. On Saturday afternoons, my sister friends and I shopped at Joplin's, stroking pastel mohair sweaters while assuring ourselves that the pleats of our woolen skirts were knife sharp. Lipstick and secret information about the heart-throb of the day were freely shared. We spent hours teasing our hair and consoling each other when pimples threatened our social life. A secret ride home in a hot rod '57 Chevy was later dissected moment by moment, with freeze-frame precision. We went to Saturday night movies together but separated in the darkness to meet unnamed boys who set our hearts afire. Relationships flowered, and we burst forth like a garden of color in our taffeta formals, wrists corsage decorated. We celebrated love and learned how to fill a senior ring with layers of white glue coated with fingernail polish so it would fit our thin fingers. And we cried together when love ended. Throughout it all, our circle of sisterhood survived, a little scratched but intact.

My collegiate sisters came from different places and offered me glimpses of other lives. We shared the thrills of fending off frostbite while wearing miniskirts and navigating icy sidewalks in stacked leather heel boots. We giggled as we threw panties at the last-ever panty raid and caught mashed potatoes in a cafeteria food fight. We sampled beer served from a pony keg out in the boonies and worried that we might not get back to our dorms before the doors were locked for the night. Professors

extolled the philosophy of Kant and Aristotle. We wondered why we should care about these ancient philoso-
phers when Bob Dylan sang his messages. Candles passed
in the sorority announced the receipt of love in the form of
a lavaliere, pin or, the ultimate, an engagement ring. Then
it was graduation, and we moved back to our own worlds.

I have been blessed with adult sisters who have men-
tored and shared my travails as a wife, mother and
teacher. We supported each other through childbirth,
breast-feeding, divorces and career changes. While our
children played in the dappled light of a spring day, we
drank high-octane fruit juice and giggled. On camping
trips we shared cooking duties, wiping s'more-coated children with cold mountain spring water while our husbands sipped the same cold water, only theirs was brewed
in the Rocky Mountains. We baked Christmas cookies and
traded them at cookie swaps. When our aging parents
orphaned us, upsetting our world order, tears and hugs
gave comfort like no words could. We released pent-up
sighs of relief when our own children successfully moved
into adulthood. And we shared advice on transforming
newly embraced daughters- and sons-in-law from
strangers into family without alienating them or ourselves. We listened to tales about recalcitrant bosses and
professional successes.

At every turn, I have found my sisters. They have
flowed through my life, renewing and enriching me with
their presence. And I can't wait to meet the next one. I
think she just moved in next door. Wonder if she likes to
climb trees?

Lee Schafer Atonna

"You know you're having a bad day when you put your
dirty clothes to bed and the kids in the hamper."

Reprinted with permission of Vahan Shirvanian.

Girls' Weekend

Well-behaved women rarely make history.
Laurel Thatcher Ulrich

Henning around, we called it. Early on, it meant getting together with a sister or two and doing girl stuff. Chicken salad and sunshine cake at George Watts' Tea Room. Browsing the exquisite and expensive china and crystal sections, choosing our registry for when the slipper finally fits. Deciding the hell with it, we'll buy our own with money earned from our creative pursuits: We will be writers and painters and researchers and teachers. Nobody to consult or compromise with; just choice and whim and change of mind.

A dozen years pass, and the hens are having a reunion of sorts. This time there are six of us, sisters by birth and marriage and friendship. We have gathered at the cottage, *sans* husbands and children, for a weekend of girl stuff. We stayed up past midnight the first night, drinking margaritas and catching up and laughing until our sides hurt, as only unchained women can.

Saturday morning, so early that the lake is as still as a held breath, three of us push the canoe away from the dock and head for the east shore, where the rich people live. Nouveau antique log homes dominate emerald lawns sloping to L-shaped docks with jet skis and catamarans anchored next to the occasional hydroplane. We sip coffee from thermal mugs and try not to bang the oars against the sides of the battered aluminum canoe.

"Who washes those floor-to-ceiling windows?" we wonder. "Probably the same crew that rakes the sand each night," we agree. "Or monograms the boat sails." "Or polishes the shells that line the pea-graveled walkway up to the tri-level deck." "Or freshens the shore-scent potpourri in the guest bath." We giggle into our sweatshirt sleeves, trying to top each other.

"Stop!" we hiss. "No waking the wealthy! It's nowhere *near* brunch and Bloody Mary time!" Too late, we notice a patriarch-type slide open a patio door and glare at us. His pajamas match, we note. "Yeah, but he's scratching anyway," observes the one in the middle. Our laughter peals across the water. "Good morning, sir!" We salute loudly, coffee cups raised.

Back at the cottage, we plan our day. A brisk walk to the public boat launch, 1.6 miles each way, followed by bagels and juice on the porch. Swimming out to the raft to work on our tans until lunch. Then two of us will bike the county trails and play tennis; three will shop. Miss Solitude claims the hammock for hours of uninterrupted reading. "That's *Ms.* Solitude to you," she updates us. We agree to meet for dinner at Remembrance of Things Pasta, and come back here for star-gazing and chardonnay.

Over plates of linguine and crusty bread, we shared the day. "*We* saw five deer and two hawks, and our tennis was so awesome we didn't even keep score," said the active ones.

"*We* hit seven boutiques and three rummage sales, and *this* one finished her Christmas shopping." The rest of us groaned.

"*I* read Oprah's book club book. The whole thing. On the chaise lounge at the end of the pier. And . . ." She paused dramatically.

"What?" We all paused, forks in midair.

"I took off my shirt."

Forks dropped into piles of pasta as we whooped in amazement.

"And that pontoon boat from the cottage four doors down came by."

"No!" we gasped.

"Verrrrry slowly," she said, solemnly.

"Oh!" we exclaimed.

"It was filled with college boys," she announced.

"Get *out!*" We were stunned. "What did you do?"

"I . . . *smiled,*" she smiled. "I mean, I was wearing sunglasses."

We applauded wildly and toasted her.

Later, under the onyx sky, our eyes adjust to the appearing stars. We listen in utter peace to the soughing breeze. A couple of bats coast from tree to tree in the nearby woods, and they don't even bother us.

The talk turns to the usual: old boyfriends, the best songs to slow-dance to, the most romantic thing our partners ever did. Lots of profound sex talk that quickly turns hilarious as we swear ourselves to secrecy. A sleepy hush falls over us like fleece.

"Look," says the eldest. "Thirty degrees northwest. It's the Pleiades."

"Tell us the story," says the youngest.

"It's about seven sisters and the end of the world. You know, Greek myth stuff and I think some Indian legend. I'll look it up when we get home."

"It's the story of us," says someone.

"Minus the one," says another, and several of us exchange glances in the dark.

We are quiet for a long time.

"Bedtime," sing-songs one of the moms. No one begs for five more minutes.

Tucked in cozy, we turn off our lights. "Good night, John-Boy. Good night, Mary Ellen. Good night, Grandma. Good night, moon." We giggle off to sleep.

Our last morning, we sweep the floors, straighten the beds, take the garbage to the van. We say good-bye to the lake, until next time, arms linked.

Henning around. Just some chicks leaving the nest for a while, in search of nothing special. And finding it. Special.

Chris Miota

7

SPECIAL MEMORIES

*H*eirlooms we don't have in our family.
But stories we've got.

Rose Chernin

Sister Dresses

How do people make it through life without a sister?

Sara Corpening

When Mother died, Dad gave up the summer house. "Come and take what you want, girls," he had said to us—and we did.

I chose the tall secretary where Mother sat so often writing letters by a sunny window. Beth chose a painting of the summer house itself. Ellen picked a statue of horses, for she and Mother had shared a love of riding. Then we put drawers full of old letters, slides and faded photos—the collective memory of a family—into a dozen boxes, and each of us chose four.

Later I sat on the top step of my porch and opened a box marked "ALBUMS." Here were photographs of my father, resplendent in his Navy uniform, and one of my mother leaning against their first car. As I leafed through the pages, the family grew, we bought our first house, the cars got bigger. Then, on the last page, there was a picture of us in our matching "sister dresses."

I could almost feel the starched ruffles and hear the rustle of the crinolines that were needed to keep the skirts nice and full. I remembered Mother's delight when she found these outfits at the children's shop in the village. There was one in my size and one for Ellen, but no size four for Beth. We were so excited when the shopkeeper told us she could order a dress for Beth that would come in time for Easter.

When the big box arrived in early April, we gathered around Mother as she lifted the dresses out one by one. They were made of clouds of dotted Swiss-white organdy with blue flocked dots. The skirts and collars were trimmed with tiny blue bows. "To match your eyes," Mother said.

We were allowed to try them on just once so we could have a "fashion show" for Father that evening. As we twirled into the dining room in our finery, he burst into applause. We daintily grasped the ruffled skirts and executed our best curtsies.

As I looked at the photograph, I could recall the warmth of the pale spring sunshine on our faces on Easter Sunday. We must have resisted putting on coats to go to church. They surely would have crushed our dresses—and besides, how then could anyone have seen how beautifully we matched?

In time, I handed my dress down to Ellen and she handed hers down to Beth. But those dotted Swiss creations were only the beginning of a long parade of matching sister outfits. I remember the year of the blue calicoes and the year we all had yellow jumpers. Even Father got into the spirit when he came back from a business trip to Arizona with Mexican dresses for each of his girls—including Mother.

Those wonderful white dresses, with rows of bright ribbons edging the wide collars and hems, had skirts that were cut in a complete circle. Father put Ravel's *Bolero* on the record player and we spun madly about the living room, our beribboned skirts fluttering like butterflies. At last we crashed, giggling, into a heap. Dad sat in his arm-chair and grinned his "that's-my-girls" smile.

I remember these first sister dresses so clearly that I'm surprised I can't remember the last ones. Maybe Mother knew we were outgrowing the idea. I think she saw how different we were becoming and just stopped buying us matching dresses.

By the time we were adults, our lives were on these very distinct tracks. Mother would shake her head in bewilderment and say to Father, "How did we get three daughters so different?" He would merely smile.

That first year without Mother, we knew Christmas would be bittersweet. For as long as I can remember, Dad had always given Mother a beautiful nightgown at Christmas—long and silky with plenty of lace. The tree certainly sparkled, but there was no big box from "Sweet Dreams" beneath it. And although we put on happy faces for the sake of our children, the little touches that Mother always added were missing.

Suddenly, Ellen drew out from behind the tree three identical white packages. On the lids, written in Dad's bold hand, were the words "From the Nightie Gnome." We opened the presents and lifted out three identical red flannel nightshirts.

Whooping with delight, we pulled them from the tis-sue paper and ran down the hall to put them on. When we came back to show off our sister nighties, Dad had put *Bolero* on the stereo. We joined hands and did an impromptu dance. As the music grew louder, we twirled around faster and faster, ignoring the widening eyes of our disbelieving husbands and the gaping mouths of our children.

I smile now at the sight we must have made: three grown women dressed in red flannel nighties whirling madly through a jumble of empty boxes and wrapping paper. When the music ended in a dash of cymbals, we crashed, giggling, into a heap.

Our husbands shook their heads in wonder. The younger children nearly keeled over with embarrassment while the older ones held their sides with laughter: Dad just cracked his "that's-my-girls" grin.

Faith Andrews Bedford

Symbiosis

All we needed to say we said with our hands and eyes. We gamblers, grudge keepers, lonely hearts know nothing but what passes between us in a moment, what is, finally, patient and wise. Sisters.

Carol Edgarian

Nine-year-old Samantha Brock sat nervously in the school bus and looked out the window searching hopefully for her younger sister, Mitzi. Most of the school-children on that route had already boarded the bus, but Samantha still saw no sign of her little sister. Her growing concern soon escalated into worry as Samantha watched the last youngster climb into the bus.

Mitzi was only six, and Samantha was very protective of her. During times like this, however, Samantha thought it took lots of determination to remain focused and ignore persistent thoughts of just how much trouble a little sister can be. Quite often she'd had to remind herself that Mitzi was, after all, only a child, and that therefore the only responsible thing she could do was remain alert to keeping her younger sister out of trouble.

A little earlier, a caravan of bright yellow school busses made its way from Harding Middle School to Watson Primary, where Samantha now sat anxiously on bus number 8. The sisters' regular bus, number 16, had broken down, and a replacement bus was sent to Harding. Samantha would have missed it herself, except that she had been sensible enough to follow some of the older girls whom she recognized from earlier rides on her bus. She knew how important it was for her to always be aware of her surroundings.

She also knew that panicking would not help her to find her sister, so she let the last little boy take his seat before she calmly but quickly walked up the narrow aisle between the long, green seats. Reaching the bus driver, Miss Cochran, who was at that instant pulling the lever to close the bus door, Samantha asked her to stop, going on to explain that her sister had not yet boarded.

The driver noticed that the child was almost in tears, so she spoke slowly and calmly, smiling like a kindly grandmother. Samantha listened closely, her eyes trained on Miss Cochran's wrinkled face. She knew how much adults like you to look directly at them when they expect you to listen to what they're saying.

However, Miss Cochran was suggesting that Mitzi had ridden home with her mother, "Something y'all have done before. Right, sweetheart?"

Samantha listened patiently without interrupting, though she knew that their mom had not picked Mitzi up today; she just knew it. She was positive that Mitzi had missed this bus because it "doesn't say number 16." Now that it was her turn to speak, she said that their mom wouldn't pick up just one of them and she certainly wouldn't do so without telling the other one ahead of time. She pleaded with Miss Cochran to let her go find Mitzi.

The driver glanced at the impatient children, bouncing up and down in their seats and shouting for her to "get rolling." Then she turned back to the small, solitary figure whose eyes were pleading quietly for help. Miss Cochran's heart was not made of stone, so she agreed, but cautioned Samantha to hurry.

The other busses were pulling out as Samantha flew down the steps and out of the bus. Pausing, she turned and thanked Miss Cochran, and in a flash she was inside the schoolhouse. Her footsteps echoed somberly as she walked the empty hall, pausing in front of each classroom doorway just long enough to check for Mitzi. Approaching the end of the hall, Samantha heard the sound of Mitzi's voice, so she hurried to the last door.

There sat little Mitzi, slumped over and swallowed up by the chair beside her teacher's desk. Between tearful outbursts Mitzi was trying to explain that she had looked for her bus but didn't find it. Suddenly, she stopped talking and turned around. When Mitzi saw Samantha, she ran to her big sister and hugged her tightly. Mitzi's tiny body convulsed as she sobbed with joy.

Samantha suppressed a gasp of relief, then took her sister's hand and led her outside. Mitzi dried her cheeks, and Samantha fought back the pool of tears that had welled up in her eyes and threatened to cascade down her face.

After the pair appeared outside, school bus number 8 erupted in a riot of childish jeers, taunting the two girls for delaying playtime at home. As Mitzi lowered her head, Samantha tightened her grip on her sister's small hand and in her bravest voice said, "It's all right, Mitzi; I'm right beside you."

Samantha looked through the open bus doors to see Miss Cochran smiling warmly. With her sister still in hand, Samantha climbed the steps and paused at the front of the aisle. Defiantly, she scanned each face in front of her until the last voice was silenced. Mitzi raised her head, followed her sister down the aisle, and sat beside her until they safely stepped off the bus in front of their home.

Samantha was thinking how it seemed like only yesterday when all of that had happened, but now, fifteen years later, she was walking towards Mitzi to comfort her once again. Minutes away from walking down the aisle and becoming a married woman, Mitzi had been no longer able to stem the flood of emotions inside her; she had burst into tears and flung herself onto a huge, overstuffed chair. Samantha thought how fragile Mitzi appeared slumped over and sobbing uncontrollably. No wonder she recalled that earlier, childhood day.

Samantha took her sister's hand and led her in front of the full-length mirror. As the pair gazed on the radiant image that Mitzi presented in the glass, Mitzi dried her cheeks.

Their eyes met in the mirror, and all at once both girls burst into laughter. Then tears again. Then tears mixed with laughter. Throwing their arms around each other, they lingered in the sweetness of their embrace.

Mitzi sniffled, then giggled and whispered into Samantha's ear: "This reminds me of the day when, well, you probably don't even remember, but, the time you found me at school when I was lost and would have missed the bus, except that you came back to take my hand and. . . ." Mitzi burst into tears again.

Samantha didn't bother to fight back the pool of tears that welled up in her eyes and cascaded down her face. She tightened her arms around her sister's delicate body and in her most loving voice, "It's all right Mitzi, I am right beside you."

Ricky Keen

A Childhood Memory

What do we live for, if not to make life less difficult for each other?

George Eliot (Mary Ann Evans)

It was November, 1957, and I was in the first grade. Each morning, Mommy let me pick out the dress I was going to wear to school, and she made sure I was clean and tidy before I left. I loved school, and I felt so grown-up and proud as I put my hand in Myra's. Myra, my sister, was eleven, and she was in the sixth grade. Myra and I went to the same school; her class was on the fourth floor, mine was on the second. We left the house together each morning, hand in hand, and Myra talked to me about everything: her friends, Hebrew school, the new sled Daddy was going to get for us, clouds . . . everything.

Well, Myra was talking about the surprise party that Mommy was planning for Daddy to congratulate him on his promotion. "We'll be at the Botanical Gardens on Sunday, and I'll make believe that I forgot something and need to go home. Now what do you think I could forget?"

Before I knew it we had walked the six long blocks and

were in the outer yard where Myra always said good-bye to me, and where all the first-graders lined up and waited for their monitor, usually a fifth- or sixth-grader, to take them to their classroom. Denise, our monitor, picked us up as usual, and led us upstairs.

Well, this particular morning, Mrs. Cohen, my teacher, had to step out for a bit. She left the room in Denise's charge, and instructed her to call each row to hang up their coats and hats.

I started to think about my teachers, and how pretty they were. *My kindergarten teacher, Mrs. Rubinstein was pretty. I liked the way she wore her shiny black hair in a flip, and her makeup was always perfect. Mrs. Cohen is pretty, although she's younger than Mrs. Rubenstein, and she looks a lot more modern. If I'm pretty when I grow up, maybe I'll be a teacher, too.*

I heard Denise say, "Row one, hang up your coats." I got up and carefully placed the loop of my coat around the big metal hook, sat down and continued thinking about jobs that pretty women had. *Airline stewardesses, movie stars . . .*

I heard Denise say, "Row six, hang up your coats," when I realized that my hat was still on my head. I quickly removed it and walked over to the closet to put it in my coat sleeve. Denise looked at me and screamed, "Benita, row six is hanging up their coats. Are you in row six?"

Very sheepishly I answered, "No, but I forgot to hang up my hat."

"I forgot to hang up my hat," Denise mimicked. "What row do you sit in?" she asked.

"Row one," I answered, "but I forgot to hang up my hat."

"I called row one before," Denise shrilled. "Since you didn't hang your hat up when your row was called, you will have to wear it all morning. Now, put your hat back on, and sit down."

Everyone was staring at me, and my face began to burn. I sat down, put my hat back on and bit my lower lip until it bled. I thought, *When Mrs. Cohen comes back, she'll let me take my hat off and hang it up. Then Denise will feel stupid.* Just then Mrs. Cohen returned. Denise walked over to her and whispered in her ear. I knew it was about me because they were both looking at me.

But Mrs. Cohen didn't tell me to take my hat off; in fact, she didn't say anything at all to me, and I sat there in my seat, in the first row, with my hat on for the whole morning.

When Myra picked me up to take me home for lunch, she took one look at my ashen-colored, pouty face and asked, "What happened to you, Beni?" I told her the story through outbursts, sobs and sniffles. She said, "You must feel terrible. But you know they were wrong. You have to tell Mommy."

But I couldn't.

I tried to eat lunch, but the food barely went down. I started to make myself feel pain in my stomach. I laid down on the sofa and gave myself the biggest bellyache a first-grader could. I couldn't ever go back to school, and I couldn't tell Mommy why. Mommy felt my head and said, "You don't have a fever, but I'll let you stay home this afternoon."

The next morning I said that my stomach still hurt, but Mommy wouldn't let me stay home unless I went to the doctor. So we went to the doctor. After Dr. Skodnick examined me, Mommy asked me to sit in the waiting room while they talked about the findings. The whole time I was there I was thinking of ways to stay home from school.

We got home about twelve noon. I was wondering why Myra wasn't home for lunch, when Mommy said, "Benita, the doctor didn't find anything wrong with you. Something must have happened at school to make you feel sick. Now, tell me what happened."

But I couldn't.

In the morning, Mommy announced that she was coming to school with Myra and me. I put on the most babyish dress I had; it was mint green with a white Baby Jane collar. Mommy knew I hated the dress, but she didn't say anything. She just checked to make sure I was neat and clean.

The march to school was solemn and silent. When we got there, both Mommy and Myra walked me to the line. Then I watched them walk up the steps to the main entrance and enter the building. My heart was pounding so loudly that I thought everyone could hear the drum beating inside me.

Denise came to pick us up as usual and led us to the classroom. We couldn't have been inside the class for more than two minutes when Mr. Rosen, the principal, appeared at the door with Mommy and Myra. Mr. Rosen asked Mrs. Cohen and Denise to step outside. That was the last time I saw Denise.

The next morning, Myra took my hand and we walked to school. "Where were you yesterday at lunch time?" I asked.

"I had a talk with Mrs. Gayrod and then I had something special to do," she replied. Mrs. Gayrod was Myra's teacher. Sometimes when Mommy wasn't at home for lunch, Myra took me to Mrs. Gayrod's room, and we ate there with her. She wasn't as pretty as Mrs. Cohen or Mrs. Rubinstein, but she sure was kind and understanding.

"I have a surprise for you," Myra added. She brought me to the schoolyard and let go of my hand. This time she didn't say good-bye. She stood in front of the line and said, "I'm Myra, and I'm your new monitor. Now line up quietly boys and girls." She walked over to me and said, "I won't let anything else happen to you, Beni. Just remember, if you need me, I'm in Room 402." Then she led us up the stairs.

Benita Glickman

Getting to Rome

Having a sister is like having a best friend you can't get rid of. You know whatever you do, they'll still be there.

Amy Li

I left home that summer with a personal mandate to find my true self. My boyfriend of six years had just broken up with me and I was determined to prove to the world that I didn't need him, or anybody else, to make me happy. Empowered and equipped with a backpack, a Eurail pass and a journal, I set out on my solo quest.

Two weeks into my trip, however, my desperate call home revealed the needy, dependent cries of the woman I was trying so hard not to be. I still cringe recalling that phone call to my family and its rare display of weakness and vulnerability. Between loud, dramatic sobs I confessed that I was lonely, I was broke and I missed home. So they sent reinforcement—in the form of my sister, Tawna, two years my junior.

I picked her up at the airport in Amsterdam and was so ridiculously grateful for the companionship that I let her decide where we would travel next. She wanted to go to Italy and she wanted to get there fast. I agreed, and made a mental note to consider the nineteen-hour train ride as a chance to reclaim my identity as Empowered Older Sister.

Tawna was still getting used to navigating with her heavy backpack as we boarded the train. Already adept at handling my load, I cringed as I watched her backpack take liberties with people's heads as we made our way down the train's narrow aisles. She was oblivious to the chaos she was stirring in her wake while I caught all the foreign looks of disapproval as we passed.

We were fortunate to find an empty car—six seats, three on each side, facing each other. We put our backpacks above our heads and giggled at the good fortune at having found such a private refuge for our trip. We stretched our feet out on our respective seats and lazily relaxed as the train pulled out of Amsterdam. A couple of stops and not even half an hour later, we had company.

Fortunately for us, he was good-looking Italian company. His name was Archangelo. I couldn't stop staring. He was beautiful—brown wavy hair, big green eyes, gorgeous olive skin and a smile that could melt my mascara. Not that I was wearing any. I had given up my pride and my makeup a few countries into my trip. So I really had no business entertaining the notion that he could be my personal tour guide once we hit Italy. My hair was in a ponytail, my Levis hadn't been washed in days and I was even sporting a few new pimples. And so, despite the fact that until this moment I had spoken to strangers only when I was hopelessly lost, I gave in to the shamelessness of it all and decided to use him to practice my Italian.

I got out "the book"—my trusty guide to Europe that my sister grew to hate—and tried to pronounce the Italian phrases the book thought one would need in Italy. Tawna squinted her eyes at me in obvious disapproval at each sentence I subjected him to. She was still wearing makeup at this point and did look cute, so she probably had a fair chance at Archangelo. And now it appeared that I was ruining it with my premature need for Italian conversation.

While at first he seemed confused—was he supposed to *answer* the questions I was throwing at him?—eventually he seemed to relax and let me do my thing. My sister shrugged her shoulders at him with an apologetic look as if to form an alliance with him against this "crazy" woman with whom she happened to be stuck traveling. She might as well have circled her finger around her ear a few times and pointed at me, so eager she was to prove me a strange bird.

Maybe it was too much for him, or maybe he was getting off anyhow, but we lost our Archangelo, our beautiful angel, after only a couple hours into our trip, perhaps in Germany. In his stead we were joined by a multilingual Dutch man with a shiny, bald head and a need for some deodorant. I was slowly beginning to lose my language inhibitions, and he had no problem practicing my Italian with me and would even humor me with responses between lecherous peeks at my sister's breasts. I eventually grew bored of my Italian studies and retreated into a book, all the while keeping a vigilant, protective eye on the Dutch man keeping a vigilant eye on my sister.

I initially welcomed the intrusion of the German couple who soon joined us. I quickly learned to resent their presence, however, when I found myself sandwiched between Tawna and the German woman. The *fraulein's* left thigh refused to contain itself to its own seat, forcing me to read my book with my arms extended straight out in front of me. There was only so much suppressing of giggles and nudging each other that we could do to entertain ourselves, and soon we grew antsy and bored.

Tawna looked out the window at the blackness of the nighttime scenery as if hoping that something, anything entertaining, would pop up out of the darkness. I tried to read but the stale, musty air in our car must have impaired my concentration; I read the same paragraph over and over. One by one the Dutch man and the old German couple fell asleep. I couldn't take it anymore. I whispered to her that I was going to try to find someplace to write in my journal. I crept over bodies and luggage, and made my escape.

I floated aimlessly down the aisles of the train until I happened upon the dining car. I was greeted by a group of people who, using Spanish I couldn't understand and gestures I could, insisted I join them for a drink. I put down my journal, and tried to summon what little Spanish I could recall from the few trips to Mexico I had taken. They were from Ecuador and countless hours later we were fast friends. I was carrying on what the wine had me convinced were long, intelligent conversations in Spanish. I told myself that being raised in California must have given me an edge.

When Tawna found me three hours later I had a new set of international friends and was laughing and speaking a language all my own. I tried to get her to join in on the fun but she just stood in the corner, annoyed. It then occurred to me that after she had traveled thousands of miles to cure my loneliness, I had repaid her by abandoning her in a car full of strangers. I bid farewell to my new friends and retreated back to our crowded, smelly car.

Back in our car, Tawna finally had something to look at out the window. I reached over and held her hand. The sun slowly rose as our train passed through the Swiss Alps. We sat silently as we looked out at snow-capped peaks tinged pink by the sun, and waterfalls, lakes and streams around every bend.

We had many adventures during those three weeks together in Europe. She'll take any opportunity to tell the story of my callous abandonment of her during our train ride to Rome. She thinks it proves how strong I really am; that I really didn't need her to "find myself" in Europe. But I know she's got it backwards. I know that it wasn't until I had my sister's hand to hold that I felt truly empowered. There are many places I "find myself," but I see myself most clearly in the reflection of my sister's eyes.

Tasha Boucher

Tasha and Tawna in Europe.

Sisters of the Attic

We shared parents, homes, pets, celebrations, catastrophes, secrets. And the threads of our experience became so interwoven that we are linked. I can never be utterly lonely knowing you share the planet.

Pam Brown

My sister and I are playing in the attic of our old house. It is night. The river roars like a line of runaway log trucks past our home. The old knotty pine house stands secure, and we are safe.

Daddy guards us. He guards well, because he sees with his ears. His people—the Cayuse and Nez Perce—taught him how, and he taught us. They love him, too. He is one-half them.

We hear the window open downstairs. My sister and I, sitting as if frozen, see with our ears too, like Daddy. We can picture in our mind what Daddy is doing.

We see the light from his flashlight on the river. It moves upriver slowly; then downriver more quickly. The beam of light loops and moves upriver again. It inches over the rocky incline, just one hundred feet from the window. "Too close. I'll stay up tonight," Daddy says, and he means it.

A bulb dangles from an orange- and green-striped electrical cord, directly above our heads. I like the shadows the spider webs make on the walls. When the light wiggles, they wiggle, too. The webs don't scare me, just the spiders who make them.

The window slides shut. My sister shrugs her shoulders. We know we are safe from the storm and the swift river, because Daddy keeps watch.

Only my sister and I are allowed to play in the attic.

The rain sounds like road gravel pelting the roof. Wearing polka-dot pajamas we sit on the floor under the attic roof, an upside-down V, like a teepee.

"I get the typewriter first!" I say as I accidentally bump the light, causing the spider webs to dance. "I'm going to write a story. You play in the Christmas stuff." I am six, and she is four and a half. That's why I can boss her.

I don't know how to type and haven't a clue what a dictionary is. If you ask me what a thesaurus is, I would tell you it is a dinosaur. I would look right at you, and you would believe me, because I believe me. You might ask, "What kind of dinosaur?" and I would tell you, "A baby one that doesn't know how to fly."

Here is a story for you. It is a summer story. I write summer stories in winter because it makes me happy. My fingers wiggle over the keys; words pour from my mouth, fly into dark corners of the attic, or hang upside down, pinned on spider webs. They are baby words that haven't grown wings yet.

"My Fort Stump" by me. My fort is an old stump. It is white and part of it is in the Zig Zag River. That's the river outside our house. I play with my tea cups there.

I also play with my dolls and my fishing pole. "Look Lavelle! There's a big fish down there! Let's get it!" I am flat on my belly crisscross on the log part of the stump.

She grabs the pole. We have no bait. "I'll get the bait, hold the pole," she says. I watch the giant fish move into the dark murky depths, under the log I lay upon.

The fish swims towards the periwinkle pool and rests in the shade, looking like a silver spear on the sandy bottom.

Lavelle comes back to the log, sits down beside me and opens her fingers. Red huckleberries fill her palm. "These look like Daddy's salmon eggs." I watch her brown hands bait the hook. Her skin is the color of dark pinecones in the summer. Mine are red and sunburned. We drop the hook and the fish swims away. Lavelle stands up and says, "I am going to get Daddy's salmon eggs out of the Frigidaire," then leaps off the log.

"Run! Go fast!" I tell her (because I am terrified to be at the river alone. I think a cougar is in the brush, stalking me, waiting to eat me. She thinks one's there too, so she runs fast . . . besides, she wants to catch the fish, too.).

Soon she is back beside me. She opens the lid, while I pinch the sharp, mean-looking hook tightly. She puts a pink salmon egg on the hook and says, "Let's catch this fish and give it to Daddy."

"I'm scared of that big fish!" I tell her, and hand her the pole. She drops the egg in front of the fish's nose! The fish swims away, makes a big circle and comes back. "He swallowed the egg!! He did! He swallowed it!" He jerks the line with a whole bunch of strong yanks, then dives deep into the dark water.

"He ate it! He ate it!" we scream. He jumps out of the

water right at our faces! He's as long as Mom's yard-stick! We both hold tight to the pole!

"I'll hold the pole; you run and get Daddy." She hands me the pole and runs. "Hurry, he's breaking the pole!" I yell.

The fish flies straight up, cutting the air in two, then hits the water, and leaps into the sky again; then dives deep down to the bottom, and moves up the river like an arrow shot from a bow, ripping the line off the reel in a loud whirrrrrrr. My arms are aching, I can't hold on much ..."

Oh, oh. These tiny finger keys are jammed. They are like a bunch of thin flat hammers all tangled. Now I have to untwist them. Oh! There's ink on my fingers, Now they are finally untwisted. Okay. Where was I?

"... I can't hold on much longer!" I yell at the top of my lungs, as loud as I can! "Daddy! Daaaddddy! Help!"

Lavelle sits down beside me. "My turn! You go play with Mom's old clothes and the Christmas stuff," she tells me.

"No! I hate it over there in the corner. There are spiders. You aren't scared of spiders, I am!"

"They're only daddy longlegs! You have to share! I'm telling Mom!"

I don't answer her. I move my fingers faster over the keys. I know she is going to tell Mom how selfish I am. I start a new story:

Fish don't like berries, just bologna. I know where there are fish. They are in the deep pools right below a waterfall. My friend has a baby deer. It has a bell around its neck. I'm scared a cougar will eat it.

"GLENDA! YOU SHARE THAT TYPEWRITER! GIVE LAVELLE A TURN!"

My fingers type faster. I only have a few seconds before Lavelle will be up the ladder, yelling "My turn!" I type faster, I talk faster and louder so Mom will hear.

Lavelle is my sister. She snuck into Mom's chocolates that Mom hid under her bed and she ate almost all of them. She took Dad's fishing eggs out of the Frigidaire, and she doesn't share. I saw her hide her food in her milk carton. She is going to have her tonsils out.

Lavelle sits down and grabs the typewriter. I crawl way back into the dark, spider web scary places. With gray insulation stuck to my pajamas, I watch Lavelle from the corner. She lifts the lid of the old machine, and lets the metal hammers hit, then puts her finger on the old spool and turns it at least five times. She clicks a little hook thing, and spins the ribbon the other way. She opens up the top and peeks in, then moves the carriage back and forth—over and over. It goes zip-flip-ring, zip-flip-ring. She hits a line of ???????? and a line of !!!!!!!! and then mmmmmmmm and then starts the alphabet real slow. A. B. C. D. E. She gets to O and likes Os so does a whole line of Os like this OOOOOOOOO. Now she is ringing the bell with her finger . . . ta-ling . . . ta-ling . . . ta-ling. She's doing this on purpose to tease me.

I have stories stuck in my head. I glare at her. I know she wants to take the typewriter apart.

"It's my turn! I'm going to tell! You're going to break it!" I whine.

"It's already broken, dumb-dumb."

I grab the typewriter. She grabs it back. I grab it back. "I don't want to play anymore," she says.

"All right. You can have it," I give in. I want her to play.

I play in the Christmas ornaments and pretend I don't care. It works. She comes to the Christmas box and finds the manger set. We unwrap the animals. We are looking for the baby Jesus. We find him. We put him in his manger bed. "I get the camel! Where's the camel?" I unwrap an angel. She has the camel.

"Does it hurt to have your tonsils out?" she asks.

I'm scared. I know it does. I dig deep looking for more angels, more angels for Lavelle. She hands me a wise man and says, "He goes with the camel." I tell her it doesn't hurt to have her tonsils out, and she can have all the ice cream she wants. She knows I had mine out when I was two so she believes me.

I sit back down at the typewriter. There is a camel and a wise man in my lap. Again my fingers wiggle over the keys . . . I think in my head because I don't want to speak sad words out loud.

Tomorrow Lavelle has to have her tonsils out. I am scared. I know it will hurt. I was two when they took mine out. Mom said the doctor is going to save them so Lavelle can see what tonsils look like. Lavelle said she would put them in the Frigidaire right by Daddy's salmon eggs. This is true, it REALLY is. I don't think Mom should let her put the—

"GIRLS! BEDTIME! GET DOWN OUT OF THE ATTIC."

The first rains of autumn are here, and the leaves are the color of butter or corn on the cob. No they aren't. They are the colors of memories, and they skip from the trees and dance across my mind, like giggles in the wind. They float down the river, just like they did fifty-three years ago. I scoop them up in my hands, and they fall through my fingers onto the keyboard. I wrap up the words and lay them beside the manger, in the attic of my soul. I give them to him. It is his gift. He can do with his gift what he pleases.

The wind blows again. I peek at the words from the attic. Just a quick tiny love peek. It is first light. The sun is spilling over the Zig Zag mountain, the morning has come. It is time. I push SEND and the words become wings. "Fly words! Do good words! Make the world a happier place!"

... My eyes fill with tears ... I don't know why ...
My fingers move again upon the keyboard.

> *Hi Sis!*
>
> *I'm sending you another story, about when we were kids; and we used to play in the attic with the old typewriter.*
>
> *Don't worry about having your gallbladder out. It doesn't hurt too long afterwards and you can eat all the ice cream you want!*

... now my eyes overflow with tears ... I am thankful for e-mail. At least it doesn't arrive tear-stained.

> *I miss you. Can you come up this summer?*
> *I love you,*
> *Glenda*

Glenda Barbre

Once Upon a Birthday

The family—that dear octopus from whose tentacles we never quite escape, nor, in our innermost hearts, never quite wish to.

Dodie Smith

I should have known something was up when my daughter Tiffany woke me at 7 A.M. She'd been away working at a summer camp, but here she was at the crack of dawn in my bedroom in Toronto saying, "Happy Birthday, Mum."

It was my fiftieth birthday, and although I'd told my husband Derek that I didn't much care about a party, I had secretly hoped that Tif would find a way to get a day off and be here with me. But why so early? Her dad was at work. Her siblings were still in bed. My fitness class didn't start until 9:30. I'd already made the fifty chocolate-covered strawberries I'd planned on serving to my fellow travelers on the aerobics floor. So I didn't have to get up yet.

"Come on," urged Tif a bit impatiently. "Get up. We have a surprise for you downstairs." As I struggled out of bed I realized her boyfriend was standing in the bedroom door pointing a video camera at me. "What is going on?" I asked. Tiffany allowed me a quick trip to the bathroom but no time to even wash my face. So when she led me down the stairs and out onto the porch, I presented my fifty-year-old self to the world in an old nightgown, with no makeup, messy hair and bags under my eyes.

When we got outside I saw our other two kids, Zachary and Samantha, on the front lawn, pajama-clad and sleepy-eyed like me. My husband, who was obviously in cahoots with Tiffany, directed me to a huge box on the front lawn. It must have been eight feet by ten and was wrapped in tissue and tied up with an enormous red bow. There was a card propped at the side that said "Happy Birthday, Mum, from Dad, Samantha, Zachary and Tiffany."

I thought, *Oh, oh, this is payback time.* When Derek turned fifty I rented fifty penguins and put them on the front lawn. I couldn't imagine what he'd put in that big box.

Turning fifty wasn't a big deal for me. The word bothered me a bit but not the fact of being fifty. I had told Derek I didn't want a party because my family—my mother and my eight sisters—all live in England and since they couldn't be here, it would mean very little without them.

"Go on, open it," they shouted. I didn't know where to begin. "Just tear the paper off," Tiffany insisted. I pulled at the tissue and opened a hole in the side. As long as I live I will never forget the overwhelming joy I felt when the side of the box fell away to reveal my mum and eight sisters from England.

Cameras were flashing from inside and outside the box. Everyone was yelling, "Happy Birthday." I could hardly comprehend what was happening. My mum's face was the first I saw. I realized there were other people in the box with her but I was so caught up with the moment, it was a few seconds before it began to register and they started coming at me. "Hi Jack," "Happy Birthday, love," "Surprise, dear Jackie." Middy, fifty-six, Brenda, fifty-four, Gorgy, forty-nine, Jenny, forty-seven, Linda, forty-five, Barbara, forty-two, Tina, forty, and Karen, thirty-seven. All of them. I couldn't believe my eyes. It was what I wanted more than anything else in all the world. All I could say was "You're all here! I can't believe it. You're here." And I couldn't stop crying.

They'd been planning this moment for two years with my husband and Tiffany. They'd arrived the night before and stayed in a hotel. Middy, the eldest, almost missed the party. She's terrified of flying and felt she couldn't get on the plane. So she went to a doctor a few months before the flight and said, "I'll ruin the whole thing if I can't get on that plane. Can you help me?" He did. He talked to her and gave her something to take before boarding the plane and more to take on the return flight. (She sent him a postcard while she was here.) My younger sister Barbara had never been on a plane before. But here they all were.

Derek and I moved to Canada thirty years ago. I was the only one in the family to leave England. So I miss them all terribly. They all live close to each other and spend lots of time together. We have thirty-three children among us, and I often feel my kids lose out because their kids are in and out of each other's houses all the time, just as though they had eight homes instead of one.

However, the ties that bind us together have never loosened over the years. We were each other's playmates and mentors and guardians from the time we were babies.

Although we remember our growing-up years with hilarity and love, life wasn't easy for our mum. We were poor. We slept four to a bed and used overcoats as blankets when it was cold. There wasn't always enough to eat, so we often had bread and sugar sandwiches for meals.

Mum took jobs in factories to make ends meet. Middy went to work to help out. Our dad was a drinker so he wasn't around much. But to tell the truth, we had a wonderful life. We were always close. We relied on each other. The older ones took care of the younger ones. When I got married I was well used to taking care of kids.

And when I think of the luxuries I have today, I wonder how mum ever managed.

For two wonderful weeks that summer, we laughed, told stories and talked all night long. Derek rented a van and we went up to our cottage in Port Severn, north of Toronto. We bunked in together just like the old days. We sat on the porch with candlelight and the moonlight over the lake and sang all the songs we'd learned as kids.

There were no husbands, no children, just us and our stories and our love for each other.

Suddenly it was time for them to leave. I could hardly bear it. At the airport when we said our good-byes I was crying so hard I couldn't speak. They were going without me. This precious gift of mine was leaving and taking nine pieces of my heart with them.

But I do feel lucky. It's rare that a family so big and so far away remains so close together. They are my best friends. They are mine. I am theirs.

A thin gold bracelet slips around my wrist today. It was their gift to me for my fiftieth birthday. Their names, one inscribed on each link, glisten at me when I look at it.

The tears in my eyes glisten back for the gift of love they have given me forever.

Jackie Case

Imprints

Both within the family and without, our sisters hold up mirrors. Our images of who we are and of who we can dare to become.

Elizabeth Fischal

Four out of my parents' five children were afflicted from birth with a rare genetic disorder called osteogenesis imperfecta (OI), otherwise known as "brittle bones." As a result of multiple fractures, OI in its extreme form causes dwarfism, severe deformity to the victim's limbs and even death. But our family is among the fortunate few as we have a very mild form of the disease. My brother only had about four fractures as a result of OI, while my next oldest sister and myself each had approximately thirty fractures. Our eldest sister, however, suffered over one hundred fractures in her legs during a sixteen-year period as well as a dozen or so fractures to her arms and shoulders. Her legs were so fragile that once, standing up at the sink to brush her teeth ended in a fracture. Consequently Debbie was confined to a wheelchair for the majority of her childhood.

Debbie is ten years my senior; being the youngest in the family, I never knew her outside of her wheelchair as I was growing up. Her chair seemed to me to be a natural extension of her, and I loved that she would give me rides around our patio while I carefully sat on her lap. Debbie's cheery disposition and her ever-present smile that stretched from ear to ear were her trademarks, and they helped us learn at a very young age to ignore the stares that we inevitably got whenever we went anywhere with Debbie. I remember hearing comments like, "That poor little girl," or "Oh, how sad!" from well-meaning onlookers, and I would think, *Debbie's not poor, and look at her smiling face—she's not sad.* I guess I was confused because we all learned to look beyond the chair to see Debbie our sister, who was usually happy and funny and nice and who could even play mean little tricks on us—like all good sisters do.

Thinking back today, we all laugh about the time Debbie and her wheelchair got stuck in the checkout line at our neighborhood grocery store. (Those were the days before many places were wheelchair-accessible.) The manager had to lift her out of the chair, place her on the counter, and then fold her chair to get it through the aisle, while all the curious shoppers stared and whispered. Debbie was naturally horrified over her predicament, but true to herself she just smiled right through it. Perhaps deep down that experience made her even more determined to walk so she would never have to suffer that kind of embarrassment again.

Defying doctors, Debbie set herself a goal before she graduated high school. She was determined to walk again. Through strength, hard work, patience and sheer will, Debbie worked toward that goal. Finally, her strength and courage paid off. The day she graduated high school, she led her senior class down the length of the War Memorial Arena walking every step of the way with a walker.

From the bleachers we watched through tear-rimmed eyes as her determined four-foot two-inch frame took step after step after step, in time with the music.

I remember my parents beaming with pride as they watched their eldest daughter walking again for the first time since she was six years old.

Then suddenly, a woman sitting directly in front of me in a white, cotton dress leaned over to her husband and whispered loudly, "They have to go extra slow because that crippled girl is leading them."

I don't know exactly what went through my eight-year-old mind at that point, but all at once my left leg straightened at the knee and my foot tapped that woman on the back of the dress. She turned around, and I jumped up hoping no one saw what a horrible thing I had just done. The woman smiled and sweetly said, "Did you want something little girl?"

My usually shy, guarded self replied without hesitation and loud enough for our whole section to hear, "That's my *sister*, and she's *not* crippled! She can walk now!" I don't know who was more horrified, that woman or my parents sitting three seats to my right. The woman quickly tried to apologize for her remark; she of course "meant nothing by it," and thankfully my mother had the grace to accept her apology.

Then, as I stood looking at this woman and wondering how she could have said something so mean, I noticed the entire audience rising to their feet and applauding. Through cheers of "Yeah Deb!" and "Way to go!" and "You did it!" we realized that Debbie had indeed met her goal. She walked before she graduated, and her entire class and all the teachers and the whole assembly of family members gave her a standing ovation when she reached her seat. Even the woman in the white dress stood up and clapped, looking back on us and smiling as if to say, "See, I'm a nice person, really I am." But I got the last word, so to speak, because when the woman turned around, she had the distinct, dirty imprint of a little girl's size-twelve shoe plainly visible on the back of her white cotton dress.

My shoe print, I'm sure, came out in the wash, but I think the imprint that Debbie and I left on that woman's soul lasted a lot longer. I know the sight of my big sister walking on her own is forever etched on mine.

Jodi Severson

My Sisters, Myself and the Seasons of Life

You keep your past by having sisters. As you get older they're the only ones who don't get bored if you talk about your memories. It's like when you meet someone who's been to India and you have too; you can talk for hours. Everyone else around you is bored but you're totally enthralled by each other's words. It's like that with sisters.

Debborah Meggah

How time changes everything, and too soon we get caught up in the worrisome trivialities of life. But one hectic afternoon, the scent of my neighbor's pine trees—that woodsy-turpentine aroma—took me back many years to a time and place when life seemed simpler.

With that whiff of pine from my neighbor's trees, I was suddenly transported back in time to the halcyon days I spent growing up with my two sisters on our grand-parents' farm in Union Grove, Alabama. In my memory, that 265-acre paradise of lush forest, cows, pigs, chickens and cotton fields remains unchanged, as does the secret place I shared with my sisters.

Our secret place was near a large pond, and we could only approach it in the proper form. We—Mary, Patti and I—would don our flying cloaks (which on ordinary days were bath towels) and race across the pasture, leaping and laughing.

From the pasture we stopped at our clubhouse, which had been used in the farm's earlier days as a place to store corn. Sometimes we slept there on our father's Army cots. It was always fun to see which neighbor's child (or children) would be there, playing; if any were girls, they came along with us.

From there, we ran to our nearest neighbor's house. They were the talk of the county because they had thirteen children. If they were around in the yard, we allowed the girls to join us. What a laughing, squealing bunch we made! We would run together through the woods, crossing the creek where Momma said a silver fox lived. Arriving at the pond, we would set to work on our glorious playhouse.

Our playhouses were architectural, if temporary, wonders, made with whatever was at hand—usually the red, long-dead needles of the pines we found surrounding the pond.

The art to a pine-needle playhouse is first to find at least five trees, grouped to form a circle, more or less. As trees whispered instructions and cicadas sang their praises, we would carefully twine bunches of the sticky, fragrant needles between the trunks of the stubby cedars and pines, working from the bottom up. The needles all stuck together making wonderfully rustic walls.

Our roofless pine needle houses usually wound up being just about five feet tall; we never felt the need to cover the sky. After finishing the playhouse, Mary, Patti and I, plus our friends, would lie on the ground and, facing the sky and encircled by the walls of our house, we would dream.

Within these walls, we planned our futures completely, down to the schools we would attend, the homes and families we would have, the places we would go and the important things we would accomplish. We shared secrets to be told to the wind or only to each other. Breezes would lift off the pond blowing cool perfume over us, laughing with us when we laughed. Those seasons were golden.

Building those pine tree houses taught me many subtle lessons about life. For we, like the trees, were sturdier if we grew close to those we loved. Like our houses built in a circle yet without a roof, our lives grew taller without the confines of a ceiling. That openness, I think, has stayed with each one of us as we've grown up, now with children of our own.

Through the building of our pine-straw playhouses, my sisters and I learned that everything is more worthwhile and more fun when we shared the job, where laughter is shared along with the work. Sharing our dreams helps make them possible. And my "architect" friends showed me the importance of sisters of the heart as well as sisters of the blood.

That was so long ago, and now my sisters—both of the blood and of the heart—and I live several hours apart, and our homes are made of brick, not pine needles, all with snug-fitting roofs.

I hope that when my sisters have rushed days like I do, that when they catch the scent of a pine tree it gives them pause and remember that each season of life, like those golden days we had growing up together, holds promise, and are reminded that living simply and living joyfully hold pleasures that endure long beyond the moment.

T. Jensen Lacey

Allies

What do women talk about? Women's conversation starts in the middle, goes to the beginning and doesn't have an end; we stop talking as we part and pick up right where we left off when we meet again.

Susan Branen

My sister and I became allies when I was three and she was seven. That's when it became us against them—the army of children our mother brought into our home to baby-sit. Not that we'd been enemies before then. Francie had always been protective of me, her baby sister, and I followed her around like a baby duck after its mother. One of our family's favorite stories is of me running after Francie with nothing on but my shoes when she'd dashed off down the street to play with the neighbors. "Wait for me!" I'd cried after her. One of our little cousins called us both "Carolannafrancie" because she'd always heard our names together and thought of us as one entity. But our survival was at stake when our peaceful, gentle lives were infiltrated by crowds of noisy, rowdy and destructive children. We were outnumbered and, as children intuitively do, we built a fortress in defense.

The invasion came about when our father was in a near-fatal elevator accident at work. It would be over a year before he'd return to work and before any money would be recovered from the lawsuit. Our mother realized it was up to her to bring in an income, but was reluctant to leave her two timid daughters with strangers while she worked. So she made the best decision she could at the time: She took children into our home. This was long before day-care centers were common and there weren't many alternatives for working mothers. Her reputation grew quickly and soon we had as many as seventeen children in our home on any given day. Mayhem broke loose in our bucolic life and reigned until we were grown and left home for college.

Francie and I were both small and noncombative, so we fought our war from a strictly defensive posture. We built a private world around ourselves that included books, Francie's passion for drawing, and Gina, our boxer dog. Taking Gina for walks up the hill and into the woods was our means of escape into that world. Under the towering, fragrant firs, the three of us would walk single file until we came to our favorite spot. It was a small opening where we'd smoothed out the spongy earth beneath an ancient fir. We'd release Gina to snuffle amongst the underbrush while we'd lean against the broad trunk of the tree to gossip, giggle and grope our way into adolescence. Francie would clear up the mysteries in my life from the wisdom she found in her books. Often she'd take her sketch pad and charcoal and draw while we talked. Sometimes we'd just listen to the silence and breathe the sweet, damp scent of the woods. At dusk we'd brush the fir needles from our clothes and trek back down the hill, timing it so we'd arrive home after most of the kids had been picked up by their parents. There we'd face the noisy wrath of our exhausted mother.

In her teens, Francie drew further into her art and books and away from people, while I reveled and struggled with intense friendships at school. But always we remained the closest of friends. We didn't dare risk the sibling rivalry we saw amongst our peers. We knew that when it came down to it, we only really had each other. Francie left for college just as I was entering high school. I stood in the room we'd shared for fourteen years, with its twin beds that we'd arranged in every imaginable configuration. On the table between the beds was the record player that had appeared under the Christmas tree one year with both our names on it, along with a little red record called "Susie Snowflake." It was all mine now; I wouldn't have to share it ever again. I wept with the emptiness of knowing that things would never be as they'd been before.

There were summers, of course, and Francie and I would pick up where we'd left off, taking Gina into the woods, walking across the bridge into the city to buy art supplies, and all the things we'd always done together. But there was a distance between us now that was undeniable. She had one foot in an adult world I couldn't begin yet to understand. I left for college at the same time she graduated, and the distance between us grew wider. Then she introduced Ron to the family, and there was the excitement of planning a wedding. Then she was gone.

Ron took a teaching job on the east coast. *We'd still be close,* I told myself, but Francie was a notoriously poor correspondent and sometimes a year would go by without so much as a letter or card. Eleven years passed without our seeing each other. Then another seven. I can count the visits over the next thirty years on one hand. But when we parted after each visit, it was as if we'd just brushed the needles off our clothes and were following Gina out of the woods.

Francie's life in upstate New York still centered on her art. She had a studio and art supply store where she could do her work and make just enough money to keep the business alive. Until three years ago, when she lost her lease. The letter I received then was long and so full of pain I longed to hold her in my arms and comfort her. Without her studio, she had no place to do her art. And without her business, she lost contact with customers who'd become friends over the years. From her pain and isolation, she began writing letters as she never had before. Ironically, at nearly the exact time that she lost her studio, I rediscovered my love of writing. I read her letters and saw the open honesty of the emotions she expressed and encouraged her to write. Writing would never replace her painting and sculpting, but it gave us a shared interest and we corresponded eagerly and frequently.

That summer she and Ron were to visit Ron's mother in Spokane on her eighty-fifth birthday. Their schedule was tight and they didn't know if they'd be able to make it to my place in Seattle. So I made plans to kidnap Francie for a weekend. I sent her a plane ticket and made reservations at a Benedictine Abbey guest house outside Olympia. I picked her up at the airport and whisked her off to our private retreat. At the abbey we sat in our room, ate with the monks and walked in the woods, talking and talking, filling in the thirty years of our separate lives. Sunday evening before we left, we took one last walk through the woods. We found a clearing and sat against an old fir tree, talking and giggling. Then we stood up, brushed the needles off our clothes and headed back to the airport, our alliance as strong as ever.

Carol Sweet

Not Just Another Birthday

*To get the full value of joy, you must have some-
one to divide it with.*

Mark Twain

There are weekends and then there are *weekends*. Those
minutes within hours within days which are completely
perfect. Such was how I spent the last few days of my
forty-ninth year, as I approached a half a century young.

I was given the best surprise of my life—a weekend at
the Calistoga Hot Springs with my best friend, my sister,
Arlie P.

From the moment Arlie picked me up at the airport
with a happy birthday balloon and a smile as large as the
universe, I knew I was in for something special.

We ate lunch in one of those elegant restaurants that
one reads about in books and watches on the silver
screen. The type of restaurant with high ceilings, spacious
grounds and gracious waiters. The type we all deserve to
eat at more often. Unfortunately, life seems to thread us
between one obligation and another. And not until we're

about to unravel do we treat ourselves to what we deserved all along.

After a fabulous meal we checked into our room at the spa. Minutes later we were sprawled out on lawn chairs, basking in the warmth of the afternoon.

We came alive with sun-drunk conversation. Our laughter filled the air, bounced off the water, hung over us like a halo.

As the heat seeped into my skin, the tensions eased from my body. I knew I had arrived at a time and place in my life with more things to be thankful for than could be packed into my tiny, unorganized suitcase.

A few hours later, we strolled down Main Street, two giddy women. We got stares from the young men. Of course, not quite the same type our daughters would get. Nonetheless, we were noticed.

We disappeared into the dress shops and gift shops. And we talked.

We talked about growing older and the passage of time. Twenty years ago our conversations revolved around diapers and sleepless nights. Ten years ago around Girl Scout cookies and Little League. Today our talk centers on college education and retirement plans. Yet while the topics may be different, we are still talking. Our sisterly bond has endured the inevitable changes of growing older. Of moving out of our twin beds and into separate worlds.

Later that night, saturated with Mexican food and beer, we crawled into bed and tried to stay awake during a TV drama. After all, we weren't that old yet. Within minutes, my sister and I were deep inside our own dreams.

Saturday morning started off with coffee, bagels and more talk. Pumped full of caffeine, we took a long bike ride during which we *tried* to talk as we huffed and puffed our way over the hills and back down along the highway.

Finally it was time for our treatments.

We were given lockers and keys and told to undress.

Wrapped in towels, Arlie and I drank flavored water, ate sweet oranges and whispered. At that moment, I was so wonderfully thankful for this sister sitting beside me. For all of our silly fights over clothes and makeup. For all of the much-cherished conversations yet to come.

Nervously, I followed the attendant down the hall into the mud room. She instructed me to place my hands on the sides of the tub, balance over the mud and then settle in. It felt warm against my buttocks and back. Soon, the girls were packing us in as if we were going to be shipped across the country.

And as long as my sister went with me, I was willing to go anywhere.

Next, we sat in hot tubs, scrubbing our finger and toe nails, sipping water. I knew my sister was getting hungry when she started eating the cucumbers floating in the drinking water. This was followed by the steam spa in which my sister kept sticking her head out the hole for fresh air.

Once we'd had enough heat, I was led down a long hallway into a small room, much like an examination room at the doctor's. Here, I spent fifteen minutes of total relaxation with cucumbers on my eyelids. Soothing music drifted into the air. My thoughts flowed randomly. I nearly fell asleep.

The treatment ended with a full-body massage. I can only say that a person has to experience this for herself. I know I can't wait for another one.

After two and a half hours of pampering, we strolled out (even stroll is too fast a word for our movements) and collapsed onto the outside chairs. The cool air played against our softened skins. Flowery scents drifted past on the wings of our contented sighs.

Eventually, we gained enough strength to walk back to our motel to get ready for my birthday dinner. Despite our food arriving late and mosquitoes joining us for dessert, it was a perfect evening.

Over Sunday morning breakfast (yes, another meal!) we looked forward to next year's treatment, the main reason for coming to Calistoga, but certainly not the most important one. Hot oils, mud baths, steam saunas, lotions and wraps can rejuvenate wrinkled, tired skin. For a bit. A day. A week. A strong bond between sisters lasts forever, keeping one's soul rejuvenated for eternity.

Janie Emaus

STONE SOUP. ©*Jan Eliot. Reprinted with permission of UNIVERSAL PRESS SYNDICATE.*
All rights reserved.

Beach Day

When I told my three older children that we were going to have a new baby, they each had a different reaction. Anny, the oldest at twelve, promptly burst into tears. She had never been good at handling change and was always the child who needed the five-minute warning whenever we had to change activities. ("Okay, sweetheart, in five minutes, it will be time to clean up the blocks and go eat lunch.") I think she also cried because, though she couldn't express it in words, she was at that stage where she had just learned what one had to do to get babies and was mortally embarrassed that her friends would know that her parents still did "that!"

Rachael, three years younger and wanting something different than just girls in the family, promptly announced that she would call the baby "Jacob." It didn't matter that the baby turned out to be a fourth daughter. Rachael called her sister "Jacob" and took every opportunity to dress her in blue until Elliana was four months old.

Kayla, four at the time, promptly announced that when the baby came, she herself would give up her pacifier so she could be one of the "big" sisters. She did, too.

Each of them had a reaction to being a big sister to this

beautiful little baby number four that clearly reflected her own unique personality. It wasn't until several years later that I realized how profoundly and distinctly each older sister had imprinted this little one, and I guess, each other as well.

A few weeks before Anny was to leave for college, I took the four girls to the beach. With twelve years between the oldest and youngest child, it was getting nearly impossible to find an activity that we could all enjoy together. At eighteen and fifteen respectively, Anny and Rachael often (and understandably) didn't want to do things that were appropriate and fun for their eleven- and six-year-old sisters. More often than not, these older two, who had grown quite close since the previous fall when Rachael entered high school, were off on their own with their own friends. Anny enjoyed having a sister at the high school with her and often was the driver when the two of them went to basketball games or movies with friends. They had a life apart from the rest of the family, largely due to Anny's sense of responsibility and the fact that she had a driver's license.

But going to the beach was one activity we could all enjoy together. Summer was almost over and everyone was feeling the approaching strain when Anny would leave for college. Already, it seemed a hole in the fabric of our family was looming. The girls didn't talk about it outright, but I knew each of them could feel it. I did, too.

The sun was high and hot as we unloaded our gear and slathered on sunscreen. But the breeze off Lake Michigan was cool and the water looked inviting. I set up a big umbrella, spread out the blanket, and prepared to park myself under it to read. The three older girls went down to the water's edge to look for shells and get their toes wet. Elliana settled down next to me with a shovel and pail and proceeded to build a sand castle. But after a few minutes, she asked if she could go down to the water with her sisters.

Unwilling to relinquish my comfortable position, I called to the big girls and motioned for them to come back. I asked them if they would watch Elli down by the water and let her gather some shells. To my surprise, they agreed without an argument.

I watched them walk away from me—four tan, perfect little bodies in various states of growth: two womanly shapes with long legs and slim hips; one still with baby fat around her middle carefully hidden under her older sister's oversized T-shirt; and one still in the sweetness of little girlhood, tiny, pudgy, deliciously unself-conscious.

They held hands.

I went back to my book for a few moments, secure that I could trust the older ones to make sure Elli did not venture too far out in the water. But then something made me put my book down and look for them.

They were walking down the beach, the two older ones in front, Kayla next, Elli trailing behind. Every so often, one of them would call to the others, bend down, pick up some found treasure, and put it in Elli's pail. Then the little procession would continue. But I noticed that Elli was not looking for shells. She was playing a different game, watching her sisters. She seemed to be hopping from side to side, following directly behind them. When they stopped, she stopped. Sometimes the older three walked with each other, side by side. But Elli always stayed behind them. She seemed happy bringing up the rear.

It took me a few minutes. Then I realized what she was doing. Elli was walking in her sisters' footprints.

The afternoon wore on. We ate and napped under the big umbrella, the girls using each other as pillows. When it was time to go, I gathered everything up and we loaded the car. I waited until we were all in the car together before I asked Elli about her game.

She told me, "I was trying to walk in only Anny's prints. But she takes too big of steps, so I had to use one of Rachael's feet or Kayla's to get to Anny's. It didn't matter whose footprint I was in but I wasn't allowed to step on the sand outside a print. That was the game."

Her sisters heard her but they didn't pay too much attention. Or so I thought. Several days later when I was helping Anny pack the last of her things before she left for school, she said, "I wish you hadn't had me first."

I thought she was expressing her fear at leaving home so I started to reassure her that everything would be okay, that she would love college and being on her own. . . . But she stopped me.

"I'm not nervous about going to school. I'm nervous about not being everything they need me to be."

I hadn't realized how seriously Anny had taken her responsibility as the oldest sister. She knew, had probably known all along, how much they looked up to her.

I wanted to tell her that she had done her job well, had given them what they needed when they needed it, that she was a good role model. That each of them would make decisions in life influenced by each other but always lead by her good example. She was a good big sister, the best big sister. I wanted to tell her all that.

"The other day at the beach. . . ." she began.

It was my turn to stop her. I said, "The other day at the beach when you were in the lead and the others followed you? When you set the pace, always looking back to make sure they were there right behind you where they were supposed to be? When I didn't get up—not once—to check on any of them because I knew you were watching out for their safety as you always do? *That* day at the beach?"

I smiled at her, knowing better than to cry.

"Do you think they'll be okay without me? They can miss me a little, but do you think they'll be okay? You know, Rachael has done some things this year in high school. . . . I promised her I wouldn't tell."

"Then don't," I said. "Evidently, you handled it."

"But she's the oldest sister here now." She stopped and thought a minute. Then she said, "Let them call me whenever they want, okay? Don't ask them why, just let them. Promise?"

I promised, aware that we were talking about some secret sister bond that existed among them completely apart from me.

I hoped my oldest daughter would realize that as they had done that day at the beach, each sister would follow in the footsteps of one of the others. But, as Elli had showed us all, it was always available to hop from one sister's prints to those of another, if needed. Because each sister, influenced by the others, would leave her own indelible mark in the sand—and on the world.

She got it. Among the socks and underwear (and her sister's sweater, probably unbeknownst to her sister) that were going off to college with Anny were four tiny pink seashells, carefully wrapped up in tissue paper.

Just a small memento from a day at the beach.

Marsha Arons

I Had Forgotten

Our real possession is our memory. In nothing else are we rich, in nothing else are we poor.
Alexandar Smitty (1630-1667)

I had forgotten that I'd once been a princess. My sister reminded me.

We were doing something that I'd heard people do and always wondered how a person could bear to do it—go through their mother's things. My three sisters and I were in my mother's cramped apartment, trying to get as much done as possible before one sister and I returned to our out-of-town homes and families, leaving whatever work remained to the other two sisters. We wanted to get as much done together as we could and share the burden as well as the grief.

We did better at the former than the latter. My sisters epitomize the "when the going gets tough, the tough get going." We worked well together, but we mostly kept our grief to ourselves.

We didn't fight about who wanted what. If two sisters wanted something, they tried to gauge who it meant the most to and that's the sister who kept it. None of it was monetarily valuable; it was all about whose memory was wrapped around it.

My mom had the same jewelry box my whole life. It was jammed with all kinds of costume jewelry, from current things back to 1940s-era items. We packaged up most of it for the give-away pile.

I pulled out a bracelet. It is one of those kind that expands to fit over the hand and then is snug about the wrist, like a watch band. It has three rows of faceted glass set in what looks like nickel plate.

"Anybody want this?" I asked, hoping, though I didn't know why, that they would all say no. I couldn't place the memory, but my gut told me there was something special connected with it.

Lorraine's face lit up. "Oh!" she said, "Do you remember this?"

"I do kind of but I don't know why," I replied.

She took it out of my hand and placed it, open side down, on top of my head. Instantly, the memory came flooding back. When I was little, Lorraine, being ten years older, would take pity on the little sister and play with me. In the attic were crinolines from fashions gone by. She would dress me in the crinolines, drape my head in colorful scarves, and anchor them with the bracelet, its sparkling glass looking like the perfect tiara. A bobby pin here and there, a little lipstick and rouge, and *voilá!* Instant princess!

All that flashed by in a moment as I looked at my dear sister, and all at once I was that little girl again, safe and treasured and loved in our cozy childhood home. Both of us blinked away tears as she wrapped me in a tight hug.

Our world would never be quite the same again. Standing on either side of our mother's bed as she died would change us somehow inexplicably forever. But we would still face that world together, our love for one another even surer.

Now when I wear the bracelet for a special occasion, inevitably someone will comment on how lovely it is. "It was my mother's," I say.

And I smile.

Nancy Swiatek Pardo

Different

People, even more than things, have to be restored, renewed, revived, reclaimed and redeemed; never throw out anybody.

Audrey Hepburn

Over the years we have discovered that being sisters and being close does not necessarily mean we agree on everything. Growing up, we differed on many things, but today we agree on what is really important, being sisters.

You can eat off her floors. You can't even eat off my table because it is covered with books—overdue and otherwise unpaid bills, scraps of paper with telephone numbers. Clothes in her closet hang neatly by function and by color. I have trouble finding a clothes hanger. Her hair always looks as though she just stepped out of a beauty salon and she did it herself. Mine is grateful for a comb in the morning. Her immaculate, pressed clothes fit perfectly and look Saks Fifth Avenue. Mine look blow-dried and usually resemble gently used off the rack. She was always beautiful and I was always plain.

Two events made us realize the importance of being

sisters—our mother's death and her terrible lung cancer. After mother's funeral, hurtful words were spoken by both of us over matters that seem now immaterial. It went like this.

"It's mine!"

"No, she would have wanted me to have it! It's mine."

Months of silence went by while we both cried by ourselves. She made the first tentative offer of reconciliation, which I joyfully accepted.

Then she went into the hospital to have a cyst on her leg removed. We silently worried that it might be cancer. It was benign. However, a routine chest x-ray showed one lung full of cancer tumors. The diseased lung was removed but the horrible malady struck the other lung.

Chemotherapy is holding the disease at bay and we have come to realize our time together here is fleeting and precious. That is not to say we always agree. We don't. Only now it goes like this.

"You take it! It's yours."

"No, you take it! It's yours."

Jane Eppinga

Heaven

As you open the newspaper, the advertisement reads:

NO HUSBANDS OR CHILDREN
NO CLEANING FLOORS OR LAUNDRY
NO BALL PARKS OR CARPOOLS
NO FAST FOOD OR STYROFOAM CONTAINERS

Those of us who spend our lives completing these tasks on a daily basis might be drawn to the advertisement as a moth is drawn to a flame. Could this be an advertisement for Heaven? No, this is simply the recipe for the best weekend three sisters could have.

My sisters and I come from a traditional family of the fifties. We were brought up in a cookie-cutter neighborhood like every other family on the block. There was a mother, father, three children and two dogs. We went to a neighborhood school and stayed within the safety of our surroundings.

As the girls grew and the family changed, our mother designed a plan in her mind that would put the CIA to shame. She would make sure that her "girls" would stay close throughout their adult life, no matter how hard she had to work. She plotted every time the girls were together. "Why don't you go out to lunch? Why don't the three of you spend a day shopping? I'll be more than happy to watch all the grandchildren," were the words that rang clear each time we were together. Mother's plan was succeeding. We actually enjoyed the time together, and we thought we were getting away with murder. After all, what could be better than a day out while Grandmommie baby-sits all the children? Boy, did we pull the wool over her eyes! But this wolf in sheep's clothing, we called Mother had formed a bond between the sisters that nobody could break.

As years moved on and Mother passed away, that feeling of being more than sisters but true friends continued to grow, as a sunflower on a summer day, always trying to reach greater heights. What would bring the sisters together more often than just holidays? When would the sisters have an opportunity just for themselves? A plan was needed. Thus, the birth of "Sisters Weekend."

Just as the title denoted, the first few trips were just that. We would meet on Friday evening and return home on Sunday afternoon. The days were filled with sightseeing, shopping and talking. The evenings were filled with delicious dinners, movies and more talking. By the third year, we found that three days and two nights were not enough for all we wanted to accomplish. We also came to the realization that if we wanted to go outside the state, we would need more time. With the support of husbands and children, Sisters Weekend was expanded for one more day. Now the sisters were ready to explore new horizons.

As if planning the invasion of a small country, arrangements are made for the weekend. We place the names of all the locations that we would like to visit on the table, like a plate of fresh fruit ready to be picked. Then the feasibility of the trip is discussed. Limitations such as time and money mean certain destinations are eliminated or

postponed to another year. Finally, a location is chosen
and the planning begins. Each year a different sister takes
charge of the reservations with input from the others.
Hotels are investigated, restaurants are selected and all
areas of entertainment such as shopping, sightseeing, his-
torical sights and night life are explored.

With all the mandatory items covered, the fun begins.
Each year, as part of the weekend, we celebrate with gifts.
Lots and lots of gifts for every occasion. We give each
other Sisters Weekend gifts, we celebrate each other's
birthdays, and if someone has reached a major goal such
as a promotion, that is also a reason for something special.
Next, wardrobes are given equal consideration. Who
wants to go away without the perfect outfit for every
occasion? Besides, any excuse to shop for a new outfit is a
good one. Finally, it is decided what snacks will be
brought and by whom. After all, the last deadly sin is to
gossip about family, friends and work without something
sinful to eat.

The day finally arrives, and the sisters all meet at a designated location. This changes each year since we are
coming from different cities. The joy comes to a crescendo
when all of us are face to face. The excitement permeates
the room and people stare as if Tom Cruise had just
entered the room. We fail to notice others around us. We
are off on our yearly adventure. Look out, here we come!

Upon arrival at the hotel, we check in as quietly as possible. This isn't always easy with all the suitcases, bags
and boxes of goodies we carry. The next few minutes are
often spent explaining to the desk clerk and bellman all
about "Sisters Weekend" and all it implies. On our fifth
anniversary, it was even more interesting. When we
arrived at the hotel, they seemed to know all about us. We
were afraid our reputation had proceeded us. Instead, all
the desk clerk would say was that he knew about us and

there was a surprise waiting for us. When we arrived at the room, we found three arrangements of a dozen red roses each. My middle sister's husband wanted to help us celebrate. We were shocked beyond belief. It looked like a funeral had taken place in our room. Since the event first started, the husbands have wanted to be a part of the celebration. Each year they contribute something to the weekend. Sometimes they treat us to dinner, send flowers or provide us with after-dinner drinks and Godiva chocolates. It's their way of always supporting the three sisters.

After settling into the room, the excitement mounts as if it were Christmas morning. The presents are handed out one by one. After all, we need to get the important things out of the way first. The gifts that are given are loving and heartwarming or funny, with hidden meanings only the sisters would understand. In only moments, paper flies everywhere as if the whirling winds of a tornado have swept though the room.

The next few days are filled with the enjoyment of being together, as if we were one. Our thoughts and dreams as well as any problems we may be facing are all discussed while shopping, sightseeing and eating. We talk way into the night about our lives during the past year. It is a time for the sisters to renew the bond that had been formed by my mother so many years ago.

The last night is always the hardest. Plans are discussed for next year's excursion, but the thought that this year's trip is over is always difficult. Tomorrow we will get on with our lives. This weekend, as short as it is, will be a moment, frozen in time, forever in our memory. We will share bits of the experience with others, but the very special moments we had will only be felt and remembered by the sisters.

Shelly Isenberg

8

INSIGHTS AND LESSONS

My sister taught me everything I need to know and she was only in sixth grade at the time.

Linda Sunshine

Little Monkey Girl

You'd think I'd cry when I think about my sister, but I rarely do. I was six months old when she died in a car accident, and I don't remember her, or the accident, at all.

When I talk about it, I feel like I'm repeating something I heard on the news, like it's something that happened to someone else. Like it's not even real.

This is what happened: My mother went to pick up my brother Alan, older than I am by seven years, from a birthday party at a friend's house. I was six months old, strapped into the car seat in the back, and my sister, four years old at the time, sat in the passenger seat. My mother went inside the house to fetch my brother and ended up chatting with the mother of the birthday boy in the front hallway, just out of sight of the car. They talked for a few minutes, then my mother said good-bye and started to leave, and then there was a loud screech and a crash.

Right away, my mother knew what had happened. She ran out to the driveway and confronted the most horrible sight she would ever see: The car was smashed into a tree at the edge of the driveway. My sister lay on the asphalt. She wasn't breathing. She was in a coma for eight days; my parents were deciding whether to turn off her ventilator when she died.

Do you see what I mean, about how the story sounds like a news report? It's all true, but I feel as if I am telling a lie. Sometimes people ask me questions after I tell the story. "Did your sister drive the car into the tree?" they ask.

"Yes," I say, "even though she was just four years old."

They say, "I hope you don't mind my asking, but . . . how did she start the car?"

"My mother left the keys on the seat by mistake," I say.

"Oh," they say. "Oh."

I've heard that three out of four couples who lose a child divorce within five years. I know my parents had a terrible time after the accident, but they never divorced. I feel proud of them every time I think of that. I can tell the story of how they stayed together, but, like the story of the accident, there are few facts and fewer details. My mother's sister came all the way from Missouri to Nevada to take care of my brother and me. She stayed home with me when my parents and brother went to the funeral. She played with me during the following months, when my mother was crying all the time, blaming herself, despondent and depressed. My father was even worse off. He started drinking heavily within weeks of the accident. He locked himself in the den and played sad, slow country songs on the record player. He and my mother fought fiercely and often, but time passed, and they received help from friends and therapists, and my father stopped drinking, and my mother stopped blaming herself, and they survived. Through it all, there I was, living in a household haunted by ghosts. There are people who have never seen their parents cry, but I am not one of them. But grief isn't all about fighting and sadness. My brother and I were showered with extra helpings of love; we received the portions of love that my sister couldn't accept for herself.

I want to tell you some things I've been told about my sister. Her name was Sarabeth. She was brave and adventurous, but no good at following the rules. She climbed trees she'd been told not to climb, and often fell and hurt herself. She ran inside the house when she'd been told not to run, and stumbled into furniture. She ran across the neighbor's gravel driveway even though she'd been warned not to, and the pebbles rolled under her feet, and her knees became a mess of tiny scrapes and cuts.

I like thinking of her as daring and mischievous. My sister, the little monkey girl, climber of trees.

I don't cry when I think about my sister. A few times, I've ridden my bike to the graveyard where my sister is buried, but the place is gigantic and crowded with gravestones, and it always takes me at least an hour of hunting to find Sarabeth's. By this time, I'm hot and grouchy and I just lay down my flowers and touch the plain, flat stone, dip my fingertips into the engraved letters of her name, and walk away. I don't cry when I tell the story of the accident, and I don't cry on the anniversary of my sister's death: April 24th. But sometimes, out of the blue, I'll read a story about two sisters or a friend will mention her own sister, and it hits me: I almost had a sister.

I wish I knew more about the little girl who lived for four whole years, about the little things that made her unique. Recently, I told my mother that I was jealous of my brother because he had memories: She looked at me for a long time, then went into the other room and returned with a box of photographs. Sarabeth is in all of the photos, and most of them I'd seen at one time or another. Sarabeth—in a diaper and tiny cowboy hat, staring up at the camera. Sarabeth's preschool class, a black-and-white assembly of smiling children, my sister on the left end of the third row back.

My mother pulled out two pictures I'd never seen before. In one, she stood next to a baby stroller with her small fingers on the handle, as if protecting it. She was only as tall as the stroller, but she stood as if she were guarding it. In the stroller was a wide-eyed baby.

"Is that me?" I said.

"Of course it's you," said my mother. "She loved pushing you around. She never ran or climbed trees when you were nearby. She preferred to help me take care of you."

I'd never seen a picture of Sarabeth and me together before. I don't think there are any others. I'd been so young when she died.

In the second photo, Sarabeth was alone. She wore a yellow-and-white checked dress and no shoes, and there was a thin red bow in her hair. "I wonder how old she was here," said my mother. "Two and a half, maybe." She turned over the photograph, then brought a hand to her mouth, then started giggling.

"What?" I said. "What's so funny?"

"You and your sister," she said, handing me the photo. "I can't tell you apart."

I took the photograph and turned it over. It was my name written in cursive on the back, not Sarabeth's.

"This is me?" I said, studying the little girl in the picture. It could have been either of us. My mind kept repeating what my mother had said: You and your sister, you and your sister, you and your sister. Then it hit me: A long time ago, I had a sister!

For one moment, holding that photo in my hand, this actually seemed real to me, and I started to cry.

Danielle Collier

I Am Mortal

I have lost a treasure, such a Sister, such a friend as never can have been surpassed—she was the sun of my life, the gilder of every pleasure, the soother of every sorrow, I had not a thought concealed from her, and it is as if I had lost a part of myself.

Cassandra Austen on the death
of her sister Jane

The wind whipped across the cemetery, swirling snow that had fallen a few days earlier—snow that blanketed the ground, a pristine white carpet for the Christmas wreaths dotting the landscape. I shivered with cold and ached with sadness. Today, under the cold clear winter sky, we were burying my sister.

She was my sister-in-law, actually, but after such a long time, that detail of our relationship seems unimportant.

Her death was a milestone for me. She was the first of my siblings, or siblings-in-law, to die. And her passing has made me very much aware of my own mortality.

I have been to many funerals in recent years. That

happens when you join the ranks of "senior citizens," when most of your friends and acquaintances are members of the "grandparent generation." But although I grieved and shared the sadness of family members as the deceased were laid to rest, I really didn't associate those deaths with the certainty of my own demise.

This time I did. Yes, I am mortal.

It seems like such a short time ago that my brother, freshly home from a stint in Germany with the U.S. Air Force, announced he had met this great girl and planned to marry her. She was *truly* a girl. Eighteen years old. I trailed her by only two years.

I was puffed up with pride as I filled the role of bridesmaid for the first time. I felt glamorous and important. And I was gaining a sister. I already had one sister, younger than I was, but at age sixteen, a ten-year-old sister was a nuisance—not someone to treasure. That came later. Suddenly, at age sixteen, I was acquiring a *new* sister. One closer to my age.

She was my sister for fifty years. And now she's gone.

Driving to her funeral from three states away, times we spent together ran through my mind like old movies. Holidays with small children everywhere, seven between our two families, eleven when my younger sister and her family moved close by. It was bedlam. Wonderful, pure familial bedlam.

Years intervened when they lived many states distant from us. Then it was our turn to follow company transfers and become "corporate itinerants." Eventually, she and my brother returned to our home state of Minnesota to live. We did not.

But there were visits. Adult visits. The children were now grown and long gone. We'd dine and talk, look at photos and talk, compare grandchildren stories and talk. Had I been fully aware, as she was near death, of how

terribly short life is, there would have been more visits.
Many more visits. More laughter, maybe more tears, as
we pored over old memorable photos together. And there
certainly would have been more talk.

I had the chance to say good-bye to her—a couple of
times. Her life seemed so tenuous, both in the spring and
summer, I was sure I wouldn't see her again after the first
time. She struggled hard, and until close to the end,
remained optimistic that she would conquer this too-
often-unconquerable disease. I was grateful to have the
opportunity to say farewell, to thank her for being my
sister for fifty years.

She and my brother observed their golden wedding
anniversary in the spring. It was to have been a gala affair;
the festivities had been planned a year in advance. Instead,
they observed the event quietly in a hospital room. When
she and my brother repeated their wedding vows, hers
were the only dry eyes there. She was buried in the beautiful dress she had selected for the planned festivities.

She showed incredible courage, my sister, as she battled
cancer that ravaged nearly every part of her body the last
nine months of her life. Her death was good in that it gave
her an escape from her suffering. We didn't want her to
leave this life—her family, her four children, her thirteen
grandchildren—and most certainly, her husband of fifty
years. But she had to. Every conceivable means for healing
had been tried—surgery, radiation, chemotherapy. All
failed, and so she died.

Because she was mortal. As am I.

Since leaving the cemetery, shivering in the cold, filled
with indescribable sadness, my life has taken on new
meaning. I find that things I see have heightened clarity;
those around me seem more important.

Perhaps, I think, *this is the last time I'll see the sky bordered in
flaming coral, streaked with gold, just before darkness settles in.*

Music I've always enjoyed suddenly fills me with such overpowering emotion, I can barely control the tears just waiting to be shed.

My husband's touch seems warmer, my grand-daughter's smile more delightful. I am more fully aware of my surroundings—all of them. I think of all the things I meant to do on life's journey. I think of all those things yet undone. I wonder which are *really* important.

During her final days, my sister realized the brevity of life and admonished others "to not hold grudges, just love each other." I don't know to whom she was addressing those words, but I'd like to think I was included.

These days, I find myself thinking of all the disagreements I've had with others over the years, and I wish I could take them all back. Some disagreements breached friendships so badly, they were destroyed. Today, I sorely miss those friendships.

I have vowed not to forget the lesson the loss of my sister has taught me. Life is short. Very, very short and far too valuable to squander on petty nothings not worth the energy they consume.

I believe I will see my sister again some day, and when I do, I will thank her for this lesson. My life, too, is short. I, too, am mortal.

Sandra I. White

Inseparable

To have a loving relationship with a sister is not simply to have a buddy or a confidant—it is to have a soul mate for life.

Victoria Secunda

My oldest was small and her sister quite tall, so folks often thought they were twins. Dressed alike in diapers and rompers or dresses and jeans, they kept me busy and delighted my soul.

They loved sleeping together under a big green quilt—my grandmother Nana's gift to me on the day of my marriage. Made of the softest cotton and thickly stuffed with down feathers, the quilt was a symphony of shapes, holding every color of green I'd ever seen. When the girls graduated from cribs to the big double bed, I gave it to them. For most of their childhood, my girls dragged that quilt everywhere. On blustery winter days, the quilt became an Indian tent where they wiggled and giggled away the cold. On warm summer days—arrayed with their dolls and assorted little friends—it became a sunny parlor for holding grand tea parties. Always, it was their refuge from monsters and hurts.

When the girls entered their teens, along went the quilt: to football stadiums, the beach and the lake. At night, they lay under its comfort to share secrets, to laugh and to cry. That old cover absorbed much mascara-stained puppy-love tears and took quite a beating, but like autumn fruit it just got softer and better with age.

College and marriage finally parted my girls, ironically, on the same day. Into separate boxes went their makeup, clothing and books. As they walked out of their room for the last time, neither girl said a word, but I did notice lingering glances and loving fingers giving a last caress to their beloved quilt.

When they were gone, I sat for a time on their bed; the room emptier and colder already.

Then, with firm resolve and Solomon wisdom, I took a deep breath and cut the old cover in half. The following Christmas, I gave each daughter her share, freshly adorned with dotted-swiss ruffles.

Now, whenever I visit their homes, I joyfully tuck my grandbabies into their bed and cover them with Nana's sun-dried quilt.

Lynne Zielinski

Animal Cracker Dresses

Only a sister can compare the sleek body that now exists with the chubby baby hidden underneath. Only a sister knows about former pimples, failing math and underwear under the bed.

Laura Tracy

I never thought having a sister was particularly enjoyable until I grew up and realized how much more annoying people who aren't related to you can be. My sister, Lori, was born four years after I was, which in kid years is the difference between two lifetimes. Growing up, I had already seen it, done it and figured it out by the time my little sister got around to it, therefore I was omnipotent and she, well, wasn't.

I wanted a buddy, like a girl version of *The Hardy Boys*. (Shawn Cassidy was my first crush.) Instead, my buddy smelled like peanut butter and was prone to running around the house sporting a bumper sticker—only a bumper sticker. I wanted someone more dignified for my adventures. My buddy created adventures rather than helped solve them. Case in point, it was the first grade, and it had taken all year for my turn to take the class hamster home for the weekend. Guess who freed Fluffy at 6:00 A.M. Saturday morning? None other than my three-year-old sister who proclaimed to a sleeping household, "De wat got out!" The adventure came in the form of my mother chasing Fluffy around the house with a tennis racket.

Payback came a year later when I persuaded Lori to take a candy cane from the supermarket unbeknownst to my mother. Once in the car, the evil truth surfaced—my mother had raised a four-year-old thief. Back into the store they marched, clutching the now sticky candy cane. I got to wait in the car. My sister did not reveal until years later the identity of her accomplice.

I was very aware of our age difference since it usually meant I was allowed to do more grown-up things like stay up late or ride the scarier rides at the fair. Lori, however, never saw an age difference and was forever attempting to copy everything I did. This was irritating because I was much too sophisticated to be emulated by a child.

When you are ten, fashion discoveries occur frequently. I thought I had found a new way to wear my hair that was sure to catch on in photo shoots around the world—the side ponytail. Never mind that in 1979, someone was bound to have done this type of thing before. There I was, sporting my new hairdo for all to admire and the only person who even acknowledged my true fashion greatness was my sister, who was more than willing to follow the trend. This became the standard for the rest of my great discoveries: miniskirts, U2, Nicholas Cage in the classic movie *Valley Girl,* and so on. She was perfectly willing to give me credit on these, which strengthened our relationship and my confidence.

Best that I can tell, sisters come in two categories: ones that look alike and ones who don't. Lori and I don't. People often commented on our lack of resemblance; she has dark hair, skin and eyes, while I am very fair. Our mother once dressed us in matching red and blue animal crackers dresses for our annual picture at Sears. That was the only day where I heard the "Oh, you two must be sisters" comment. To this day I inspect her for something that I can recognize as mine and say, "See we *do* have the same elbows!"

In spite of our opposing looks, we happen to have the same voice. Hers is capable of singing, mine is most assuredly not, but otherwise identical. This was an instrument of torture for my boyfriends in high school through college. Often there would be the prerequisite quiz at the beginning of every conversation, "What color jacket did Mr. Peters wear today in economics?" "Aha! Mr. Peters teaches trigonometry, put your sister on!" To this day when I leave a message on voice mail for my husband, and I call later to check my messages, it takes me a minute to realize it's me and not Lori telling my husband I am running late.

My sister and I have this thing where we will send our mother the same birthday, Mother's Day or Christmas card without knowing, despite living a thousand miles apart. We also tend to call her or each other at the same time even though we are in separate time zones. I don't feel it if she burns her hand on a hot stove, nor are there any plans to start our own Psychic Sisters Network anytime soon, but it is comforting to have a strong connection with my sister. We have started collaborating on cards before we send them to ensure our mother gets a well-deserved variety.

Sisters teach you many things, and mine is no different. The most important thing I learned from Lori is how special our relationship is. I hit her once during one of our "You wore my shirt" brawls and the look that came across her face was not one of pain, but of betrayal and devastation. I had crossed the line and become a bully rather than a role model and trusted ally. The regret I felt that day provided me with a clarity in which I saw the full meaning of our relationship. Lori had always grasped the importance of our friendship; I did not understand it until that day. I gave her the somewhat stretched shirt as an apology. She accepted and we never fought again . . . that day.

We shared a room until I was ten. When nights became spooky we shared a bed as well. We shared bowls of dessert, until I spit chocolate pudding back in the bowl. Ultimately we shared a lifetime. Our mother taught us to love each other and reminded us daily that each of us is the only sister the other would ever have. I have learned that she is the only sister I could ever want.

Cricket Hardin Vauthier

The Greatest Gift

I'm five years old, and my mother is on her hands and knees, washing the kitchen floor. I'm telling her about a new girl in school, and she suddenly looks up at me and says, "Who are your two best friends?"

I'm not sure what to say. I've been friends with Jill since I was three or so, and I really like Jaime, a friend in kindergarten.

"Jill and Jaime."

My mother stops scrubbing the floor and starts to take off her yellow rubber gloves. "Well, what about Karen and Cindy?"

My sisters? "I don't know who their best friends are," I say.

"No," she says. "I'm saying, why aren't they your best friends?"

She seems upset, like I hurt her feelings. "But they're my sisters."

"Yes, but they can still be your best friends. Friends may come and go, but your sisters will always be there for you."

At the time, the idea of my two sisters being my closest friends seemed strange to me. We fought all the time over toys, food, attention, what to watch on television—you name it, we bickered about it at some point. How could my sisters be my best friends? They weren't the same age as I. We all had our own friends in school.

But my mother never let the three of us forget it: Sisters are lifelong friends. Her wish—like most parents'—was to give us something that she never had. Growing up an only child, she longed for siblings. When she gave birth to three daughters—separated by only four years—the ful-fillment of her dream had only just begun. She had given us each a gift—our sisters—and she wanted to make sure we did not take that gift for granted. She would fre-quently tell us how lucky we were. But there were other, more subtle ways that she encouraged us to grow closer. She never showed favoritism to one daughter over the other, as not to cause jealousy or bitterness between sis-ters. She constantly took us places together—skating, shopping, swimming—so we developed common inter-ests. And when we were teenagers, Mom always pun-ished us equally, giving us yet another bonding experience.

We didn't always get along beautifully and fought just like any other siblings. But somewhere in between Mom's lectures, the family vacations and the shared memories, we realized that our mother was right. Today I share things with my sisters that I do with no one else. My sis-ter Cindy and I ran the New York City Marathon together, side-by-side, even holding hands when we crossed the finish line. When my sister Karen got married, I was her maid of honor. Cindy and I traveled through Europe together and even shared an apartment for two years. The three of us trust each other with our greatest secrets.

It was twenty-three years ago that my mother first asked me who my two best friends were. Today she doesn't have to. She already knows.

Christine Many

Thanks for the Miracle, Sis

My Dear Sister Sally,

This is a thank-you note shared in public because—as you say—it may hold out hope to others.

When I left you in the rehab center in mid-November, a week and a half after your second stroke, at age forty-six, you were paralyzed on your left side, confined to bed, confused about what was happening. Doctors said you could die, or at best subsist with extensive brain damage.

Thank you for proving them wrong.

Oh, the joy of having you and our younger sister, Jill, meet me at the airport in mid-January, just two months later! Precious, upright you—leaning on your cane, your hair freshly cut and styled; tears running down your face. Were your cheeks wetter than mine?

We came to make sure that you would be safe at home alone until your son got home from school and your husband home from work. Those few days showed us you would, and taught me far more than I can tell you.

Yes, you still have weakness in your left arm and a slight hearing loss. You mispronounce some words and get confused if we talk too fast, but *you* are intact: your keen intelligence, your delicious sense of humor, your thoughtfulness, your generosity, your sweet soul. More folks should be as whole as you are.

And now we see a new side to the shy and sometimes fearful middle sister who preferred to stick close to home, while Jill and I ventured forth getting into trouble. Thank you for your example in courage, fortitude, and the ability to keep putting one foot in front of the other in the face of great odds.

I watch you exercising several times daily to strengthen your left arm: stacking dice and paper cups, moving a dish towel around the table in figure eights, laboriously picking up paper clips and small screws to drop into a cup.

I saw you punch numbers into the automatic teller machine to get your bank balance, then do it all again when you forgot the sum. And I was suddenly ashamed that some days simply getting out of bed seems like too much work for me.

Thank you for the laughter. When you went to have your blood checked weekly to make sure your blood thinner was working, you said you had an appointment at the "vampire's." When you looked at the bleak hospital photos I'd snapped of you attached to snakelike tubes, you said, "I was *really* having a bad hair day!" Boy, are you a lesson in lightening up.

Stopping by your office gave us the opportunity to see how much others care about you (something some folks never discover until a funeral). Your coworkers told me how helpful you'd been when their relatives suffered strokes. They talked about your enthusiasm and generosity when they had babies or adopted a family at Christmas. Such an outpouring of love!

Several times you apologized for "being trouble." Don't you know how grateful we are, dear Sally, to finally be able to give back to you? Who else but you would present

Christmas gifts in January—gifts you'd purchased long before the stroke, now wrapped in paper bags with bows because you couldn't manage gift-wrapping?

Thank you for pointing out what's truly important—and for saying that you've dropped from your list nagging your teenager about his room. "I used to worry about things I thought were problems—like being fat," you said. "Fat isn't a problem. Being healthy is the most important thing in the world." Let me remember that the next time I climb on the scale.

And thanks, too, for the lesson in gentleness with yourself. When you pulled your shirt on inside-out and we called it to your attention, you didn't beat yourself up for making a mistake, as the rest of us do so often when we don't do something perfectly. You simply said, "*Oops*, I flunked shirt!" and fixed it.

I'm the wordsmith, but you say things better. Like when you read through all the nice letters that readers sent when I wrote about your stroke. "People are really nice, aren't they?" you said through tears. And over cocoa, you remarked, "I'm so glad I didn't die. I woulda missed you guys."

We would have missed you, too, Sal. But I want you to know: as painful and as frustrating as this whole experience has been for you and everyone who cares about you, it has been rich in love and lessons. I'm thankful for that.

Because of you, I'll be more patient with the person walking slowly in front of me or trying to figure out change. Who knows what odds that stranger contends with, that stranger who is someone's father or mother or sister.

And I'm so glad you're mine, my miracle sister. I love you, Sal.

Janny

Jann Mitchell

No Time to Say I Love You

Everyone needs reminders that the fact of their being on this earth is important and that each life changes everything.

Marge Kennedy

Sweat beads gathered on my forehead at just the thought of the first day of high school. I thought for sure that I was going to be singled out and embarrassed in every class and then be laughed out of the school. In first hour, when I was called to the office, being singled out became the least of my problems.

My twenty-year-old-brother, Brian, stood filling out papers for me to leave. He turned to face me and my heart sank. His face was pale and blotchy, like someone had carelessly thrown red paint on a white sheet of paper. His eyes were swollen and red. This being the first I had ever seen my brother cry, I knew that something bad had happened. He grabbed my hand and leaned down until his face was level with mine.

"Amanda has been in a car accident, and she is in the hospital," he said.

Every inch of my body went numb as I absorbed what my brother was telling me.

My sister? In a car accident? How could that happen? At age seventeen, Amanda was the safest driver I knew.

Without a thought in my head, I pulled away from my brother and sprinted down the hallway.

I had to get to my locker, my class and out of that school as fast I could. Yet nothing was fast enough. It felt like everything around me had slowed to a painful crawl just when I wanted it to speed up.

Yelling over my shoulder that I would be out to the car in a minute, I opened the door to my classroom. My teacher didn't ask what I was doing; she knew. She knew just by looking at me that I was leaving even without a note. Nothing she could do was going to stand in my way.

People watched from class windows as I ran down the hall in a panic to my locker and then out of the school doors. I would get in trouble for not waiting to get a note from the office, but I didn't care. Nothing mattered more than getting out of that school and to where my sister was.

Brian and I drove to the trauma center at Mid-Michigan Regional Medical Center. We ran into the room, and then I saw her.

She was laying on her back on a bed with her head and neck in braces. Her face was covered from the eyebrows up and you could see blood everywhere. She was hooked to several different machines to monitor her body reactions. Her entire body convulsed with the effects of the trauma.

My mom and dad stood at her side crying. Our pastor, youth pastor and what seemed at the time to be half of our church congregation were also in the room.

I walked like a zombie to her bedside.

Nothing could explain the feeling that coursed through me when she looked up at me with blood-filled eyes. In her eyes, where I expected to see fear, I saw strength.

Then her eyes softened, and she spoke. She said one thing to me while she was lying on that bed.

She looked up at me and said in a strained voice, "I love you, Renee." I couldn't handle the emotion that filled me at the realization that I rarely told my sister I loved her. I tried to answer her, but she wasn't listening anymore.

The doctors were taking her away to the x-ray room, and she was watching them carefully.

As they wheeled her broken body down the hallway with her blood seeping into the bandages and onto the white sheets that covered the portable bed, every inch of my being wanted to scream out to her that I loved her, but I couldn't. I couldn't move, speak or even cry until she was around the corner and I could see her no more. Then the tears came.

I knelt on the floor and cried in the corner. I cried tears of hopelessness and frustration.

Though everyone kept telling me she would be all right, something in their voices spoke loudly of the doubt that everyone was secretly harboring in the back of their minds. All I wanted was for the doctor to say, "She's going to be fine."

He didn't. Every moment that passed allowed the doubt to grow stronger and bigger, like a dense black cloud that refused to allow the sunlight to come through. Finally, he walked tentatively down the hall and stood quietly in front of us.

I tried to read his face what he was going to say, but I couldn't. He started to tell us about her head.

When the tie-rod on her car broke, the car hit the side of the ditch and flipped end over end, clearing the ditch and landing on the other side in a small patch of trees.

Her head struck an object, which was assumed to have been the dashboard, with the front part of her face. The impact drove all of the skin on her forehead back into her hair. Pieces of skin still remained in that cursed car.

I knew that head wounds were very dangerous and that they could result in many different injuries. At that moment, I really wished that I had paid more attention to my teacher when we talked about head wounds in health class.

It was then that the long-awaited words came. The only words, from the only person that I could accept them from—the doctor. Amanda was going to be okay.

My soul leaped and my heart raced as I realized I still had a sister. She would never look the same and would require hours of plastic surgery, but she was alive, and that's all that mattered to me.

A year later, I still have a sister, and even though we fight and nag at each other, every time that I see her face and I spot the large scar that stretches from her hairline across her forehead, down her eyelid and back up to her hair, I remember to tell her that I love her. I remember when I almost didn't have the chance to tell her again how much I really do love her, and I thank God I still can.

Renee Simons

Lessons from My Angel

You don't get to choose how you are going to die. Or when. You can only decide how you are going to live. Now.

Joan Baez

The drive to the hospital is long, too long. I am bringing my twenty-seven-year-old sister home. My sister—blue eyes, blonde hair and a smile that lights up a room. We found out five months ago that she has a brain tumor. She got better, then got worse. Now they tell us that she will not make it, that the most they can hope for is to shrink the tumor as small as possible in order to buy her a little more time. I walk into the hospital and find her in the physical therapy room. Angel's right side is paralyzed from the tumor, so they are helping her try to strengthen that side. So far she can lift her right arm up a couple of inches. Sweat is streaming down her face at the effort. "C'mon arm!" she grimaces at the strain. This is as close to a complaint as I have ever heard from her.

I sit back and watch her. I find myself doing this a lot these days. Trying to capture and freeze moments to file away and save for "later." She simply amazes me. In her shoes, I would be doing a lot of crying, serious complaining and endless whining. Not her. I have never heard her, not even once, ask "Why me?"

At home, she loves the room I have fixed up for her. We tape the countless cards to the wall where she can see them. She smiles at them. It comforts her knowing many people care. Nighttime is finally here, and I am exhausted. It has been a long day of lifting and constantly helping her. But I feel good. I am taking care of my sister, and I am honored to do it. It's getting late, and I get my kids to bed and help her dress and get into bed.

Helping her into the bed breaks my heart. She trembles from head to toe. Her right arm dangles—dead and useless—and is bruised from shoulder to fingertips from constantly hitting things she can't feel with it. I swing her legs onto the bed and we smile into each other's same-color blue eyes. I hold back the tears until I get upstairs.

My husband is asleep, and I am finally alone, so I let the waves of pain wash over me. Seeing her so helpless and weak and suffering is like a shard of glass in my soul. I can't take it anymore.

Sobbing, I begin to pray. I am no longer asking God, I am now yelling at him, begging, pleading angrily to not let her be like this. I run out of words and just say *Please, no*, over and over, crying until I am sick. Worn out, I head downstairs, knowing I need to sleep so I can have the strength to get through another day like today.

I pause outside her room and peek in to make sure she's okay. She is awake and sees me. "You okay?" I ask for the six-hundredth time today. "I'm fine, I just can't sleep." She tells me the steroids that reduce the swelling in her brain keep her awake. I plop down in the rocking chair next to her bed and put my feet up, scrunching them under her pillow. I settle in, and we begin to talk. She shocks me with what she says next.

"I know you're worried about me. I don't want you to worry. I'm really okay." She goes on to tell me how the worst is behind her, that things are getting better. She says she will get well. I look at her skeptically and wonder if the tumor has made her dense. She ignores my disbelief and continues in her efforts to comfort me. She tells me that she knows why she is sick, and that it's necessary to bring our family closer together. She doesn't mind and feels it a privilege to endure something that will effect changes in others. She tells me of the many, many blessings that have already come about because of her cancer. So many people—strangers—praying. Her faith has grown in leaps and bounds. Her life has been touched by so many people she calls her angels.

What she doesn't realize is how many people have been impacted by her. When she was in the hospital, she would have Mom buy dozens of roses and bring them to her. She would then take the bouquets apart and one by one take them to every single patient on her floor. She would also give them to the kind, wonderful nurses who took care of her. She spreads light wherever she goes. It's an awesome sight.

We talk all night, deep into the morning. Finally, as the gray turns to pinks and brilliant oranges shimmering through her window, she is tired enough to sleep. I leave her room and climb into my own bed for a couple of hours of rest. I feel lighter and more peaceful than I have in a long time. I smile and know God arranged our long talk.

The days go by, and we get into the routine of things. Daily radiation and physical therapy. Countless medications. Hair falling out and the subsequent buying of hats. Cutting up her food, putting the toothpaste on her toothbrush. Even my tiny son, Noah, at two years old, helps her to get across the room by pushing on her bottom.

Everyone helps, and my husband is amazing. He lifts her gently out of the van and picks her up when she falls and I don't have the strength. My sister is right; this has brought out the best in everyone.

Sometimes I lose the peaceful feeling I got when we talked. Sometimes I feel numb; other times I can't stand the pain of seeing her suffer, of seeing her one good hand tremble with the stress of bringing a bite of cereal to her mouth, shaking till the cereal falls off the spoon. It still breaks my heart. Last night was one of those times.

I had started her shower and left the door open a crack so I could hear the water shut off—my signal to help her out and get her dressed. In the kitchen, I heard a giant SPLOOSH, then a thud and a crash.

Heart pounding, I rushed into the bathroom to find her lying on her back in the tub, shower curtain on the floor and water everywhere.

"Are you okay?" I shrieked yet again. She muttered that she was fine and apologized for the mess. It was then that I cracked, looking at my young, vibrant sister, lying like a stuck turtle on its back, her body a rainbow of hundreds of bruises, her head shiny and bald, thin strings of the remnants of her hair clinging wetly to her face. I helped her up and didn't let her see my tears and my body shaking with uncontrollable sobs. I would give anything, *anything* at all to wave a magic wand and make her strong and well again.

I got her ready, and she was fine. Falling happens quite a bit. We'll get her a shower chair. She keeps saying she's fine.

A little later, we are sitting on the couch. My husband is down in his office, working, the kids are in bed and Angel and I are sitting on the couch, just vegging in front of the TV. She looks at me very intensely and suddenly says, "Stop worrying about me."

I turn to look at her and realize I'm not hiding my

feelings very well. She begins to cry and says, "I am so blessed. I have been so well taken care of. Everything I need, I have. I WILL get well, so stop worrying so much. Get on with your life and start LIVING again!"

I let a few tears escape and feel the knot in my stomach ease a bit. Her faith and her indomitable spirit are an inspiration. I decide right then and there that for her, I will do it. I will, of course, still worry and feel pain at her suffering, but I will also try harder to equal her faith. I will laugh more and live more. I smile, and my face feels weird. I realize that it's been a long time since I've smiled. I do it again, and she laughs. We both laugh together, and I say a silent prayer of thanks for this gift that is my sister. My Angel.

Susan Farr Fahncke

Comrades in Arms

Sisters are the easiest people in the world to forgive. Except when they are the hardest. It's a question of balance.

Source Unknown

Life can be a challenge when you're just over two years old and a "little mother" to your thirteen-month-old sister. Even at that tender age, I knew being an older sibling and the first child in the family meant I had certain inescapable obligations. Making sure my little sister, Shelley Lynn, did everything she was expected to do was a chore I accepted willingly and perhaps a touch too enthusiastically—as evidenced by the black and white photo my mother took one spring morning in 1952.

Dressed in identical mint-green cotton dresses, Shelley and I were posing, for some long-forgotten reason, in the front yard of our home in Weidman, Michigan. We were supposed to face the camera, hand in hand, and smile like good little sisters. But Shelley decided life would be more interesting if she turned to her left. She ignored our mother's plea to face the camera, so I took my turn at persuading her. And persuade I did—with a vengeance. Although I don't remember this exact incident, I remember others like it: times I tried to bend Shelley to my will and came away with bite marks, a much-deserved smack in the chops or sometimes (once in a while, but not very often)—sweet victory!

This time, however, victory eluded me. Shelley put up a mighty struggle and I tried my darndest to subdue her. Apparently, being in the presence of our mother was enough to discourage us from fisticuffs (this time) and we settled instead for choke holds and pinching. The picture shows me, a full head taller than Shel, standing behind her with my arms wrapped tightly around her tiny neck. Struggling for breath, she's trying valiantly to pry my arms loose and break the choke hold I have on her with her own two chubby arms clawing at mine. I'm determined; she's determined; it's a stalemate. The grimaces on our faces tell it all.

Back in those days, casual shots—or at least those depicting murder—were probably considered a waste of valuable film. To her everlasting credit, our mother abandoned all caution and snapped the picture of our sisterly struggles, preserving for all time a scene that would be repeated, again and again, throughout our childhood and teen years. Fortunately, she wasn't witness to all of them. It might have killed her.

Although we weathered the usual upheavals during our adolescence, we managed, somehow, to string together enough periods of tentative truce and testy tolerance to forge a strong bond of sisterhood. (Not that we didn't test that bond, mind you. We did our level best to scratch each other's eyes out on several occasions. The WWF would have been proud of us.) Of course, that sisterly bond would not become apparent until years later, after our independence had been won from schoolteachers, parents and the frustrations of sharing a small bedroom for several years. But bond we did. In fact, relations between us have been much calmer in recent years. We haven't smacked each other in decades and I can't remember the last time I pulled a handful of hair from her head. To her credit, I haven't sported bite marks or a black eye for an equally impressive period of time. We have grown up. We now pride ourselves on our genteel manner and civilized ways. I guess you could say we've come a long way, baby.

I've discovered, in fact, that she's quite a wonderful person—loving, gentle, responsible and, for the most part, reasonable. I am still the serious, responsible older sister, endowed with certain rights and responsibilities, not the least of which is my right to insist that she do things my way. Shelley, however (still one year and three weeks younger than I), sometimes insists on running her own life. And that's not all bad.

Our differences, however, are many. She is dark and petite; I am light and taller. To look at us, you'd never know we're related. She's the artist; I'm the writer. I like to throw ideas out and let the chips fall where they may. She's organized, loves structure and, as a result, gets a lot more done than I do. I started my family at a young age and had three children—one right after another. They are all on their own now, pursuing marriage, careers and lives of their own. Shelley had her children several years later and spaced them out. She's still in the midst of home-work, slumber parties, track meets and parent/teacher conferences. I'm waiting for grandchildren; she's still waiting for her turn in the bathroom. I've worked outside the home for years. Shelley's worked even harder as a stay-at-home mom/art student and obtained her degree from one of the most prestigious art colleges in America— somewhere in between swimming lessons, broken arms, allergy shots and first dates. But despite our differences, the similarities we do share boil down to this: We love our families, we love our lives and the paths we've chosen for ourselves, and we love each other. These likenesses seem to have held us in good stead.

Again and again, Shelley reminds me of the strong bond of sisterhood we share—during the bad times, as well as the good. During a particularly difficult period in our lives a few years ago, when tempers were short and miscommunications and misunderstandings plagued us, Shelley—with God's help—came to the rescue. For the last few months and for long-forgotten reasons, words had been hard to come by, gestures of love even harder to express. Tensions were mounting, and I didn't know how to fix things. We found ourselves, once again, at a stalemate. I prayed for a resolution to our problems but couldn't figure out how to make things better between us. Was our close and loving relationship slipping away forever? Would our stubbornness, our inability to communicate, our pride prevail? Had God given up on us? Or had I?

One evening, she arrived at my front door and handed me a small white box. Inside was a delicate golden pin in the shape of a bow; a small heart-shaped locket dangled from it. Tentatively, I pried open the locket and inside, facing one another, were miniature pictures—one of her, the other of me—when we were not much older than we were in the other photo. This time, there were no grimaces, no struggles—just the innocent smiles of two little girls—sisters—looking back at me. All the misgivings of the previous months melted away. There we were, pressed together for all time in a delicate heart—just as we lived in the hearts of one another. Even though I had remained muddled and inactive, God had softened Shel's heart and given her the perfect solution to our troubled times.

We need one another. Separate, we are fine; but together, we are spectacular.

We don't all have to face the same direction in life to enjoy its many delights or take joy in one another. That fading photo and delicate heart-shaped locket are poignant reminders that we can always look at things from a different angle.

Of course, I'm not making any promises. I may have to step in once in awhile and take charge of the situation. After all, I have a longstanding tradition to uphold, and when you're one year and three weeks older than your baby sister, you most certainly have a thing or two you can teach her. Even if you have to put her in a choke hold to do it.

Deborah Dee Simmons

Deborah and Shelley "posing" for their mother.

Taking Care of Each Other

On my sister's fourth birthday, she got a fire engine. She flung herself across it, scooting around the linoleum, her frilled panties visible and her curls bouncing. She was the justifiable center of attention—it was her birthday. I recall feeling resentment and anger and wanting that darn fire engine. I'd never had a penchant for fire trucks before.

After a second, she got off the engine, distracted by a new doll. With a slight smile she shoved the truck in my direction. My resentment melted.

We played out similar scenes throughout our childhood. The Chatty Cathy doll from the eighth birthday party became joint property. My sister was a pretty child; she danced well, excelled in athletics and had a herd of friends. I was a brooding bookworm.

She recalls different days. She still has the delusion that she only passed algebra because of me. One of her favorite stories from high school centers on needing a ride and calling one of my erstwhile boyfriends to fetch her.

But from the moment she shoved that fire truck across the floor, we shared. She may have been younger in years but she set a pattern of a lifetime of sharing. She took care of me even though she was "the baby."

Sitting in the middle of boxes and bags after the death of both of our parents we had the horrible task of dividing the knickknacks and mementos of our family. We started with sticky notes. Going around the house, we each affixed notes to whatever we wanted. We even created a third category—"I don't want this, but I don't want it sold so if you don't want it, I'll take it." It was a sad task. Mom and Dad would have been proud. We'd heard of siblings driven apart by desire for a duvet or lust for a love seat, but we grew closer in our grief.

My parents left a lot of things. But they only left us each one sister.

No conflict. Tears, memories and laughter— "Why did Mom save the canceled checks for all our toddler finery?" And "Well, we have proof they paid the light bill in 1958." "And, in '59." I also now know my sister can't be repossessed. I saw the paid hospital bill for her birth.

My sister is the organized one. She took charge of canceling the cable, dealing with Social Security and arranging a real estate agent. I'm the emotional one. I fulfilled the Jewish tradition of attending daily services to say the Mourner's Kaddish, a prayer honoring our departed parents. My sister carved safety out of chaos by organizing it. I created more chaos by ranting and crying.

We each did what we needed to do to seal the open wound left by being orphaned.

While we were sifting through the flotsam and jetsam of their forty-five years together the phone rang. It was one of the organizations Mom made charitable donations to frequently. "She's passed away," my sister said.

Then I heard her say, "Oh my sister handles that," before she handed me the telephone. The caller wanted to pray for my mom.

I muttered something and got off the phone barely able to control my giggles. "What was that for?"

"Well," she said. "That's how we share it: I do bills, and you do prayer."

I looked at the mess we'd made pulling decades of old clothes out of closets, piling them up on every surface. "Do you ever want to go to synagogue with me? I mean I could understand if you felt uncomfortable because it's been so long."

She continued making notes on her pad for the estate sale. "No. I don't think so," she said. "I don't think that it would meet a need for me."

I watched her organize, categorize and fill the page with careful documentation.

"I do know it will be there if I ever need it," she added. Her voice was soft. Her words hung like specks of dust in the still air of the house no one lived in any longer.

Since that day I've had moments when I feel alienated from my religion. Sometimes when I get caught up in my daily concerns, it seems like services are just another chore to be checked off. I'm not a world-class house-keeper; in fact, I expect the board of health to condemn my kitchen soon. Yet, every year I undergo the laborious task of cooking and cleaning for Passover, doing what I need to do to keep Judaism alive.

When I wonder what it's for, why I repeat the rituals and say the prayers during moments when I don't feel particularly spiritually inclined, I recall that afternoon between the bags and boxes.

I have to do my small bit to keep Judaism going—my sister might need it one day. We've always taken care of each other. That afternoon among the boxes she took good care of me.

Diane Goldberg

My Other Mother

Shared joy is double joy, and shared sorrow is half sorrow.

Swedish Proverb

I hated her.

There was no getting around it: I despised the very ground she walked on. She was tall and beautiful, and I was not. She treated me like slime, and I let her because she was bigger. She teased and belittled me and made me feel inferior. I was last to get my way and the first to get in trouble, or that was how it always seemed.

I hated her. And I tried desperately to convince myself how much I meant those words.

One day, while still in the midst of sibling rivalry, our parents announced their divorce. How could this be? Oh, sure there were some fights but nothing too bad. Just normal everyday stuff, but then how were we to know what was normal? Before I could really accept this, my mother was gone. I was twelve, the baby, and had never felt so much like one until that horrible day.

Suddenly, I was very alone.

How could they do this to me? I lost friends as, back then, no respectable parent could possibly allow their darlings to associate with an unsupervised child from a broken home. I ruined my clothes, as I'd never had to wash my own before. I burned my meals, as Dad worked late, and I was hungry. I hated everything around me. I hated my mom for leaving, my dad for letting her, and myself for being so helpless. I guess I didn't have much left in me to hate Dana so much anymore.

Many afternoons I would come home to an empty house, watch television, burn my own dinner and cry myself to sleep. Dana had her own life, an older life, full of friends and sports and parties. Her boyfriend practically lived at our house. They used me as the butt of their jokes, but I just didn't care anymore.

One day after they teased me to tears, I ran to my bedroom and threw myself on my bed, sobbing my despair. I don't know if I've ever cried harder than I did that day. I pined for my old life; I'd take the fights if things could just go back to being normal. I cried until I had nothing left but deep exhaustion and those awful hiccups that come with a long cry.

Then something pressed its weight beside me. I turned over and saw Dana sitting on my bed. I opened my mouth to shout at her to leave me alone! But the look on her face stopped me.

I buried my face and whimpered, "Go away," with a pathetic amount of conviction.

Dana reached out and brushed the hair from my face. "I'm sorry," she whispered.

I held my breath, wondering if her boyfriend was standing near the door, just waiting for the cue to burst out laughing and prove they were playing yet another cruel joke. But Dana stretched out beside me and rubbed my back. "What's wrong?" she asked, and the sincerity I heard in her voice opened a flood of fresh tears.

"I hate this! I want Mom to come home! I hate you and you hate me, and I hate everything!"

"No you don't," Dana said. "You don't hate me."

I wanted to shout, "Yes, I do!" I tried to shout it, but the words stuck in my throat. Truth was I didn't hate Dana. I wanted to, but I wanted her to love me more. What was it about an older sister that made a young girl pine for her acceptance? Why was it I had a hurt so deep and aching that I wished Dana could make it disappear? She was the closest thing I had to a mother, yet I despised the fact she couldn't see how much I needed her. I guess I hated the fact that she didn't need my guidance and love as much as I yearned for hers.

"And I don't hate you," she added.

"Yes you do," I said. "You're so mean to me."

"I'm your big sister, I'm supposed to be mean to you," she chuckled, as if I was supposed to know this. "That doesn't mean I hate you." She wrapped her arms around me. "I love you, Stace."

I didn't care that tomorrow she would probably go back to being mean and spiteful. I didn't care that it would be years before Dana would tell me those words practically every day and mean them. I didn't care that it would take ten years and a six-hundred-mile gap between us for me to wish we could see each other daily. Right then I wanted to believe her; I needed to. I rolled into her hug and let her hold me.

I'll never forget that day. Sometimes it seems like yesterday. She was there to hold me when I needed someone to do so; today she is still there.

Stacey Granger

Love Covers a Multitude of Mistakes

Sisters are so special. The connection can run the full range of emotions: from a full-blown, hairbrush-throwing fight to the comfort of a counseling session with shared tears and lots of hugs. My sister and I experienced many fights and many nurturing moments through our lives. But my most significant childhood memory displays true loyalty on my sister's part.

I remember the day as if it were yesterday. The scars have disappeared, but my feelings about my sister truly took a turning point on that late summer afternoon—the day after my sister Michelle's twelfth birthday.

Michelle and I were as different as night and day. I was the "little sister" and always looked up to my big sister with envy. She was tall and skinny, with long, beautiful blonde hair and teeth as straight and bright as a white picket fence. Somehow she always looked delicate and dainty even after she came home from a long day at school. I was a different story altogether. I was short, chubby and had a two-inch overbite. If you ever saw me cleaned up and put together it was only on Sunday morning when my mother curled my short hair and put a dress on me. That look only lasted about the first thirty minutes of church, before I found a way to tear my stockings and scuff up my patent leather shoes.

September 27, 1982, was Michelle's twelfth birthday. She had been begging for a ten-speed bike for a long time. My parents couldn't always give us what we wanted financially, but the love we shared could fill one thousand mansions. This particular year, they had saved their money and bought Michelle a bike. Not just any bike—a beautiful, pale-as-the-sky, blue ten-speed bike. Her very first bike with gears. The seat was high and dainty, the handlebars were curved and cushioned with pink rubber. There was nothing childish about this bike. This bike had "woman" written all over it, and I was jealous.

Michelle rode up and down the driveway showing off her new gift. Her hair flowed behind her, and her smile showed she was proud of her biking skills. I waved and smiled and acted as if I was truly happy for her. And I was happy for her, in a deep dark secret kind of way. I knew that she came home from school forty-five minutes after me. I also knew this would be plenty of time for me to take joy rides on her bike before she arrived. So the smile was real. It just maybe had a tinge of envy and deceit behind it.

I had to go to my room that night to plan. I had a few obstacles to face the next day. First of all, since I was younger and shorter than Michelle, I'd have a hard time getting on the bike. But if I walked it to the front porch steps, stood it up, and stood on the second step, I would be able to get on the bike. Next, I began to search through my shoes for the biggest soles. I found a good ol' pair of thick, wooden clogs. Luckily they had a strap on the back, and the sole was a good two inches. My next obstacle would be sneaking the bike out for a ride when my mother wasn't looking. Considering my sneaking skills, this would be easy as pie. I was ready. Plan completed.

The next day in school, I could hardly concentrate. I

was so excited about the adventure I would face that afternoon. I could almost feel the wind blowing through my hair and the smile that would last a lifetime.

I got off the bus and ran all the way to my house. I threw my stuff down and yelled to my mom, "I am going to go bike riding with my friends." This is what I usually did in the afternoon, except I had a big-seated purple and pink bike with plastic fringes coming out of the handlebars and "baby" written all over it. My excitement was almost about to explode through the top of my head. My friends would be calling me the coolest kid on the block. They'd all look at me with envy.

Envy would now lurk in their eyes.

I took the bike to the front of the house, stood on the second step and sure enough, I could reach the seat. My feet barely reached the pedals, but I knew I could always straddle the front bar or stand up and ride if my legs became too tired. I was on, settled, then off into the big world of biking adventures. I rode about a half a mile down a straight road to my friend's house. This is when the first problem occurred to me. How was I going to stop? My feet could barely reach the pedals, much less the ground.

I soon searched out where I could ride up to something, anything, like a tree stump or step or rock to put my foot on. In my desperation, I jumped off, the bike skidding a few feet to the left but luckily I didn't even drop the bike. It was a perfect stop. My friend and I went for a ride; she couldn't believe I had the nerve to ride my sister's new bike. She had three older brothers, and I told her she didn't understand my sister and our connection.

The ride had been simple up until now. "It is time for an adventure," my friend said. "Let's test out the brakes on the bike."

Within minutes I found myself at the top of "the hill."

This was not just any hill; this hill was the biggest hill for miles. It was straight down and graveled. Once you started this ultimate ride there was no stopping. You had to get to the bottom of the hill to be able to stop or you would skid and slide and possibly injure yourself pretty badly.

There I was, and time was slipping away from me. My sister's bus would be pulling up within minutes at the end of the street. So I had to either ride or walk the bike down. I had a crowd of kids cheering for me now. "Sheri! Sheri! Sheri!" So I clenched my hands tightly around the handlebars, somehow hoping to reach an angel to watch over me. I took a deep breath and I was off . . . the first few seconds, I was steady . . . then as the bike picked up speed, it began to wobble a little, then a lot and too soon I lost control. The back wheel skidded off to the side, slinging me onto my right thigh. I slid down the rest of the hill on my right leg with my left leg straddled over the bike. All courage was lost, there was no turning back now, I screamed and cried and yelled "HELP!" The rest of what I thought would be an adventure turned out to be a nightmare. My leg was covered in blood, my body shook with fear. I was covered in dirt and small pieces of gravel. My face was completely smudged with wet dirt from the million tears I had already shed.

Suddenly, I heard someone yell my name, "Sheri, it's okay I am coming!" Blinded by my own tears, I could not see anyone. But I knew that voice—it rang clear to me. It was my sister. Her bus had already arrived, she dropped her belongings and was running full force to save me. Delicately she picked me up, placed me on the handle bars, and she rode me all the way home. She spoke not a word. Just pushed those pedals as fast as she could all the way home to my mom.

My mother rushed to the front door to meet us—she had

heard my crying. My sister ran in the house to get the Band-Aids, alcohol, washcloths and later even a cold drink.

My sister never fussed at me for scratching her new bike or for riding it without permission. She didn't even tell me how stupid it was for me to try to ride down "the hill." She only loved and nurtured me. This is what sisterhood is all about. There are times to fight and times to love, times to laugh and times to hug, times to play and times to pay for your mistakes. And my sister chose all the right decisions. My consequence was much beyond what I deserved. My knee was sore and scabbed and unbearable to move for days. My sister was my hero. Her loyalty and character has never changed over the years. She's still a sister who rises to the occasion to encourage me when I doubt, strengthen my weaknesses and sometimes even tell me I am making a bad decision. But her best quality is to just be a "sister." Not a mom, not a doctor, not a psychologist, but just simply a "sister."

That September afternoon, my sister was just that—a sister. I learned many valuable lessons that day and still apply them to my life today. Love covers many mistakes. When pain is absolutely unbearable and you become blinded by the many wrong bike rides you've taken, listen for love. You may not see the person running toward you, but you can listen. Listen to the beat of your own heart. And if it is love, you will hear it. If someone wrongs you, still love. Always love. For we are somehow all sisters in this great big world of problems. So learn to listen to your heart by loving those in need, those who need encouragement, and most importantly, love the unlovable. For love covers a multitude of mistakes.

Sheri Jennings

Hey, I'm Telling!

One day when I was a little girl, my mom asked my sister and me if we wanted to go with her to the grocery store. Immediately we began fighting over who got the front seat, and my mom settled it by making us both sit in the back. After a few minutes, we started bickering again.

"Hey, you're on my side!" "You touched me."

Looking back at that childish fighting, I realize something beautiful has happened to us. We have grown close. And that closeness has lasted a lifetime.

My sister and I are in our forties now and our childhood battles are over—we don't "tell" on each other anymore. Yet comments we made when we were kids still ring true today.

"You *are* on my side!" "You *have* touched me."

Penny Perrone

Who Is Jack Canfield?

Jack Canfield is one of America's leading experts in the development of human potential and personal effectiveness. He is both a dynamic, entertaining speaker and a highly sought-after trainer. Jack has a wonderful ability to inform and inspire audiences toward increased levels of self-esteem and peak performance.

He is the author and narrator of several bestselling audio and videocassette programs, including *Self-Esteem and Peak Performance, How to Build High Self-Esteem, Self-Esteem in the Classroom* and *Chicken Soup for the Soul—Live.* He is regularly seen on television shows such as *Good Morning America, 20/20* and *NBC Nightly News.* Jack has co - authored numerous books, including the *Chicken Soup for the Soul* series, *Dare to Win* and *The Aladdin Factor* (all with Mark Victor Hansen), *100 Ways to Build Self-Concept in the Classroom* (with Harold C. Wells), *Heart at Work* (with Jacqueline Miller) and *The Power of Focus* (with Les Hewitt and Mark Victor Hansen).

Jack is a regularly featured speaker for professional associations, school districts, government agencies, churches, hospitals, sales organizations and corporations. His clients have included the American Dental Association, the American Management Association, AT&T, Campbell's Soup, Clairol, Domino's Pizza, GE, ITT, Hartford Insurance, Johnson & Johnson, the Million Dollar Roundtable, NCR, New England Telephone, Re/Max, Scott Paper, TRW and Virgin Records. Jack is also on the faculty of Income Builders International, a school for entrepreneurs.

Jack conducts an annual eight-day Training of Trainers program in the areas of self-esteem and peak performance. It attracts educators, counselors, parenting trainers, corporate trainers, professional speakers, ministers and others interested in developing their speaking and seminar-leading skills.

For further information about Jack's books, tapes and training programs, or to schedule him for a presentation, please contact:

Self-Esteem Seminars
P.O. Box 30880
Santa Barbara, CA 93130
Phone: 805-563-2935 • Fax: 805-563-2945
Web site: *www.chickensoup.com*

Who Is Mark Victor Hansen?

Mark Victor Hansen is a professional speaker who in the last twenty years has made over 4,000 presentations to more than 2 million people in thirty-two countries. His presentations cover sales excellence and strategies; personal empowerment and development; and how to triple your income and double your time off.

Mark has spent a lifetime dedicated to his mission of making a profound and positive difference in people's lives. Throughout his career, he has inspired hundreds of thousands of people to create a more powerful and purposeful future for themselves while stimulating the sale of billions of dollars worth of goods and services.

Mark is a prolific writer and has authored *Future Diary, How to Achieve Total Prosperity* and *The Miracle of Tithing*. He is coauthor of the *Chicken Soup for the Soul* series, *Dare to Win* and *The Aladdin Factor* (all with Jack Canfield), and *The Master Motivator* (with Joe Batten).

Mark has also produced a complete library of personal-empowerment audio and videocassette programs that have enabled his listeners to recognize and use their innate abilities in their business and personal lives. His message has made him a popular television and radio personality, with appearances on ABC, NBC, CBS, HBO, PBS and CNN. He has also appeared on the cover of numerous magazines, including *Success, Entrepreneur* and *Changes*.

Mark is a big man with a heart and spirit to match—an inspiration to all who seek to better themselves.

For further information about Mark, write:

MVH & Associates
P.O. Box 7665
Newport Beach, CA 92658
Phone: 949-759-9304 or 800-433-2314
Fax: 949-722-6912
Web site: *www.chickensoup.com*

Who Are Patty and Nancy Mitchell?

Patty Aubery is the vice president of The Canfield Training Group and Self-Esteem Seminars, Inc., and president of Chicken Soup for the Soul Enterprises, Inc. Patty has been working with Jack and Mark since the birth of *Chicken Soup for the Soul.*

Along with her sister, Nancy, Patty is the coauthor of *Chicken Soup for the Surviving Soul, Chicken Soup for the Christian Soul, Chicken Soup for the Expectant Mother's Soul, Chicken Soup for the Christian Family Soul* and *Chicken Soup for the Christian Woman's Soul.* She has been a guest on over 150 local and nationally syndicated radio shows.

Patty is married to Jeff Aubery, and together they have two wonderful children, J. T. and Chandler. Patty and her family reside in Santa Barbara, California.

Nancy Mitchell Autio is the director of story acquisitions for the *Chicken Soup for the Soul* series. She graduated from Arizona State University with a B.S. in nursing. After graduation, Nancy worked at Good Samaritan Regional Medical Center in Phoenix, Arizona. Four months later, she moved back to the Los Angeles area and became involved with the *Chicken Soup* series.

Nancy says she is most thankful for is her move back to Los Angeles. "If I hadn't moved back to California, I wouldn't have had the chance to be there for my mom during her bout with breast cancer." Out of that struggle, Nancy helped coauthored *Chicken Soup for the Surviving Soul* and other *Chicken Soup* titles. Little did Patty and Nancy know that *Surviving Soul* would become their family's inspiration when their dad was diagnosed with prostate cancer in 1999.

Nancy, her husband, Kirk and their daughter, Molly, reside in Santa Barbara.

You may contact Patty or Nancy at P.O. Box 30880, Santa Barbara, CA 93130 or by calling 805-563-2935.

Who Are Heather and Katy McNamara?

After a stint as a freelance contributor, Heather became the editor-in-chief for Chicken Soup for the Soul Enterprises in 1996. Two years ago, she coauthored the well-received *Chicken Soup for the Unsinkable Soul*. Katy owns a shop in Santa Monica which caters to the scribe in all of us, focusing mainly on fountain pens and papers from all over the world.

Both girls' love of literature grew from their third-grade public school teacher, Mrs. Lutesinger, who read to them every day—the same third-grade teacher who inspired their siblings Laura and Danny.

"We feel so lucky to have grown up in a family that rates reading as enjoyable a pastime as tag or television," the sisters concur.

When the idea of a "Sisters" book first came up, Katy leapt at the chance to participate. "Patty and I were partners in crime in high school, and we essentially coerced our little sisters Heather and Nancy to pal up—so the opportunity to work together sounded like too much fun to pass up—and it was!"

"My sisters have definitely helped shape me into the person I am," Katy continues. "Laura's fiery spirit, her sense of independence, and most of all, her love for adventure continue to inspire me while Heather's integrity, outstanding sense of humor, and joie de vivre make me smile every day."

Heather adds that she feels truly blessed by having three siblings who make her laugh. "Best of all," Heather continues, "I count my brother and sisters among my best friends."

Today Heather and Rick live in a rural outpost of San Fernando Valley, where they enjoy the panoramic view of the valley, their garden, and their three dogs—all adopted strays. Twenty miles away, Katy shares a 1924 cottage in historic Topanga Canyon with her sweet mutt Rosie, comedic cat Sassy, and all-around great guy, husband Paul.

You can reach Heather or Katy by contacting P.O. Box 30880, Santa Barbara, CA 93110.

Contributors

Rhonda Adkins misses Roxie very much. Justin is twenty-one, married and with a baby boy on the way. Shaun is nineteen and working full time. Jerry and Rhonda have been married now for five years. They enjoy spending time with the boys and also Jerry's two sons, their wives and three granddaughters. Justin's son will be the first boy in the family! You can e-mail her at *jradkins@comcast.net.*

A resident of Stonington, Connecticut, **Marci Alborghetti** writes about spiritual, social and business matters and has had three books published: *COMPASSION, The Miracle of the Myrrh* (for children and families), and *Freedom from Fear: Overcoming Anxiety Through Faith.* For more information about the books, or to reach Marci, please e-mail *inklin@ntplx.net* or call 860-535-251

Jade Albert is a world-renowed children's photographer. Her work appears regularly in national magazines and in major advertising campaigns. She recently collaborated on her first book as a photographer for *About Face* by Cindy Crawford (HarperCollins). Jade divides her time between Manhattan and Shelter Island, New York.

Marsha Arons teaches high-school English and is a freelance writer and lecturer. She specializes in writing stories, essays, articles and promotional material for a wide audience. Marsha began her relationship with *Chicken Soup for the Soul* in 1993 and her name appears on the covers of many of the books to which she has contributed. Marsha's stories, articles, and essays have appeared in such national magazines as *Reader's Digest, Good Housekeeping, Redbook, Woman's Day* and *Woman's World.* In addition, she has worked for several years for several Jewish publications including *JUF News, Chicago Jewish News, The Intermountain Jewish News,* and *Jewish Image* magazine. Besides teaching, writing, and producing videos, Marsha's career includes speaking engagements. She addresses diverse groups, relating many of her most-beloved stories as well as trying out her new ones on live audiences. She is married and the mother of four daughters ranging in age from eleven to twenty-three. Marsha lives in Skokie, Illinois.

Karen Asp is a freelance writer who specializes in health, fitness and women's issues. Her work has appeared in *Health, Cooking Light, Family Circle, Shape* and *Fitness.* She's currently writing her first novel and plotting with her sister new ways to give her parents Christmas presents. For information, visit *www.karenasp.com.*

Lee Schafer Atonna celebrates life with her husband of thirty-three years, their two grown sons and two "grand" puppies. A graduate of Northern Arizona University (B.S.Ed.) and the University of Toledo (M.Ed.), she teaches kindergarten. She loves music, laughter, hiking, reading, Arizona sunsets and taking solitary forays into creative writing.

Lisa Baillargeon is a loan officer in Massachusetts. Lisa enjoys reading, writing, snowmobiling, vacationing and spending time with her husband and four children. She writes poems for all occasions and children's rhyming stories as a hobby. She can be reached at *mlbrgn2@aol.com*.

Chera Lee Bammerlin received her English and communications degree from Nebraska Wesleyan University in 1996. After teaching high school for five years, she is now pursuing freelance writing and photography while living and working on the family ranch in Keya Paha County, Nebraska. She can be reached at *cheraleeb@msn.com*.

Glenda Barbre developed a love for writing while still a child in the Mt. Hood National Forest. As her life unfolded she begin writing for devotionals, among them *Ripples of Joy* and *All Is Calm All Is Bright* compiled by Cheryl Kirking. Her work has appeared in *Guidepost's Angels on Earth,* and *Reminisce* magazine's *We Made Our Own Fun.* She writes a monthly feature for *The Gazette* newsmagazine in Sandy, Oregon. She is working on true childhood stories of growing up in the Mt. Hood National Forest, as well as comedy poetry and Christian devotionals.

Cindy Beck received her bachelor of arts, summa cum laude, from the University of South Alabama in 1998. In her spare time, she enjoys reading and writing. She is recently married and lives with her husband Nicholas in Alabama. Please reach her at: *CindyDBeck@aol.com*.

Faith Andrews Bedford is fifty-seven and has been married for thirty-eight years to Robert F. Bedford. She has three children, ages thirty seven, thirty-three and twenty-eight and two grandchildren, ages three and six. Bedford recently had her story, "Grandmother's Shell" published in *Chicken Soup for the Grandparent's Soul.*

A retired high school principal, **Rita Billbe** owns Angels Retreat resort on the White River in north central Arkansas. Her interests include writing, singing in her church choir, reading and planning a family reunion each summer. E-mail her at *angelret@flippinweb.com* or see the Web site *www.whiteriver.net/angels-retreat.*

Dee Berry is a hobbyist writer and member-in-good-standing of Frank's Writing Workshop. She wishes to thank "the gang" and her husband, Neal, for their honest and kind critiquing. She is a devoted gardener, who often finds inspiration amongst her lavender and roses, or hip deep in compost.

Tasha Boucher lives in Los Angeles. She recently completed her master's degree in counseling at Cal State Northridge. She has taught creative writing workshops to at-risk youth, and also she enjoys writing, traveling, photography and being a mentor to Datasha, an incredible teenage girl she has had the pleasure of knowing for the past six years. Tasha can be reached at *tasha_boucher@hotmail.com*.

Dawn Braulick lives in Montana with her husband and eight children. She works in an automotive repair business. Dawn enjoys the ocean, drag racing and her family. She is currently writing her first novel. Please reach her at *DragonDawnB.@aol.com.*

Diane Burke lives in Florida with her husband, grown son, daughter-in-law, three grandchildren, parents, uncle and sister. She has a second son and five other siblings with their families in various states across the country. She is currently working on a collection of short stories entitled "The Family Trap (Or I'll give you $50.00 if you prove I am adopted.)." Her e-mail address is *wburke3@cfl.rr.com.*

Muriel Bussman became a registered nurse in 1948. She retired in 1992 after many happy years in pediatrics and obstetrics. She went back to college and received a liberal arts degree at age fifty and then began writing. Her family consists of three daughters and three sons and six grandchildren.

Jackie Case is a stay-at-home mother of three children. This birthday gift shall remain special as our youngest sister, Karen, after a short illness passed away the following year. Karen's family misses her and will never forget her.

Rebecca Christian is a writer, editor and humor speaker who writes plays and essays as well as doing commentaries on public radio. Her musical comedy revue, "Mothering Heights," (with Tracey Rush) was recently published by Dramatic Publishing. Contact her at 4535 Waveland Ct., Des Moines, Iowa, 50312; (515) 274-9976; *christia@raccoon.com.*

Elayne Clift, a writer in Saxtons River, Utah, teaches at several New England colleges and universities. Her latest book is *Escaping the Yellow Wallpaper: Women's Encounters with the Mental Health Establishment.* For her other titles, visit *www.sover.net/ecl.ft.SandraDowns.*

Danielle Collier is a freelance writer living in the Midwest. She has published fiction and nonfiction and is currently working on her first novel.

Alice Collins, wife for forty-one years (but who's counting), is the mother of four adult sons and one daughter who have gifted her with ten adorable grandchildren. Alice writes two weekly Chicago area columns penned with the humor and sentiment of family life. She can be reached at *Acoll999@aol.*

Andrea D'Asaro's personal essays appeared in *Meridian Bound,* a collection of Philadelphia authors, and in the *Philadelphia Inquirer, Redbook* and on *NRP's Weekend Editor.* Andrea teaches writing at Arcadia University in Glenside, Pennsylvania, and coaches MBA students at the Wharton School of the University of Pennsylvania and Drexel University. She earned her master's in journalism from Temple University and lives in Elkins Park, Pennsylvania, with her husband and two sons.

C. Michele Davis is a freelance writer whose articles have appeared in magazines ranging from *Baby Talk* to *Mature Living,* as well as newspapers and law enforcement publications. She recently completed her first young adult novel. To see a listing of her previously sold and currently available work, go to *www.MicheleDavis.com.*

Janie Emaus writes novels, short stories and poetry for adults and children of all ages. Her career began by making up stories for her sister at the age of four. Her work has appeared in children's magazines, literary journals, educational videos and newspapers. Janie can be reached at *zarnt@aol.com.*

Delia Ephron, author and screenwriter, has written many books for children and adults, including the recent novel *Hanging Up*. Her film work as a writer and producer includes the movie *Hanging Up*, as well as *You've Got Mail*, *Sleepless in Seattle* and *Michael*. She lives in New York City.

Jane Eppinga's writing credentials include more than two hundred articles for both popular and professional publications. Her biography of *Henry Ossian Flipper, West Point's First Black Graduate*, was part of a package presented to President W. J. Clinton as a successful appeal to have Henry Ossian Flipper posthumously pardoned. Her other two books are *Arizona Twilight Tales: Good Ghosts, Evil Spirits, and Blue Ladies*, and *Images of America: Tucson, Arizona*. E-mail her at *janee@flash.net.*

Susan Farr Fahncke is a freelance writer living in Utah. Author of *Angel's Legacy*, she also writes for inspirational books and magazines and runs a Web site of inspirational stories. You can find her stories in other *Chicken Soup* books. E-mail: *Editor@2theheart.com*. Web site: *www.2THEHEART.com.*

Hope Fillingim, now thirteen years old, enjoys soccer, basketball and hanging out with friends. She and her sister Hannah are the best of pals, even though they still find time to disagree. Hope lives in Rome, Georgia, with Hannah and her parents. And she gets straight As in school.

Nancy B. Gibbs is the author of *Celebrate Life, Just for Today*. Her stories have appeared in more than thirty books and several magazines, including *Chicken Soup for the Nurse's Soul, Stories for the Heart, Guideposts* books, *Angels on Earth, Woman's World* and *Family Circle*. She is a mother and grandmother who can be reached at *Daiseydood@aol.com.*

Benita Glickman teaches ESL, mentors new teachers and writes curriculum for the Office of the Bronx Superintendency. She received the Alice Minnie Hertz Heniger Award for children's literature. Her poetry appears in numerous publications including the *Aurorean, By Line* and *Black Bear Review*. She can be contacted at 55 Knolls Crescent, Bronx, NY 10463-6354.

Diane Goldberg lives with her husband and a geriatric beagle in the southeast. She has lunch with her baby sister several times a month; they giggle far too much for grown-ups. She writes dark fantasy and horror as d. g. k. Goldberg, you can find out about that part of her world at *www.dgkgoldberg.com* and you can e-mail her at *dgkgoldberg@dgkgoldberg.com.*

Eileen Goltz graduated from Indiana University and the Cordon Bleu Cooking School, Paris, France. Eileen writes, runs a catering business, and does recipe development and food styling. Her first cookbook, *Perfectly Pareve* (Feldheim), was released in November 2001. She is married, has two sons and can be contacted at *ztlog@aol.com*.

Stacey Granger is the author of several books including *The Portable Mother, The Portable Father,* and *The Workout Cop-out* and is a previous contributor to the *Chicken Soup* series as well as many other anthologies. She lives in Maryland with her husband and their six children. She can be reached at *staceya ganger@aol.com*.

Pamela Haskin lives on a homestead in the Alaska Bush with her husband of twenty-three years. As an award-winning author and motivational speaker, she encourages others to choose, then go live, their dream. She plans to publish a book about her time in the wilderness. You can reach her at *PamelaHaskin@worldnet.att.net*.

Jonny Hawkins has been cartooning professionally for sixteen years. His work has appeared in *Reader's Digest, Guideposts, Harvard Business Review* and more than 250 other publications. He can be reached at 616-432-8071 or by regular mail at P.O. Box 188 Sherwood, MI 49089 or e-mail: *jonnyhawkins2nz@yahoo.com*.

Deborah Hedstrom-Page is a writer, teacher and researcher with a degree in English/communication. She has published nine junior-age books, compiled two gift books, and coauthored a devotional for caregivers. In addition she has published more than three hundred magazine articles in publications such as *Guideposts, Moddy Magazine* and *Country Women*.

Ina Hughs has been a full-time journalist since 1973 and is currently a writer for *The Knoxville News Sentinel* in East Tennessee. She has published two books—*A Prayer for Children* and *A Sense of Human*—and has contributed to numerous anthologies and journals, including *Chicken Soup* publications. She lives in a cabin on the Tennessee River. Please reach her at *Hughs@knews.com*.

Shelly Isenberg received her B.S. from the University of Central Florida and a masters in educational leadership from Nova Southeastern University. She is currently an assistant principal in South Florida and has just completed the intern principal program. Shelly loves working with children and the great outdoors.

Molly Bruce Jacobs lives in New Mexico. Her essays have appeared in magazines and newspapers, her short stories in literary journals. She has won numerous awards for her essay "A Letter to Annie." Born in Maryland, and a graduate from Columbia Law School, she is writing a memoir about her sister Anne. She may be contacted at *m.b.jacobs@att.net*.

Robin Janson-Shope received her B.S. degree with honors, at W.W. Whitewater in 1975. She teaches middle school near Dallas, Texas. With more than one hundred magazine articles and short stories in print, she also enjoys swimming, garage shopping, reading and working with teens. She is presently working on Christian romance/mystery novels. She can be reached at *hi2robin@attbi.com*.

Sheri Jennings received her B.A. in elementary education from High Point University in 1998. She is currently children's director at First Wesleyan Church and a full-time, stay-at-home mom. Sheri enjoys drawing, painting, biking, reading and writing. She writes inspirational cards, poems and songs and plans to write inspirational books. Please reach her at: *FWCNursery@aol.com*.

T. Jensen Lacey has published more than five hundred newspaper and magazine articles. Two Native American history books, *The Blackfeet* (1995), and *The Pawnee* (1996 Chelsea House), and two books of state history, *Amazing Tennessee* (2000) and *Amazing North Carolina* (2002) (Rutledge Hill Press). Lacey's young adult novel, *Growing Season*, is available through *www.1stbooks.com* or through bookstores. Lacey's Web site is *www.tjensenlacey.com*.

For information about **Ruth Latta**'s books and writing services, please visit her Web site at *www.cyberus.ca/rklatta/ruthlatta.html*.

Ricky Keen graduated from high school at Portland, Tennessee. He received a scholarship to attend college at Western Kentucky University in Bowling Green, Kentucky. Ricky enjoys reading and writing short stories. "Symbiosis" is his first published short story.

Martine Klaasen and her sister continued taking turns uniting about their daily woes in their diary. Eventually they switched to e-mail as a more high tech way to stay in touch. And while an ocean still separates the two sisters, they remain close sisters and friends for life.

Alora Knight, eighty-one, when seventy-eight started her business Poetic Pictures—making colorful frames for the poems being marketed. She also collaborated with daughter, Marsha, on children books. She has been published many times and is a member of ASCAP. Her poetry is on several Web sites. She enjoys reading, gardening and volunteering.

After raising her family, **June Cerza Kolf** spent twelve years doing hospice work and began her writing career. She has published six books relating to grief and terminal illness and is a frequent contributor to inspirational magazines. Her most recent, *Standing in the Shadow*, is for suicide survivors.

Jennifer Koscheski lives in Colorado with her husband, John, and three of their four children. Her oldest son is a marine. Helping in her husband's business and mothering consumes most of her days, but she also enjoys many hobbies, including writing encouraging letters to family, friends and sometimes strangers. She may be reached at *Jenn122861@aol.com*.

Leona Lipari Lee is an RN with degrees in psychology and English and the author of *How to Survive Menopause Without Going Crazy, Taxing Tallula, The Sisters: Lost in Brooklyn* and *The Sisters: Found in San Antonio*. Contact her at *Lee3731@bellsouth.net*.

Connie Lounsbury is a frequent contributor to *Guideposts* and other magazines and is published in *Stories for the Kindred Heart* and *More God Allows U-Turns*. She won first place in the 2001 Writer's Digest Writing Competition, inspirational category, and is working on a self-help book and her second novel. Contact her via e-mail at *ConnieL@soncom.com*.

Judy Lynne Lucia writes short stories, essays and is currently writing a novel based on the death of her teenage son. Judy is a facilitator for Survivors of Suicide and a member of the Light for Life Foundation. She enjoys biking, gardening and raising butterflies. Please reach her at *JudysWorld10@aol.com*.

Carol McAdoo Rehme believes sisters are where you find them. She is a four-time mother whose life after kids includes a career as a full-time storyteller, speaker and author. A frequent contributor to the *Chicken Soup* series, she writes for other inspirational books as well. Contact her at: *carol@rehme.com* or *www.rehme.com*.

Carolyn Magner Mason is a freelance writer from Tuscaloosa, Alabama. The mother of two daughters, she writes a weekly parenting column for *The Tuscaloosa News* and has been published in *USA Today, Writer's Digest, Overdrive Magazine* and other regional newspapers. She can be reached by e-mail at *emagner@randallpub.com*.

Gwen Macsai, a National Public Radio writer and producer, chronicles each weigh station along the interstate that rushes us from girlhood to womanhood in a series of first-person essays as witty, well-timed, and as outrageous-as-successful stand-up routines. She covers it all from the unwavering loyalty girlfriends deserve and demand to the humiliations of junior high school. Acutely observant and fearless, she muses on how the music of adolescence calibrates your brain for all time, and how dating boys does little to eliminate the propensity for having crushes on other girls. Gwen's book, *Lipshtick*, is available at *www.amazon.com*.

Cammie McGovern received the Nelson Algren Award in short fiction. Her fiction has been published in *Redbook, Seventeen, Glimmer Train, TriQuarterly* and other journals. She lives with her husband and two small children in Amherst, Massachusetts.

Destiny McIntosh is eleven years old and goes to Alliston Union Public School. Her best friend is Amber Cote, who is also eleven. Destiny has a little sister Kennedy, who is three years old and the person that inspired her to write this poem.

Betty McMahon has been writing for newspapers and magazines for the last twenty years. As part of her business, Z Communications, she writes marketing and advertising materials for corporate clients as well. She is also currently at work on two books, a self-help book and a mystery.

Christine Many is a writer and editor based in New York City. She has written for *Reader's Digest, Ladies' Home Journal, Sports Illustrated for Women* and other publications. She can be reached at *christinemany@yahoo.com*.

Liz Mayer is an environmental studies graduate from the University of Waterloo, Ontario. She is a freelance writer, researcher and publicist who specializes in magazine features, promotional copy and Web-site content. Liz enjoys literature, film, travel and running. Please reach her at *liz@xynapse.ca.*

Walker Meade started writing at the age of fourteen. His first story was published in *Colliers Magazine* when he was twenty-two. He wrote short fiction for the *Saturday Evening Post, Gentlemen's Quarterly, Good Housekeeping, The Ladies Home Journal* and nonfiction for *Cosmopolitan, Redbook,* and *Reader's Digest.* Later he took a position in publishing and became managing editor of *Cosmopolitan* and then managing editor of Reader's Digest Condensed Book Club. His last position in publishing was as president and editor in chief of Avon Books, which he continued to do for ten years. His first novel titled *Unspeakable Acts* is available from *Amazon.com.*

Carla Merolla's work has appeared in several national publications. She also teaches creative writing near her New Jersey home and is working on her first novel. Please reach Carla at: *cmswim@aol.com.*

Chris Miota teaches in the Communications Division at Alverno College in Milwaukee, Wisconsin. She writes for magazines and literary journals and has edited several books, and she is currently working on a collection of short stories. She sees herself singing the blues in a slinky red dress atop a shiny black piano in the future. RSVP: *cmiota@hotmail.com.*

Phyllis Nutkis is a teacher and writer in Skokie, Illinois. She is the author of many professional articles on education, and she conducts workshops and lectures on early childhood education. You may contact her at *Edwriter100@aol.com.*

Christa Holder Ocker, a frequent contributor to the *Chicken Soup* books, is a happy grandmother who draws the inspiration for her stories from living a life filled with love, happiness, sorrow and passion. She can be reached via e-mail at *ockerc@optonline.net.*

Nancy Swiatek Pardo has been a secretary for twenty-five years and currently works in downtown Chicago. She is a commissioned Stephen Minister and serves as lay pastor at First Presbyterian Church of Arlington Heights, Illinois. Nancy enjoys reading, needlework and spending time with family and friends. Her email is *pardonan@attbi.com.*

Diane Payne earned her M.F.A. in creative writing and has a memoir being published by Red Hen Press. She teaches English at the University of Arkansas-Monticello. Diane's daughter, Ania, enjoys hearing Aunt Connie stories. Being an only child, she doesn't understand how these things happen. Contact her at: *dianepayne@earthlink.net.*

Darla Perkins has worked as a classroom aide for mentally and physically challenged children for twenty-four years. She is currently employed by Springfield City schools in Ohio. Darla enjoys reading, biking, walking and canoeing. She is a roller coaster enthusiast. Someday she hopes to ride in a hot air balloon.

Penny Perrone is a freelance writer with a background in the mental health field and an M.S. in community health. She has recently completed an inspirational, healing-type manuscript for those overcoming overwhelming obstacles and is in the process of finding a publisher. Penny's e-mail is *PennyPennedIt@worldnet.att.net.*

Rhonda Rhea is a pastor's wife, mother of five, conference speaker and an inspirational humor columnist for *Homelife Magazine* and other Christian newspapers in the U.S. and Canada. She has also written scads of feature articles and her first book, *Amazing Grace,* is due out in early 2003. She can be reached by e-mail at *Rhonda@RhondaRhea.net.*

Ann Marie Rowland lives and writes in the woods of northern Michigan. She is a singer/songwriter who enjoys reading, spinning, knitting, natural history, gardening and talking to her sister. She is working on a devotional book for women. Contact her at P.O. Box 492, Gaylord, MI 49734.

Jodi Severson earned her B.A. degree from the University of Pittsburgh. She resides in Rice Lake, Wisconsin, with her husband and three children and is employed by the State Public Defender's Office. She writes in her spare time, and is currently working on a children's book about osteogenesis imperfecta. Please reach her at: *seversonj@mail.opd.state.wi.us.*

Vahan Shirvanian went from gunnery instructor (Air Force) to *The Saturday Evening Post* in 1946 and became a contract artist for that magazine. His work has appeared in hundreds of other magazines as well. He has been named Best Cartoonist of The Year six times.

Phoebe Sisk received her B.A. from Austin College in 1988 and her M.S.B.A. from Boston University in 1992. She recently left a *Fortune* 500 corporate communications position to care for her son Elijah, and she is now a freelance writer. Phoebe lives with her husband Kevin in Dallas and plans to publish her first children's book in 2003.

Deborah Dee Simmons is a freelance writer whose work, including a newspaper column, anthologies and award-winning poetry, has appeared in numerous online and print publications. She's completed a children's book series and the first volume of another series of her humorous and inspirational stories. She can be reached at: *dsimmons@ionia.k12.mi.us.*

Renee Simons is a junior in high school. She loves reading and doing photography. She plans to attend University of Findlay to receive her pre-veterinarians license and then transfer to Michigan State for her veterinarians license. You can reach her at *ronie102@yahoo.com.*

Melinda Stiles taught English in Wisconsin and Michigan for twenty-one years. She retired and moved to Idaho to write. Her stories have appeared in *Kalamazoo Gazette, Woven on the Wind, Reminisce, Pass/Fail* and *Chicken Soup for the*

Teacher's Soul. She can be reached at *thel@salmoninterne.*

Kelly L. Stone is a licensed professional counselor and holds a master's degree from Florida State University. She has worked in the field of children's mental health as a counselor and program director for more than thirteen years. She resides in Atlanta and is currently working on a novel. Reach her at *k_stone@bellsouth.net.*

Gail Strock, a freelance writer, enjoys finding humor in everyday experiences with her family and friends. She's been an agricultural correspondent for *Lancaster Farming* for eleven years and has published other stories and thoughts of faith. Her e-mail address is *gstrock@acsworld.net.*

Amanda Athey Swain earned both her B.A. (1995) and master of instruction (1999) with honors form the University of Delaware. She teaches seventh-grade language arts in Sussex County, Delaware, where she lives with her husband and children. Amanda enjoys playing and reading with her children and plans to continue writing.

Carol Duncan Sweet, of Asheville, North Carolina, works as a contract fundraising coordinator for various nonprofit organizations. Born in Oregon, she has traveled extensively and taught English in Korea and the Czech Republic. In addition to travel and spending time with friends, her passions include ballroom dancing. E-mail her at *mhatter2@earthlink.net.*

Nora Stueber-Tamblin resides in Adams Basin, New York, where she and her husband own Gearings Farm Market. Her writing is published in Illiad Press, Sparrowgrass and The National Society of Poetry. From this presented story, Nora and her family united, creating and publishing *Brown Paper Bags,* their life story in foster care. E-mail her at: *etamblin@aol.com.*

Michelle A. Tessaro is a homemaker and freelance photographer. She resides in Memphis, Tennessee, with her husband Paul and her children Melody, David and Kathryn. She enjoys the outdoors, family activities and phoning her sisters. Michelle comes from a family of five girls and three boys. Contact her at *michbunji@aol.com.*

Victoria E. Thompson received a B.A. degree from UCLA and an M.S. and M.A. from California State University, Los Angeles. She has written articles for various periodicals and has had several productions of her original plays. She has worked as an actor for more than thirty-five years on episodic television, movies and several soap operas. She has worked extensively on the stage both in the United States and in Ireland. Please reach her at *tvhcek@earthlink.net.*

Cricket Hardin Vauthier is a general manager for a *Fortune* 500 company and freelances when she finds the time. She is a 1992 graduate of the University of Texas and lives in Dallas with her husband and two sons. She can be reached via e-mail at *chvauthier@aol.com* or at 214-507-6834.

Penny and **Vicky Vilagos** are motivational speakers who specialize in inspiring team excellence. They are members of the Canadian Olympic Hall of Fame and the Canadian Association of Professional Speakers. Their upcoming book is entitled *Triumph Through Teamwork: Achieve your Dreams with the Power of Teams.* To arrange a speaking engagement, in English or French, call 1-866-426-5122 or e-mail *info@VilagosInternational.com.* Web site: *www.VilagosInternational.com.*

L. J. Wardell works as an engineer and research scientist. Her work and hobbies take her all over the globe. Lois enjoys both technical and travel writing as well as photography. Her current work involves the study of active volcanoes. You may reach her at: *wardell@nmt.edu.*

Elisha M. Webster is a student at Appalachian State University in North Carolina. She is a psychology and English major. She receives nourishment from her fabulous friends and family, the ocean, mountains and shadow puppets. She wants to be the Lupin Lady when she grows up. Reach her at: *LupinGal@excite.com.*

Chadd Wheat is a consultant and writer from Lebanon, Indiana. He is married, has a son, a daughter and an insolent cat. Though he has a bad case of wanderlust, he has an unreasonable fear of flying (he prefers to travel by rail). His humorous pondering can be seen at *www.chaddwheat.com.*

Sandra I. White retired from the training and development field in 1998. Since then, her time is divided between writing and volunteer work. Her first novel is scheduled for publication in the spring of 2002. In addition to writing, she enjoys reading and painting. She can be reached at: *swhite66@prodigy.net.*

Julie D. Workman graduated with honors in home economics from Vincennes University in 1992. Since, 1995 she and husband, Joel, have served in the pastorate and mission field. They have three small children and reside in Denver, Colorado. Julie's sister, Cindy, now lives in Indianapolis with her husband and three boys.

Stephanie Wyndance is a pen name used by freelance writer Sharla Taylor. She can be reached at P.O. Box 1513, Collierville, TN 38027-1513 or 901-853-6007. Visit her Web site *www.athomewithwords.com* to learn more about her résumé writing business or visit *www.sharlataylor.com* to read more of her short stories online.

Lynne Zielinski's articles, stories, essays and book reviews appear in national magazines, newspapers and anthologies. She believes life is a gift from God and what we do with it is our gift to God. Lynne freelances out of Huntsville, Alabama, and can be reached at: *ArisWay@aol.com.*

Greta Zwaan has been active in writing for the past fifteen years, having one book published and presently pursuing two more. Writing comes easy to her but being a pastor's wife and involved in the church and volunteering at the local school her time is very limited. Greta's hobbies are collecting cookbooks (up to 12,050 so far), writing and refinishing furniture. She is also an avid gardener. She hopes to finish her second book this year.

Permissions

We would like to acknowledge the following publishers and individuals for permission to reprint the following material. (Note: The stories that were penned anonymously, that are public domain, or that were written by Jack Canfield, Mark Victor Hansen, Patty and Nancy Mitchell or Katy and Heather McNamara are not included in this listing.)

Revenge of the Fifth-Grade Girls. Reprinted by permission of Carolyn Magner Mason. ©1999 Carolyn Magner Mason.

A Gift of Love. Reprinted by permission of Cindy Beck. ©2000 Cindy Beck.

Spit Promises. Reprinted by permission of Dawn Braulick. ©1995 Dawn Braulick.

Diane's Walk. Reprinted by permission of C. Michele Davis. ©2001 C. Michele Davis.

A Promise to Roxanne. Reprinted by permission of Rhonda Adkins and Carla Merolla. ©1997 Carla Merolla. Appeared in the November 4, 1997 issue of *Woman's World Magazine.*

Are You Sure? and *Hey, I'm Telling!* Reprinted by permission of Penny Perrone-Foiles. ©2000 Penny Perrone-Foiles.

Pictures and *Sugar River.* Reprinted by permission of Phyllis L. Nutkis. ©2002. 2001 Phyllis L. Nutkis.

Happy Mother's Day! Reprinted by permission of Victoria E. Thompson. ©1995 Victoria E. Thompson.

We Chose to Be Friends and *Getting to Rome.* Reprinted by permission of Tasha Boucher. ©2000 Tasha Boucher.

Playing Cupid. Reprinted by permission of Chera Lee Bammerlin. ©2001 Chera Lee Bammerlin.

My Family Was Separated. Reprinted by permission of Nora Steuber-Tamblin. ©2001 Nora Steuber-Tamblin.

Comfort Zones. Reprinted by permission of Melinda Sue Stiles. ©2001 Melinda Sue Stiles.

Seeing Everything. Reprinted by permission of Diane Payne. ©2001 Diane Payne.

Swing Set and *Beach Day.* Reprinted by permission of Marsha Arons. ©2002 Marsha Arons.

Sister's Song. Reprinted by permission of Rita Elaine Billbe. ©2001 Rita Elaine Billbe.

Voices. Reprinted by permission of Julie D. Workman. ©1994 Julie D. Workman.

Chicken Soup for the Soul.

Improving Your Life Every Day

Real people sharing real stories — for nineteen years. Now, Chicken Soup for the Soul has gone beyond the bookstore to become a world leader in life improvement. Through books, movies, DVDs, online resources and other partnerships, we bring hope, courage, inspiration and love to hundreds of millions of people around the world. Chicken Soup for the Soul's writers and readers belong to a one-of-a-kind global community, sharing advice, support, guidance, comfort, and knowledge.

Chicken Soup for the Soul stories have been translated into more than 40 languages and can be found in more than one hundred countries. Every day, millions of people experience a Chicken Soup for the Soul story in a book, magazine, newspaper or online. As we share our life experiences through these stories, we offer hope, comfort and inspiration to one another. The stories travel from person to person, and from country to country, helping to improve lives everywhere.

Chicken Soup
for the Soul.

Share with Us

We all have had Chicken Soup for the Soul moments in our lives. If you would like to share your story or poem with millions of people around the world, go to chickensoup.com and click on "Submit Your Story." You may be able to help another reader, and become a published author at the same time. Some of our past contributors have launched writing and speaking careers from the publication of their stories in our books!

Our submission volume has been increasing steadily — the quality and quantity of your submissions has been fabulous. We only accept story submissions via our website. They are no longer accepted via mail or fax.

To contact us regarding other matters, please send us an e-mail through webmaster@chickensoupforthesoul.com, or fax or write us at:

Chicken Soup for the Soul
P.O. Box 700
Cos Cob, CT 06807-0700
Fax: 203-861-7194

One more note from your friends at Chicken Soup for the Soul: Occasionally, we receive an unsolicited book manuscript from one of our readers, and we would like to respectfully inform you that we do not accept unsolicited manuscripts and we must discard the ones that appear.

Chicken Soup for the Soul.

Woman to Woman

Women Sharing Their Stories of Hope, Humor, and Inspiration

Our **101** BEST STORIES

Jack Canfield & Mark Victor Hansen

edited by Amy Newmark

Women have always been wonderful sources of inspiration and support for each other. They are willing to lay bare their souls, even to perfect strangers. Put two random women together in a waiting room, on an airplane, in a line at the supermarket, and the sharing begins, often at the deepest level. Women share hope, humor, and inspiration with each other in these 101 favorite stories from Chicken Soup for the Soul's library.

978-1-935096-04-7

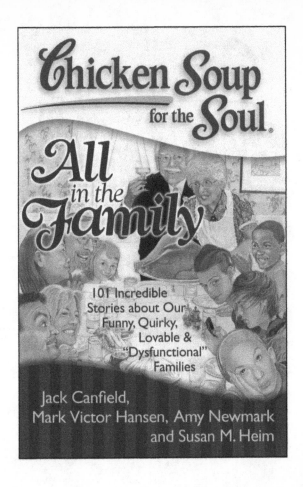

Full of stories about wacky yet lovable relatives, holiday meltdowns, and funny foibles, along with more serious stories of abuse and outbursts, this book is usually hilarious, and occasionally poignant. It is a quirky and fun holiday book, and a great bridal shower or wedding gift! Norman Rockwell's famous Thanksgiving family painting appears on the back cover and is lovingly parodied on the front, showing that all our families are just a little dysfunctional!

978-1-935096-39-9

Chicken Soup for the Soul
for the Soul
Family Matters

101 Unforgettable Stories about Our Nutty but Lovable Families

WARNING: MAY CONTAIN NUTS

Jack Canfield,
Mark Victor Hansen,
Amy Newmark and Susan M. Heim
Foreword by Bruce Jenner

Nearly everyone thinks their own family is "nutty" or has at least one or two nuts. With 101 stories of wacky yet lovable relatives, funny foibles, and holiday meltdowns, this book is usually hilarious and occasionally poignant. This book shows readers that we all have the same family matters and what really matters is families. It is a quirky and fun holiday book, and a great bridal shower or wedding gift!

978-1-935096-55-9

Chicken Soup for the Soul®

Count Your Blessings

101 Stories of Gratitude, Fortitude, and Silver Linings

Jack Canfield,
Mark Victor Hansen, Amy Newmark,
Laura Robinson & Elizabeth Bryan

This uplifting book reminds readers of the blessings in their lives, despite financial stress, natural disasters, health scares and illnesses, housing challenges and family worries. This feel-good book is a great gift for New Year's or Easter, for someone going through a difficult time, or for Christmas. These stories of optimism, faith, and strength remind us of the simple pleasures of family, home, health, and inexpensive good times.

978-1-935096-42-9

Chicken Soup for the Soul.

Devotional Stories for Women

101 Daily Devotions to Comfort, Encourage, and Inspire Women

Susan M. Heim & Karen Talcott

With a foreword by Jennifer Sands, Christian author and speaker

Throughout time, women have shared their joys and sorrows, thoughts and feelings, experiences and life lessons with one another. The tradition continues in this charming book with 101 stories of friendship, faith, and comfort that affirm God's unconditional love and His wisdom. Women will find encouragement, solace, and strength in these personal stories and prayers that cover everyday trials, tests of faith, marriage, parenting, service to others, and self-esteem.

978-1-935096-48-1

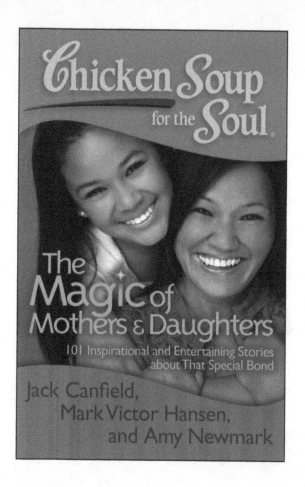

Mothers and daughters. They are, at the same time, very similar and completely unique. This relationship—through birth, childhood, teen years, adulthood, grand-children, aging, and every step in between—can be the best, the hardest, and the sweetest. Mothers and daugh-ters will laugh, cry, and find inspiration in this collection of stories that remind them of their shared love, apprecia-tion and special bond.

978-1-935096-81-8